Recruiting Immigrant Workers: Korea 2019

OECD
BETTER POLICIES FOR BETTER LIVES

This work is published under the responsibility of the Secretary-General of the OECD. The opinions expressed and arguments employed herein do not necessarily reflect the official views of OECD member countries.

This document, as well as any data and any map included herein, are without prejudice to the status of or sovereignty over any territory, to the delimitation of international frontiers and boundaries and to the name of any territory, city or area.

Please cite this publication as:
OECD (2019), *Recruiting Immigrant Workers: Korea 2019*, Recruiting Immigrant Workers, OECD Publishing, Paris.
https://doi.org/10.1787/9789264307872-en

ISBN 978-92-64-30786-5 (print)
ISBN 978-92-64-30787-2 (pdf)

Series: Recruiting Immigrant Workers
ISSN 2225-7950 (print)
ISSN 2225-7969 (online)

The statistical data for Israel are supplied by and under the responsibility of the relevant Israeli authorities. The use of such data by the OECD is without prejudice to the status of the Golan Heights, East Jerusalem and Israeli settlements in the West Bank under the terms of international law.

Photo credits: © Jonathan Evans/Immagine ltd.

Corrigenda to OECD publications may be found on line at: *www.oecd.org/about/publishing/corrigenda.htm.*

Foreword

This review of Korea's labour migration policy is the ninth of a series conducted by the OECD Secretariat as a follow-up to the 2009 High Level Policy Forum on International Migration. The rationale for this initiative was the recent growth in labour migration observed in many countries and the likelihood that recourse to labour migration would increase in the context of demographic ageing. Prior to the global economic crisis of the late 2000s, many countries had made substantial changes to labour migration policies with a view to facilitating recruitment from abroad. With the introduction of these changes, more prominence was accorded to the question of their effectiveness, and more broadly to the objectives of labour migration policy in general. Although the economic crisis put a damper on labour migration movements, it did not stop them entirely, and interest in labour migration policy is unlikely to diminish in the near future.

The central objective of labour migration policy is to help meet those labour market needs which cannot be satisfied through tapping domestic labour supply in a reasonable time frame, without adversely affecting the domestic labour market and without hindering development prospects in vulnerable origin countries. Although the objective itself can be easily stated, specifying the criteria for assessing the success of policy in achieving it is a complex matter. It involves evaluating how well labour market needs have been identified and whether migration has had an impact on the labour market, both of which are analytically difficult.

This series of reviews addresses the question of whether labour migration policy is effective in meeting labour market needs without adverse effects, and whether the policy is efficient. To address these questions, this review aims to analyse two key areas: i) the labour migration system and its characteristics, in terms of policies in place and the labour migrants who arrive; and ii) the extent to which it is responding to the current and forecast needs of the domestic labour market, as well as any impact on the latter.

Korea faces a similar discussion as other OECD countries regarding effective labour migration policy, and it is in this context that Korea requested that the OECD review its labour migration policy. The temporary foreign worker programme introduced in Korea in the mid-2000s has led to a significant share of jobs in manufacturing SMEs being taken up by these workers. At the same time, Korea's globalisation strategy has aimed to attract more high-skilled foreigners and mobile talent, but numbers remain low.

This review asks the question of what should be the role of discretionary labour migration policy in the specific context of the country, given the profound structural changes underway in the Korean labour market and the challenges in ensuring human resources to maintain productivity and social cohesion in the future.

Acknowledgements

This review, the ninth in a series, was conducted by the OECD Secretariat as a follow-up to the 2009 High Level Policy Forum on International Migration. This review was written by Jonathan Chaloff, with statistical support from Veronique Gindrey and Jongmi Lee. Contributions were provided by Marina Belmonte, Wookyung Jung, Christina Kim, and Jongmi Lee. It benefited from valuable comments from Jean-Christophe Dumont. Delegates to the OECD Working Party on Migration discussed a draft of this Review in June 2018 and provided comments. The OECD Secretariat would like to thank the Ministry of Employment and Labour for its support for the Review. In addition, the Secretariat would like to thank the Ministry of Justice as well as Human Resources Development Korea for comments.

Table of contents

Tables

Figures

Boxes

Acronyms and abbreviations

BK21	Brain Korea 21
BLS	Basic Livelihood Security
CEPA	Comprehensive Economic Partnership Agreement
CPIK	Chinese Program in Korea
CPS	Current Population Survey
DGI	Departure Guarantee Insurance
EAPS	Economically Active Population Survey
EEA	European Economic Area
EITC	Earned Income Tax Credit
EMS	Employment Management System
EPIK	English Program in Korea
EPO	European Patent Office
EPS	Employment Permit System
EPS-TOPIK	Test of Proficiency in Korean for EPS
FDI	Foreign Direct Investment
FIMS	Student Information Management System
FLFS	Foreign Labour Force Survey
FWPC	Foreign Workforce Policy Committee
HRD Korea	Human Resources Development Service of Korea
ICT	Information and Communication Technology
IQEAS	International Education Quality Assurance System
ITS	Industrial Trainee System
KBiz	Korea Federation of Small and Medium Business
KDI	Korea Development Institute
KEDI	Korean Educational Development Institute
KEIS	Korea Employment Information Service
KESS	Korean Educational Statistics Service
KIPA	Korea Invention Promotion Association
KIS	Korea Immigration Service

KLI	Korea Labor Institute
KOICA	Korea International Cooperation Agency
KOSBI	Korea Small Business Institute
KOSIS	Korean Statistical Information Service
KOTRA	Korea Trade-Investment Promotion Agency
KPC	Korea Productivity Centre
KSGC	K-StartUp Grand Challenge
LMT	Labour Market Test
LPI	Low-Pay Incidence
MEST	Ministry of Education, Science, and Technology
MoEL	Ministry of Employment and Labour
MoJ	Ministry of Justice
MW	Minimum Wage
NEET	Not in Education, Employment or Training
NHI	National Health Insurance
NIIED	National Institute for International Education
OASIS	Overall Assistance for Startup Immigration System
OPT	Optional Practical Training
PBS	Points-Based System
PES	Public Employment Service
PIAAC	Programme for the International Assessment of Adult Competencies
SBA	Seoul Business Agency
SEVIS	Student and Exchange Visitor Information System
SILCLF	Survey on Immigrant's Living Conditions and Labour Force
SMBA	Small and Medium Business Administration
SME	Small- and medium-sized enterprise
SOL	Shortage Occupation List
TaLK	Teach and Learn in Korea
TFW	Temporary Foreign Worker
TSS	Temporary Skills Shortage
UI	Unemployment Insurance
USPTO	United States Patent and Trademark Office
WCU	World Class University
WHD	Wage and Hour Division
WHM	Working Holiday Maker

Executive summary

Labour migration is used as one of several responses to labour demand in certain sectors of the Korean labour market. Korea has an ageing population, a rapidly shrinking but unprecedentedly high-educated youth cohort, and a dual labour market with a large number of low quality jobs. Jobs in SMEs in the manufacturing sector are particularly unattractive to resident workers and hard to fill. Migration to Korea has grown in two decades, bringing the number of resident foreigners to about 3% of the population; in 2016, foreigners comprised 3.7% of the economically active population, below the OECD average. About half of all immigrants are from China, many of them arriving through work-visit programmes for ethnic Korean foreign nationals. The transition to permanent residence is high in this group. This review addresses the question of whether Korean labour migration policy ensures that international recruitment helps meet needs in the labour market which cannot be met locally. It examines key issues in the design of the Korean labour migration system, explores obstacles to labour migration for highly qualified foreigners and mobile global talent, and identifies where Korea can consider changes to make improvements.

Temporary foreign workers from other countries admitted for low skill jobs account for almost one in five foreign residents. One in ten Korean employers with five or more employees rely on filling some vacancies with foreign workers. To recruit from abroad for low skilled jobs, they must use the Employment Permit System, Korea's temporary labour migration programme There were almost 300 000 workers under the programme in Korea in 2018, and about 50 000 incoming workers, making it one of the largest programmes among OECD countries in absolute terms and relative to the size of the labour force. The programme primarily serves SMEs in the manufacturing sector, where these workers account for 10% of total employment.

The programme design has a number of unique features. It is based on bilateral agreements with 16 countries of origin, who co-manage selection. Candidates must pass a Korean language exam to be eligible. From a roster, Korean authorities select a list of potential candidates for employers. This procedure has largely eliminated the rent-taking and worker indebtedness that plague similar programmes elsewhere. The programme is managed by the government at no cost to employers, offering regular follow-up and intervention; services to workers; and support for return.

Safeguards for local workers from competition and substitution effects lie in three mechanisms: annual admission quotas, which cap entries; a mandatory advertising requirement prior to recruitment; and the distribution of employment permits favouring employers who hire local workers. The quotas keep demand for workers higher than supply. The labour market test – vacancy listing – is relatively undemanding in international comparison. The penalty/points system for attributing workers needs to be evaluated to examine its effect on local hiring and retention; turnover is high among resident workers due to low wages and difficult conditions. Further, most foreign workers reach maximum overtime, while residents work fewer hours.

The cost of employment is not considered as a mechanism to favour recruiting locally: the programme is designed to supply workers at minimum wage for non-skilled work. Workers may not voluntarily change employers without employer consent, which limits their ability to bargain for higher wages even as their productivity increases or as demand increases. The definition of the programme as exclusively non-skilled is in possible contradiction with measures to improve the skills of workers. Selection of candidates has been refined over the years to favour better qualified candidates: 20% have tertiary-level qualifications and most incoming workers have certified skills. The maximum duration of stay in Korea has been increased from three to five to almost ten years, meaning that many workers acquire language and vocational skills which increase their productivity, without being able to bargain for higher wages. Increases in minimum wage may have important effects on the programme, reducing employer interest or increasing the demand for skills. Several restrictive windows have been put in place to allow the most productive, highest paid and most skilled workers to transition to a temporary renewable work permit, although most workers are unable to qualify.

Korea has modernised its migration policy framework to reduce barriers to recruitment of highly skilled foreigners. Professional employees of foreign firms investing in Korea are treated particularly favourably, and few restrictions apply to recruitment for skilled jobs: no labour market test applies, and access to permanent residence is possible through accelerated procedures, including a points-based selection for talent. Notwithstanding this openness and some high-visibility initiatives to subsidise top talent, Korea has attracted few highly skilled foreigners and has retained even fewer. Workplace culture and a highly competitive labour market for tertiary-educated represent obstacles. One channel for recruitment is international students, who are more likely to be adapted to the Korean labour market and culture and to remain. Korea has increased enrolment at a rate faster than the OECD average, in part to respond to falling youth cohorts, but only 2% of higher-education students are international students.

The permit framework includes more than 170 subcategories of admission, of which more than 100 allow different forms of employment, each with its own eligibility criteria and conditions for changing status. The current division of permits into "professional" and "non-professional" categories means that many medium-skilled jobs are not labour market tested, although there is a list of authorised occupations.

In summary, the existing framework for labour migration has been successful in providing substantial labour input to a specific segment of the labour market in several sectors of the Korean economy, resolving many of the problems common in temporary labour programmes. However, it could be improved, including to adapt to changing skills demands in the country and profiles of labour migrants.

Assessment and recommendations

A favourable labour market situation

The employment situation in Korea is favourable, with low overall unemployment, of under 4%, although participation rates are low for women and for some groups, especially for women with children and young people, even those with higher education.

but a profound demographic transformation underway

Due to a sharp decline in fertility rates in the 1980s, Korea has one of the fastest aging populations in the OECD. The working age population reached its peak in 2016, at 37.6 million, and is declining by 0.2% per year; by 2030 it is expected to have fallen by 10%. The old-age dependency ratio – the number of people over 65 to the number of people 15-64 – is currently 19, one of the lowest in the OECD; it is expected to increase to 89 by 2065, when Korea will have the highest rate in the OECD.

and high educational attainment of youth cohorts

Korea has the highest share of young people enrolling in universities in the OECD and the highest share of people age 25-34 with tertiary degrees, 70% (OECD, 2017[1]). The share of young Koreans with less than secondary education is nominal. Further, according to PIAAC, the skills of Koreans even with only secondary education are among the highest in the OECD, indicating a very skilled young workforce.

Korea has seen the supply of younger less-educated workers diminish

Over the decade 2005-15, the combined effect of shrinking youth cohorts and higher educational attainment led to a sharp decline in the number of less-than-tertiary educated of 65%, from about 4 million people aged 25-34 to 1.4 million. This is by far the sharpest decline of any OECD country.

The less-educated workforce also counts many older workers, and overall is rapidly aging. In 2010, 88% of the less-educated workforce was over 45 years old. While workers over age 50 have a high participation rate in Korea, of almost 70%, older workers cannot compensate for the shrinking share of young workers without higher education qualifications entering the labour force. By 2025 the number of low-qualified young workers is expected to fall below 1 million. If there is not a drastic decline in the demand for less skilled workers, it will be increasingly difficult to fill these positions.

Korea still has a large number of jobs requiring little education and low skills

Export-oriented manufacturing was the driver of economic growth in the decades through the 1990s, and continues to be very important. Its share of employment stands at about 15%, having fallen less than in most other OECD countries in the past decade. The service sector has grown substantially and now accounts for 70% of employment. The agricultural sector has a small share of employment, generally low skilled. In the construction sector, which accounts for 7% of employment, many of the jobs are still low-skilled.

Most of these jobs are low-quality jobs

Since the 1990s, the labour market in Korea has become highly dual, with jobs in large firms and in the public sector offering security, higher wages and better working conditions, while those in small and medium enterprises offer less attractive conditions. In manufacturing especially, large firms have outsourced low-productivity elements of their supply chain to SMEs which operate under strong competitive pressure. Turnover is high in these firms and wages are low.

Korea's foreign population has grown quickly over the past two decades

Most of the immigrant population in Korea has foreign nationality. The foreign population with longer-term permits was almost 1.5 million at the end of 2016, or about 3% of the population. This number is twice the level in 2005 and well above the 1 million foreign residents identified in the 2010 Census. The number of foreigners holding short-term permits was about 350 000 and illegal overstayers numbered 200 000, primarily former visitors and tourists. In 2016, legally resident foreigners comprised about 3.7% of the economically active population, lower than the OECD average.

The foreign population comprises temporary workers of different nationalities and a growing permanent resident population

Of the foreigners in Korea in 2016, 38% were overseas Koreans. The temporary Work-Visit visa (H-2) (16%) was composed almost entirely of Korean Chinese and 74% of the F-4 visa for overseas Koreans (24%) was Korean Chinese. Temporary foreign workers who arrived under the bilateral programme for non-professional workers comprised 18%. Marriage migrants, primarily women who married Korean men through matchmaking services, comprised 8%. Marriage migrants accounted for about 15% of all foreign residents in 2010 but their share has since grown less rapidly than that of other groups, especially Korean-Chinese with permanent residence. Other permanent residents accounted for 9%. Students comprised 5% of foreign residents.

Korea has been active in developing a migration policy

Immigration policy in Korea is determined by the Immigration Policy Committee, a committee under the Prime Minister in which the lead ministry is the Ministry of Justice. This Committee, starting in 2008, has developed five-year Basic Plans on migration and integration, mapping priorities for labour migration; the third Basic Plan 2018-22 was released in 2018. The Basic Plans have largely addressed migration management and the integration framework, without specifying the role that foreign workers are expected to play in specific sectors of the Korean economy and labour market, especially the role of less-skilled temporary migration and the need to carefully monitor and manage it. The Basic Plans have highlighted internationalisation of higher education, access to the global talent pool, and attracting investors.

Employer use of foreign workers has increased in low quality jobs, initially without a strong policy direction

Starting in the late 1980s, foreign workers started to be employed in these jobs. Initially, Korea admitted foreigners under an internship programme, which grew sharply in the 1990s and was rife with abuse. There was widespread rent-taking by intermediaries in the recruitment process in origin countries, and many highly indebted interns arrived and were employed not as trainees but as workers without respect for conditions of labour law, while others sought employment outside the terms of their permit. There was also a high overstay rate. By the late 1990s, there were almost 200 000 overstaying foreign workers, and about 100 000 interns.

In the mid-2000s, Korea instituted a formal policy for temporary employment of foreign workers, EPS

The watershed moment for foreign worker policy in Korea was in 2004, with the introduction of the Employment Permit System (EPS). This policy had two main components. The first was a programme for admission of temporary foreign workers for up to three years, through bilateral agreements, with workers assigned to employers in a fixed number of sectors through quotas. The second was a programme for admission of ethnic Koreans abroad – primarily Chinese – to visit and work in Korea for up to almost five years, subject to restrictions on their employment in certain sectors.

The programme has expanded since introduction to account for a large share of employment in certain sectors

Since its introduction, the number of workers employed under bilateral agreements has risen to 294 000, or 10% of the manufacturing sector employment, and has become an integral part of the labour force of SMEs in manufacturing and agriculture, despite the restrictions placed on which firms are allowed to recruit foreign workers and a ceiling, at the firm level, on employment of some categories of foreign workers. The programme for ethnic Korean Chinese rapidly reached its ceiling of 303 000, although it has fallen in recent years as many participants have changed status to permanent residence. About 10% of employers with more than five employees rely on filling at least some vacancies with foreign workers; this share has remained steady in recent years and reflects the use of foreign workers by a specific type of firm in Korea.

The programme provides low-cost workers to firms that struggle to remain competitive

Low-skilled temporary worker programmes may allow certain firms to delay or maintain a low level of investment. Korea has made the decision with EPS to provide firms with a certain quantity of low-skilled workers, albeit with safeguards against a negative effect on resident workers. EPS is designed in such a way as to limit competition for available foreign workers, which could drive up wages; about two-thirds of participants earn minimum monthly wage, and hourly wages are lower than the Korean average in SMEs in the manufacturing industry. Many OECD countries have similar programmes in seasonal agricultural jobs, to maintain the viability and low prices of this sector; some have programmes for household care workers or other seasonal or one-time needs. Korea is rare in the extent of the programme and in the design of the programme.

One policy concern is to increase the cost of employing foreign workers in order to protect resident workers. One proposal under consideration is to introduce a levy to increase employer cost. However, real wage increases would also increase costs, and this could be achieved through the points-based system by distributing work permits to the highest-paying firms.

The EPS model is a government-to-government model with all phases of employment overseen

EPS is unique among OECD countries in its scale and comprehensiveness. Potential candidates must pass a basic Korean language test in order to enter a pool managed by the government in the origin country. For each position in Korea, three potential candidates are identified, who must pass a physical strength and capacity test. The list of candidates sent to employers reflects employer preferences for nationality, gender and age, as well as specific skills. Employer preference for nationality is respected up to a point, since EPS also ensures that all participating partner countries are included in the recruitment. Employers choose one of the candidates. However, asking employers to express a preference by nationality, age or gender in the recruitment process is not in line with Korean antidiscrimination standards and should be addressed. The Korean government agency administering the programme, HRD Korea, brings workers to Korea and provides ongoing support to EPS workers, with initial training and pre-return and post-return training, as well as supporting employers and workers during their stay.

Foreign workers are assigned to employers based on a number of different criteria

Admission quotas are set below the demand for foreign workers. Employers must labour market test their demand for foreign workers, and only if they are unable to fill the position after a mandatory advertising period and after reviewing workers sent by the public employment services are they allowed to recruit. Employers apply to use the EPS system for workers and, in two to four annual draws, are assigned a number of permits for employment corresponding to the number of

EPS workers they may employ. Initially, permits were divided among employers in the sector; since 2014, permits have been allocated to employers based on a points system ranking prior compliance and the share of EPS workers among their workforce. Lower shares of foreign workers are rewarded with more workers, although firm-level ceilings are quite high, with small firms allowed to have almost all their workers through EPS. The points system also penalises employers for severe abuses of workers. Employers who have been sentenced to at least imprisonment for sexual violence, etc. will be prohibited from getting issued a certificate of visa issuance for foreign workers for five years. For employers who have been punished for assault, sexual violence, etc., the punishment they have faced will be weighted in the PBS, rather than automatically disqualifying them from receiving further workers. The government should make efforts to prevent unpaid wages through safeguards, such as deducting points under the PBS.

There is no sector mobility and limited job mobility for EPS workers

EPS workers, once admitted, are expected to stay with their initial employer unless they are subject to illegal employment practices or firm closure. Workers may request up to three voluntary changes of the employer during their work period for legitimate reasons, with the employer's consent. Employers may be unwilling to release their workers due not only to the high initial investment in participation in the programme and in training workers but also to the shortage of labour. However, in cases of unpaid wages and working condition violations, there is no limit on the authorized number of workplace changes. There are no limits to changing workplaces due to violation of the employment contract such as the employer's violation of working conditions and unfair treatment. Job mobility has been a point of contention. The mechanism for job changes should be examined. With the introduction of a points-based system, for example, it would be possible to allow workers to transfer to higher-ranked employers who have not fulfilled their allotment; this would be transparent and would encourage greater compliance with programme regulations.

Job mobility provisions could improve compliance

While illegal employer practices allow job change, poor but legal working conditions prevail in these sectors – explaining the high turnover of Korean workers. Mobility constraints in EPS eliminate incentives for employers to improve the competitiveness of working conditions. Employers may also provide lodging and board, for which they are allowed to deduct costs; there is no incentive to improve housing conditions. A proposal to allow workers in agriculture to change employers in the case of poor housing conditions or excessive rent charges could be implemented and extended to other sectors.

The EPS has reduced the abuses associated with temporary labour migration programmes

Prior to its introduction, low-skilled labour migrants paid high rents to intermediaries and their debt made them vulnerable to abuse and more likely to illegally overstay. Migrant recruitment costs have been substantially lowered through EPS. Low wages are prevalent in SMEs in the manufacturing and services sector for Korean workers. EPS does not require employers to report payment of minimum monthly wage, but evidence suggests that EPS workers earn the minimum monthly wage – and about one-third earn more than that. Reported working hours of 60 hours per week however raise the concern that overtime is not consistently being paid. Competition among firms for EPS workers could be further supported to grant workers more protection, authorising more employment permits to firms than available workers and allowing workers a slightly greater degree of in-sector and in-region mobility.

Measures to reduce illegal overstay have been partially successful

One of the main concerns regarding low-skilled foreign workers is the risk of overstay; EPS was introduced partially to prevent overstay. The rate – 16.3% in 2016 – is comparable to temporary work programmes with similar characteristics in other OECD countries. Korea uses two main mechanisms to discourage overstay. The first is the Departure Guarantee Insurance, a payroll contribution paid by the employer. The insurance pays severance at departure, and the worker receives these funds at the airport or within 14 days of returning home. Court cases have ruled that overstayers have a right to this fund. The fund could be structured to ensure that it is fully paid for timely departure and withheld progressively for longer overstay. The second mechanism is to place pressure on the origin country to suspend recruitment; this has been used to effect with several origin countries. Softer measures include working with returning workers to help them find work with Korean firms in their origin country, and publicising this possibility. These could be expanded.

Compliance and transparency could be reinforced using new technology

While EPS workers earn at least minimum wage, there is as noted some concern over non-payment of overtime. In addition, foreign workers in Korea participate in four separate insurance schemes, of which they contribute to two, while employers contribute to the other two. Insurances include a set-aside which is returned to the worker upon departure. To improve transparency, the existing app for EPS workers should allow workers to predict, calculate and track their individual accumulated deposits and severance pay rights.

Duration of stay has been increased from three to five to ten years

When introduced, the maximum stay was three years, considered a sufficient time to recover the investment in training by the worker, the programme administration and the firm. However, many workers acquired firm-specific skills and improved their language ability and productivity, so that at the end of the first three-year period, employer pressure led to an introduction of a 22-month extension. When this deadline was reached, provisions were made for "diligent" workers (those who remained with their employer for the entire period) to return to Korea, as well as workers capable of passing a more advanced language test. These workers would return home, for three months for diligent workers and six months for other returning workers, before re-entering Korea. When the first workers approached the 10-year mark, no further extensions were granted. Of all permits in OECD countries, EPS has the longest temporary low-skilled work permit duration where no settlement or family reunification is allowed, more than Israel (five years) or the United States (three years).

Provisions for returning workers have been enthusiastically taken up

The provision for diligent workers has been taken up by employers and workers; employers have preferred to retain their veteran employees, rather than start again with new EPS workers. The skills and language ability, as well as familiarity with firm practices, acquired during the five years of diligent work appear to be of value for employers. It would be reasonable to expect a wage threshold for returning workers, especially if the firm does not undergo a new labour market test for the vacancy for which they worker is returning. A higher re-entry wage would also be a means to encourage employers to hire resident workers, since there is no labour market test for employing a diligent worker.

More opportunity to remain for more skilled EPS workers

In principle, EPS workers are not allowed to change status. In 2011 a small window for status change was opened to allow workers who had acquired specialised skills, received a higher salary, and held higher education qualifications to change status to an E-7 visa; this visa is indefinitely renewable, allows family reunification and a pathway to permanent residence. About one in five EPS workers holds tertiary qualifications in the home country, suggesting initially a large pool of potential users. However the skills certification and salary requirement proved too high for most workers and take up was minimal. In 2014, the bridge to the E-7 was further widened, with education and skills criteria reduced. Fewer than 300 EPS workers qualified for this status change in 2015. In 2017, a further bridge was introduced, favouring future status change. Higher-productivity EPS workers should be encouraged to use these bridges.

The shift towards more selectivity may mean that future EPS workers will be more productive

After more than a decade of imposing only a basic Korean language test and a strength test, Korea introduced in 2016 the possibility for EPS candidates to increase their chances of selection through additional "points" for experience or certificates of training or government-issued qualifications in the fields sought after. High points can even substitute a poor Korean language test result, which otherwise blocked experienced candidates. The shift towards selecting more experienced and skilled workers for EPS will likely increase their value to employers – important if the new higher minimum wage introduced from 2018 to 2020 is to be respected. However, this higher value for employers may also mean more of them will transition from temporary to renewable long-term status. The use of a points system for low-skilled workers is a novelty in OECD countries. Going forward, it is possible that there will be a tension between the objective of the EPS, to provide low skill workers, and the increased efforts to select foreign workers according to their adaptability and to support the development of skills of participants. The wage effects of higher productivity should be monitored.

Bringing higher-skilled and higher-productivity workers into EPS represents a change in the non-professional model, which justifies the sector and job mobility restrictions. Higher skill EPS workers will find it easier to shift to permits such as E-7, which allow job mobility. The occupational restrictions that currently ensure that they do not compete unfairly with skilled Korean workers would no longer apply, which raises the question of whether a labour market test would be appropriate at the transition from EPS to long-term stay.

The seasonal worker programme in agriculture needs to be monitored closely

EPS was not designed for seasonal employment. Concern over potential overstay long prevented introduction of a seasonal agricultural workers programme until a 2015 pilot, involving local authorities, who could sponsor seasonal workers themselves or allow foreign residents (marriage migrants) to nominate their relatives. Several hundred workers came through the programme. This is an unusual model for seasonal workers; most countries try to avoid ties between seasonal workers and local actors or residents, to ensure departure. While overstay was not a problem in the pilot, allowing local residents to propose nomination to the local authority raises the risk of rent-taking from which the EPS programme has so far been largely insulated. The programme is less designed to meet labour demand than to provide a work-visit permit to relatives of migrants. If the programme is to expand, Korea should consider the seasonal work models used in Canada and Spain for example, where bilateral agreements are in place and repeat rates are high.

The EMS Work-Visit programme has gradually lost restrictions and workers have gone primarily into the service sector and construction, with many transitioning to permanent residence

Ethnic Korean Chinese have been coming to Korea for employment on different grounds since the late 1980s; most speak Korean. The system became the Work-Visit for ethnic Koreans in 2007 with numerical restrictions on sectors of employment, these quotas were eliminated in 2009 (except for the construction sector). H-2 workers are allowed to be employed in about 80 occupations. In 2013, 38% of H-2 workers were in the manufacturing sector, while 27% worked in the restaurant and hospitality sector and 17% in construction. In 2010, H-2 visa holders were granted access to the F-4 long-term residence visa if they met criteria on one of three grounds (age, employment in a rural sector, and passing a vocational certification). It was relatively easy to qualify for vocational certification, since some were easily obtained even if the worker had no intention of working in that occupation (although occupational restrictions apply to F-4 visa holders). As a result, the number of F-4 visa holders rose from 190 000 in 2012 to 373 000 in 2016, while the number of H-2 Work Visit residents has fallen below its ceiling, although it remains in the mid-200 000s. Ethnic Korean Chinese now account for 30% of long-term foreign residents. However, half of the adult Korean-Chinese foreigners are over 50 years old, compared with 15% for other foreigners; 52% are women. As this group is aging both in Korea and in China, it cannot be considered a long-term source of foreign labour. At the same time, the language requirement for ethnic Koreans has been lifted; since those coming from countries of the former Soviet Union have poor Korean language skills, any increase in flows from these countries will have implications for the integration of this group.

Foreigners are ineligible for a number of key benefits offered working Koreans

Foreigners, with the exception of those belonging to a household that includes a Korean citizen, do not have access to income support (the Basic Livelihood Security Programme) or to the EITC, the primary forms of income support for low-income working Koreans. While this may have made sense as long as workers were in Korea for short periods with no prospect of settlement, for the growing number of long-term and permanent-residence holders (there are more than 600 000, including family members of Korean nationals), equal access to income support appears important, especially since wages remain low for so many of them.

Highly qualified foreign workers are recruited mostly for export-oriented positions rather than to meet general skills shortages

Due to high educational attainment and an oversupply of qualified young people, there is no broad shortage of highly skilled workers. However, Korea has a favourable framework for work permit authorisation for qualified foreigners, with a large number of separate programmes. The strategy for attracting highly skilled foreign workers focuses primarily on supporting export activity, FDI and knowledge transfer, rather than securing skilled labour force. In some cases, such as employees of firms investing in Korea, processing work permits is instant and paperwork is simplified. Korea has introduced a number of special visas for investors, including for start-up firms. Large-scale investors acquire immediate permanent residence and the right to bring their families as permanent residents.

International student enrolment has started to grow again, but the higher education sector should be under close observation

Korea has an excellent tertiary education system producing highly qualified university graduates. Universities have a strong incentive to boost international enrolment as they face a decline in native numbers and because the Ministry of Education considers "internationalisation" in its quality index. Korea is attractive to foreign students, most of whom come without government scholarships. Although the share of international students in higher education in Korea is still low (about 2%), it rose sharply in 2014-17, from 85 000 to 124 000, after several years of plateau due to stricter verification of admission criteria. Many (41%) are language students or non-degree students.

In 2013, only 6% of graduating international students found a job in Korea; the job market for international graduates is difficult because few firms are seeking their profile. There is concern that many foreign students come to Korea for employment during their studies only, and many of the lower-ranked universities have little incentive to impose close selection on international students. This has been improved and a new compliance system put in place. Use of international rankings should take into account foreign student performance rather than enrolment.

A large number of permit categories are offered to qualified foreign workers, each with its own requirements and processing standards

Even excluding visitors, short-term stays and diplomatic categories, Korea has about 170 permit sub-categories for study, employment, and family. Different family categories account for about 40, and study for about 15, leaving a large number of categories for investors and workers. Korea has a number of longer-term residence categories – F visas – all of which qualify as residence for naturalisation. Some F visas grant permanent residence without employment restrictions but others do not, and the benefits of each visa in terms of duration and family reunification vary. Status changes among these visas are not uncommon. These visas could be simplified by eligibility criteria and associated rights and requirements.

This is partly due to occasionally overlapping initiatives by different ministries

Co-ordination of migration initiatives occurs through a 5-year Basic Plan setting out priorities and assessing achievements, with an associated budget. Ministries launch and promote their own initiatives, leading to the creation of specific and sometimes overlapping visa categories and initiatives for specific groups (high-level scholars, status-changing investors).

The division of permits into "non-professional" and "professional" should be reviewed.

Korea separates its permit categories into non-professional and professional. Only the E-9 non-professional permit requires a labour market test. The E-7 visa, the catch-all category for employment in one of more than 80 occupations, is not labour market tested, even if it covers about 20 occupations requiring lower skill levels where a 20% firm-level ceiling on foreign workers applies. Korea should consider separating the E-7 visa into a labour-market tested permit and a high-skilled labour-market test-exempt permit, as in many other OECD countries. Further, a large share of what are classified as "professional" visas are actually foreign-language teachers, who are low-paid and work in instable employment, often unemployed and using a bridging visa between jobs. Some free-lancers bridge to other sectors using a job-search visa. In light of this, the language teacher visa should be a bridge to permanent residence only in the presence of meeting an appropriate income threshold.

Summary of the main recommendations for Korea

Reorganise permit categories in light of long-term migration strategy

- Clarify the role of immigration in meeting short-term and structural labour needs in the medium term, to clarify to employers their options for recruiting and to students their post-graduation options.
- Simplify the wide range of permit grounds to clarify temporary non-renewable, temporary renewable and permanent permit classes. Separate and simplify permanent residence visas, through possible extension of the current F-2 points system.
- Consider separating the E-7 permit into labour-market tested medium-skilled permits and labour-market test-exempt higher skilled permits.
- Points-based selection for different permits (F-2, E-7, investor permits, etc.) could be opened to applicants from any prior status meeting criteria, rather than apply to specific status change channels.

Reinforce mechanisms to prevent employers from becoming dependent on lower-productivity E-9 workers and to provide incentives for improving working conditions

- The points based system could take into account recent hiring behaviour of employers, penalising those who lay off resident workers after hiring E-9 workers
- The government should make efforts to award more permits to firms which improve the quality of jobs.
- Penalties should be imposed on employers who abuse workers.
- Firms with higher scores under the PBS could be allowed to recruit more foreign workers than lower-scored firms.
- If mechanisms to increase cost to employers and favour hiring of resident workers are implemented, higher wages should be preferred to employer levies.
- E-9 workers who are skilled, or have acquired skills and abilities in Korea, should have opportunities to work in professional fields and change residential status.

Improve equal treatment for foreign workers

- Do not ask employers for age, gender and nationality preference for EPS workers.
- Allow foreigners with permanent residence equal access to income support benefits.

Improve the potential of labour migration programmes to meet a wider range of needs

- Together with a clear 10-year limit to E-9 employment, inform participants and employers of criteria for bridging from E-9 to E-7. Consider allowing transition through points to be accumulated during the years of E-9 employment.
- Expand the seasonal agricultural worker programme cautiously, allowing local authorities to sponsor seasonal workers on condition of low overstay rates. Future development, based on interinstitutional co-operation between national and local authorities, could lead to establish bilateral agreements for seasonal workers with key partner countries granting repeat spells of employment.
- Reinforce outreach to employers, especially larger employers, to support employment of international students
- Evaluate the outcomes of investors under the D-8 and other investor visa programmes in terms of the economic impact of investments and the effective residence of investor visa holders. Make renewal conditional on business outcomes but maintain favourable bridge to permanent residence.

Promote the integrity of the system and improve compliance

- Maintain caution on enrolment of international students, requiring proof of entrance criteria and devoting particular supervision to language courses where students are granted, and use, labour market access.
- The departure guarantee insurance should be able to be tracked as an individual account.

Collect detailed data and conduct analysis to inform future reforms on a number of important issues

- Consider creating a Secretariat at the Foreign Workforce Policy Committee to commission and analyse empirical analyses of the impact of foreign workers on the economy and labour market, and to propose policy measures in response to queries or mandates from the government.
- Examine firm data for firms allocated foreign workers to understand the effect on employment and wages of Korean workers in these firms, and the survival rates of these firms, relative to firms which did not request, and those which did not receive, foreign workers.
- Track the outcomes of international students more closely.

Chapter 1. Context for Labour Migration

This chapter discusses developments in Korea that have implications for the role of labour migration. The development of the Korean economy is presented, in terms of its segmentation. The demographic trend of an aging population and a shrinking youth cohort is described. The chapter notes the high rate of tertiary education among young Koreans, and the relatively low education and skill level of the generation of Koreans currently heading into retirement. Vacancy data suggests continued demand for workers in firms offering low-quality jobs requiring little education. The chapter notes that young Koreans are an ill-fit with the jobs being vacated by retiring older workers.

The statistical data for Israel are supplied by and under the responsibility of the relevant Israeli authorities. The use of such data by the OECD is without prejudice to the status of the Golan Heights, East Jerusalem and Israeli settlements in the West Bank under the terms of international law.

Korea's economy: growth and sectors

From one of the least developed countries in the world in the late 1950s, Korea has become one of the most developed. From a situation of widespread unemployment and poverty, wages rose rapidly across the Korean economy between the 1960s and 1980s, and near-full employment (unemployment rates of 2-4%) was achieved by the late 1980s. In 2016, Korean GDP per capita was less than 10% below the OECD average, and Korea ranked in the upper half of OECD countries in terms of GDP per capita.

Figure 1.1. Korea's economic development has been impressive

Thousands of US dollars at constant prices and 2010 PPPs (Panel A) and percentages (Panel B)

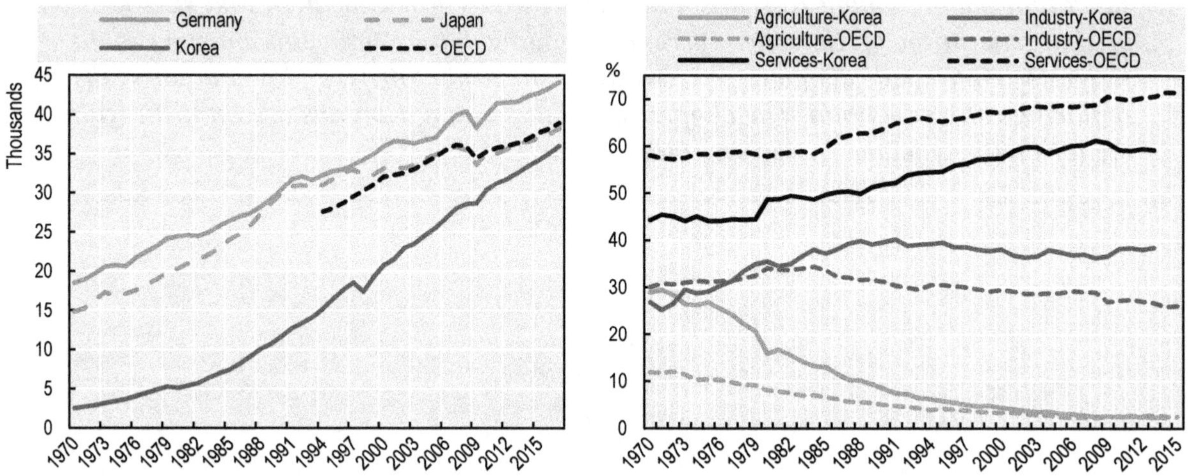

a) Weighted average of the 35 OECD countries.
b) Unweighted average of 33 OECD countries (Israel and Switzerland were excluded due to unavailable data).

Source: OECD Productivity Database, http://stats.oecd.org/Index.aspx?DataSetCode=PDB_LV, Productivity and ULC – Annual, Total Economy, "Level of GDP per capita and productivity" for Panel A; and OECD Annual National Accounts Database, http://stats.oecd.org/Index.aspx?DataSetCode=SNA_TABLE6A, Detailed Tables and Simplified Accounts, "Table 6A. Value added and its components by activity, ISIC Rev. 4" for Panel B.

The employment rate in Korea has been rising for the past three decades, from 57% in 1986 to 63.9% in 1997, prior to the crisis of the late 1990s, when it fell to 59.2%. The 2000s saw employment rise again, to 63.9% in 2007, and only a one point decline during the crisis of the late 1990s. It is now at record levels, of 66.3% in 2016. However, these high employment levels hide a wide gap in the employment rate between men and women. Since 2000, the employment rate for men has been largely constant, close to the OECD level; while the employment rate for women has been slowly rising but remains almost 20 points below that of men, twice the gap of the OECD as a whole (Figure 1.2). Further, contrary to other OECD countries, Korea's gender employment gap increases with the level of education. In 2015, the gender employment gap (the difference between male and female employment rate as a share of the male employment rate) for tertiary-educated women was 30%, the highest among OECD countries. The gap for less educated women was smaller, less than 20%, and below the average for OECD countries.

Figure 1.2. The employment rate for women is much lower than for men

Percentage of the working-age population, 2000-16, by gender

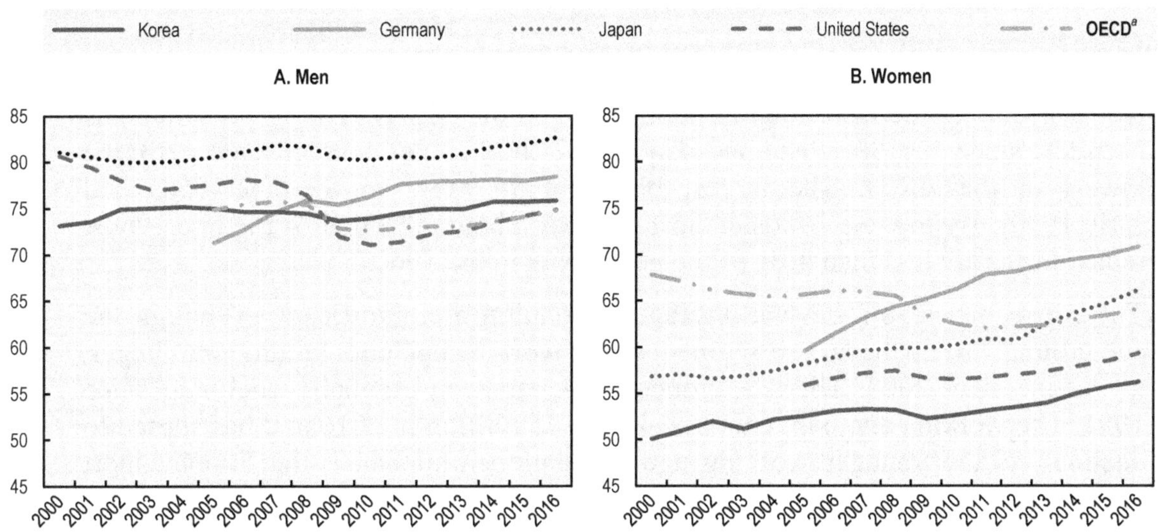

Note: a) Weighted average of OECD countries.
Source: *OECD Employment Database*, www.oecd.org/employment/database.

In terms of sectors of employment, in 2016 services were the main type of sector, accounting for 60% of employment. The manufacturing sector accounted for 14.6%. However, the share of employment in manufacturing fell by just 0.3 percentage points from 2006 to 2016, compared with about 2% in other OECD countries, indicating the continuing importance of manufacturing.

Regardless of sector, however, employment in Korea has increasingly been characterised by a dual labour market. Large enterprises and the public sector offer higher wages and better working conditions than small and medium-sized enterprises. SMEs often have low firm survival rates and offer low-quality jobs (minimum wage or worse, poor working conditions, high turnover).

A distinguishing feature of employment in Korea is the outsized role of SMEs (firms with fewer than 300 employees) in terms of employment. This is particularly true in the service sector, where SMEs comprise 90% of employment and 85% of added value. In the manufacturing sector, SMEs account for 81% of employment, but only 41% of added value. In other words, productivity in manufacturing SMEs is about 5.5 times lower than in large manufacturing firms. This gap is the largest among OECD countries. By comparison, in Japan the ratio is about 1.3, while in the United States, SMEs in manufacturing are more productive than large firms.

Employment in large firms has been declining since the 1990s, from 22.6% in 1993 to 13.6% in 2014. In manufacturing, the decline in large firm employment has been more severe: from 35.3% in 1993 to 19% in 2014. There has been a corresponding boom in the number of small (10-19 employees) and very small (1-9 employees) firms. Self-employment is quite high, at 25.5% in 2016, when compared with the OECD average of 15.8%. The majority of the self-employed are former wage workers, often early retirees.

Demographic context

Korea is among the fastest aging populations in the OECD. The fertility rate has been low since the 1980s, and has stood at 1.2 children per woman since 2013, the lowest in the OECD. The largest birth cohorts were in the late 1960s and early 1970s. By the late 1980s, cohort size was about 60% that of the late 1960s; today, births are less than 40% of the peak years in the 1960s.

The consequences on the working age population are significant. Although the age group 25-49 is the largest segment of the working age population, it has begun to decline since 2008. The age group 15-24 has been gradually declining since 1991. The working age population peaked at 35 million in 2016 and has started to decline. As the younger working age population diminished, the 50-64 cohort already exceeded that of the 15-24 group by the early 2000s. The 50-64 is projected to soon approach the size of the 25-49 population. However, even the 50-64 population is predicted to decrease beginning 2024. Following projections from Statistics Korea, the share of the working-age population is expected to decline from 73.1% in 2013 – the highest in the OECD - to 63.1% in 2030 and 49.7% in 2060. At that point, the population over the age of 65 is projected to comprise 40.1% of the population, and the population under 15 to comprise just 10.2%. The projection model used here does not, however, include migration.

According to UN projections, the old-age dependency ratio in Korea will increase more than in any other OECD country between 2015 and 2060 (Figure 1.3).

Figure 1.3. Korea will have the largest increase in its old-age dependency ratio between 2015 and 2060

Number of people of retirement age (65+) per 100 people of working-age (20-64), in 1970, 2015 and 2060

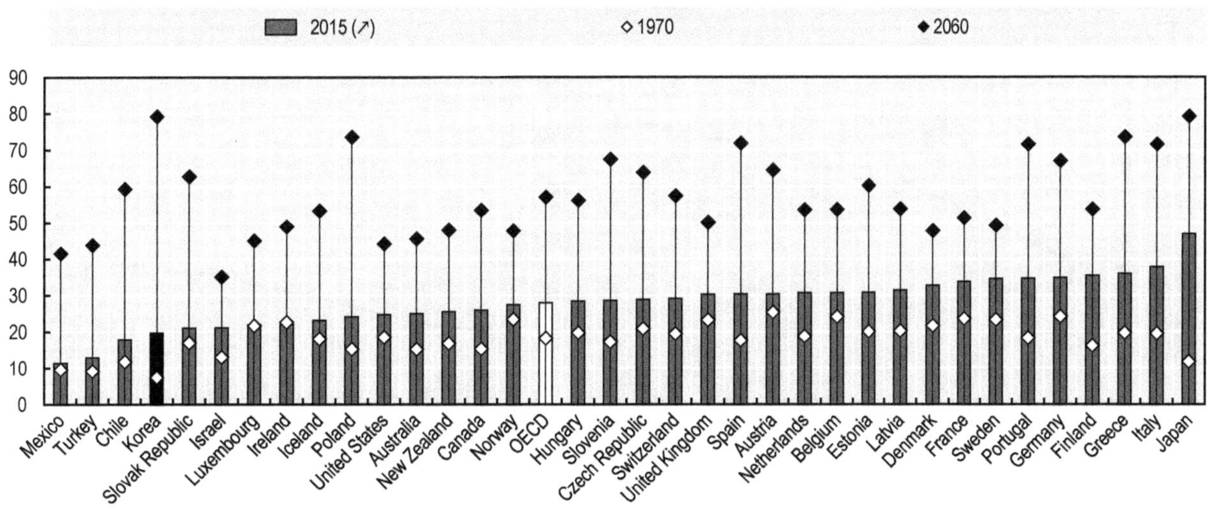

Source: Calculations from United Nations, World Populations Prospects - 2015 Revisions.

A highly educated youth population

In addition to the rapidly aging population and imminent decline in the working-age population, another particularity in Korea is the extremely high educational attainment of the labour force, especially the younger age cohorts. Korea has the highest proportion of people aged 25 to 34 with tertiary education among OECD countries, and a large share of students progresses into tertiary education. The high school graduation rate is the highest among the OECD countries, above 93%. According to the Ministry of Education, 77.3% of general high school graduates and 32.8% of vocational high school graduates were enrolled in post-secondary programmes in 2017. This represents a decline from 2009 (when the share was 85% and 74% respectively). Until recently, both general and vocational high schools had encouraged students to pursue post-secondary studies.

The highly educated are expected to account more than half of the people in the labour force by the mid-2020s (Figure 1.4). The surge in tertiary educated became evident from the beginning of the 2000s – the number of highly educated exceeded the low educated in 2003 and the medium educated in 2012. At present, 86% of the active population has at least upper secondary education or above, of which 52% is tertiary educated.

According to projections by KEIS (Park et al., 2015[1]), this trend is expected to continue (Figure 1.4, Panel A). The KEIS projections even appear conservative, since the actual trend line is steeper through 2016 for both less educated and more educated workers.

Figure 1.4. Decline in active population is only in the least-educated segment

Economically active population, observed and projections, 2000-30, by education and age.

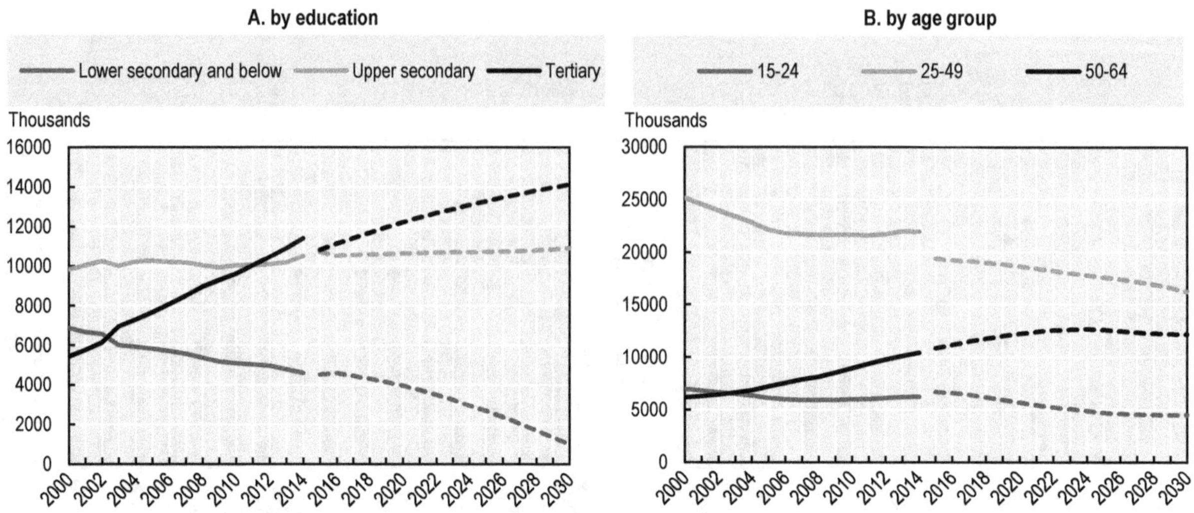

Note: Panel A; Values until 2010 are real observed value. Panel B: Observed until 2014.
Source: Panel A: Society with 100-year life expectancy, Prospects and Counterparts on Employment and Job 2010, KEIS (Park et al., 2015[1]). Panel B: EAPS (2000-14); Population Projections for Korea: 2010-30 (Based on the 2010 Census), Kostat

When looking into working-age population divided by age and education level, the evolution is even more striking. Figure 1.5, based on the 2015 Census, shows that the age cohort entering the labour force has very different characteristics from that which is leaving the labour force. Regarding educational attainment, generations entering and leaving the working-age population have opposite characteristics. Among those 55 to 64 years of age, 39% have less than upper secondary education. The low-educated accounted for an overwhelming majority among those 65 and older in 2015, who were leaving or have largely left the labour market by now. There are now few similarly low educated workers to step into their shoes.

Significant gender disparity concerning education attainment is another feature of this generation compared to the younger population (82.8% of women aged over 65 do not have high school degrees). On the other hand, the educational attainment is quite different for the middle-aged working population. Among those 45-54, the upper-secondary educated are the majority for the first time, and the tertiary educated exceed high-school graduates among those aged 35-44. The situation changes markedly for the youngest generation. 70.8% out of those aged 25-34 are tertiary educated and the gender disparity disappears. As for those aged 15-24 who are entering the labour force, not only does the overall size of the population diminish, but there is a further tendency towards higher education. Considering that population in schooling is included in this group and 68.9% of the upper secondary graduates are enrolled in post-secondary school (Ministry of

Education, 2017[2]), it is likely that the 15-24 cohort would follow a similar pattern as the 25-34 cohort.

Figure 1.5. Younger cohorts are much better educated than older cohorts

Distribution of working age population by age and education in 2015

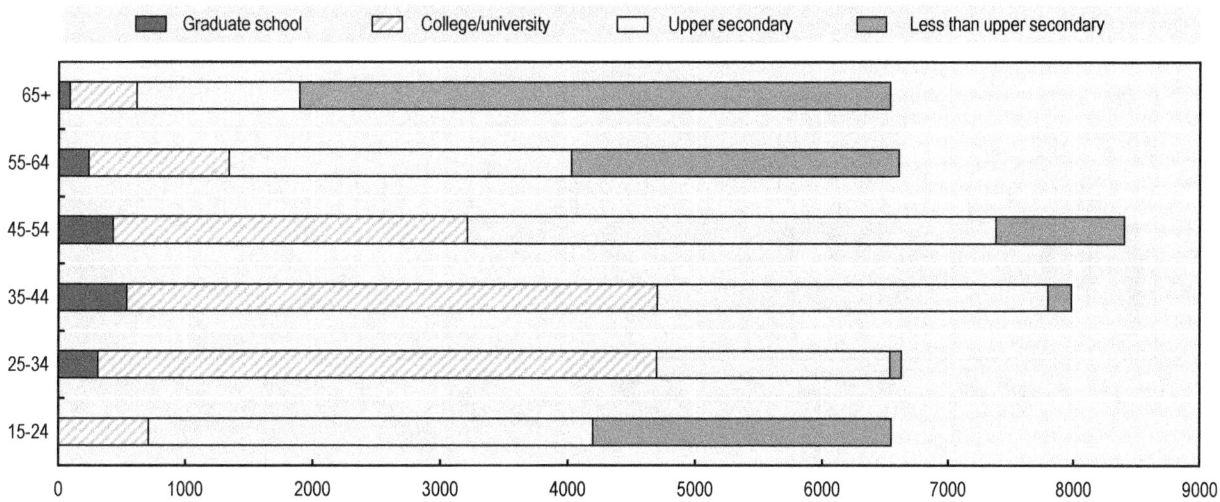

Source: Kosis, 2015 Census.

There are now few young people to take low-skilled jobs. The combined effect of rising education levels and shrinking youth cohorts is that there are relatively few young people with less than tertiary education. Indeed, the population entering working age with less than tertiary education is much smaller than it was just a decade earlier. The number of people aged 25-34 in Korea with less than tertiary education fell from 4 million in 2005 to 1.4 million in 2015. The dramatic change in the Korean labour force occurred in a very short time span; no other OECD country has seen a similar contraction over such a short period (Figure 1.6). Further, over the same period, the number of people aged 25-34 with tertiary education increased from 4.2 million to 5.7 million. As a result, there is a significant gap between the qualifications of vacancies that the older generation is creating with their retirement, and that of the jobs for which the younger generation has trained and which it is willing to fill. Young high-skilled Koreans face a job market in which there are not enough high-skilled jobs, but they have not shown a great interest in taking up employment – especially in manufacturing jobs in SMEs – where skill demands are basic, conditions are poor and wages are low.

Figure 1.6. Korea has seen the largest decline in the OECD in its less-than tertiary educated youth cohort over the past decade

Change in the population age 25-34 with tertiary education and less than tertiary education, 2005-15

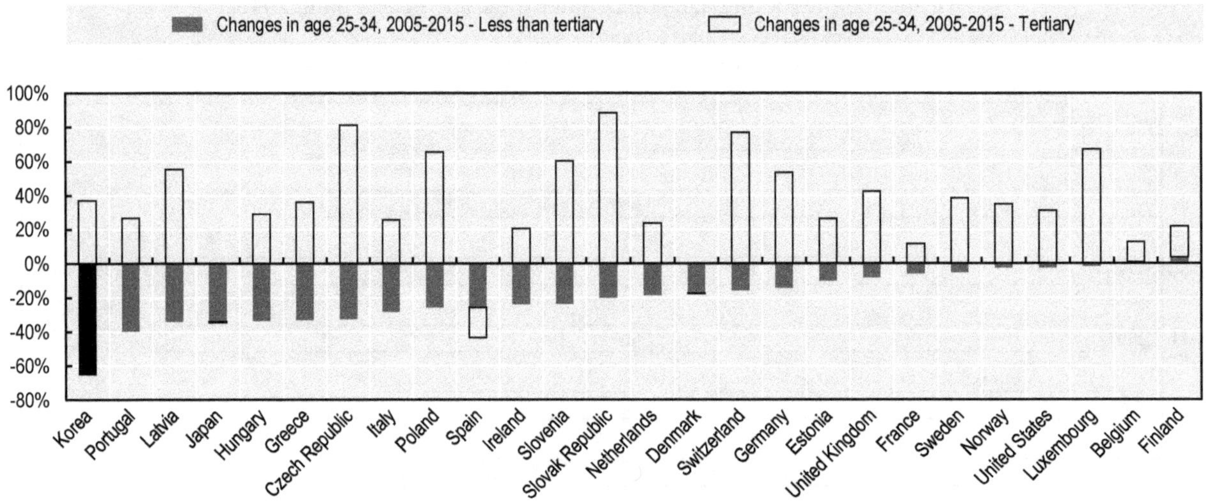

Source: Labour Force Surveys.

Even among the non-tertiary educated, young Koreans have very high skill levels. According to PIAAC, Korean young people are among the most skilled in the OECD, with literacy and numeracy scores comparable to the highest levels within the OECD (OECD, 2013[31]). Remarkably, literary proficiency among Korean young people with less than secondary education is very high, comparable almost to those with tertiary education and much higher than similarly-educated young people in other OECD countries. This suggests a very high quality education system, and that even non-tertiary educated Koreans may be overqualified for jobs requiring only basic skills and involving routine tasks. Also notably, the gap in PIAAC literacy and numeracy scores between the younger (16-24) and older (55-65) groups is very wide – 50 points – pointing to a large gap between the skills of younger and older workers. This is the largest gap within the OECD countries, and again raises the question of who will be willing to step into the jobs vacated by the older, retiring generation.

Current labour market conditions and labour shortages

Current labour market conditions in Korea are favourable in comparison with other OECD countries. The proportion of working-age population (15-64) in employment was at 68.3% in 2015, although the absolute size of the working age population, as noted, has begun to diminish. Employment levels remained high during the global financial crisis of the late 2000s. In 2016, the Korean harmonised unemployment rate dropped to 3.7%, the second-lowest in the OECD following Japan, although it crept up to 3.8 by mid-2018. The inactivity rate, while falling slightly from 31.3% in 2016 to 30.7% in 2018, remains however among the highest in the OECD. This is driven by particularly high inactivity rates of women (56.1% in 2016); among men, Korea's participation rate was above the OECD average.

The situation for youth on the labour market in Korea is noteworthy for its low unemployment rate and low activity rate. In 2017, the unemployment rate was 9.8%, slightly below the OECD average of 11.9%. However, the participation rate of young people is relatively low in international comparison, especially in light of their high education attainment. The NEET (not in employment, education or training) rate in Korea, 18% in 2017, is slightly higher than the OECD average, but higher-educated Korean youth are more affected than those with lower education, the opposite of the situation in most other OECD countries. Young people in fact postpone entry to the labour market, investing further in their human capital in an attempt to pass selection exams and secure employment in the primary labour market – large firms and the public sector. The inactivity of highly-educated young people also suggests an unwillingness to accept jobs for which they are overqualified.

The participation rate among older workers, on the other hand, is relatively high. Many Koreans aged 50 or above have retired from their jobs in the primary labour market but, due to low income, must seek income through poor quality jobs in small enterprises or in self-employment in their "second career" (OECD, 2018[4]).

Therefore, the labour force reserve largely comprises highly educated young people who are delaying their entry into employment, and women who have left the labour force (due to childbearing, but also to a "glass ceiling" preventing them from finding a job in the primary labour market).

The number of vacancies posted on Worknet, the employment information service run by the Ministry of Employment and Labour for job matching, has been steadily increasing, from 841 000 in 2004 to 2.5 million in 2013. Of those vacancies, 88% were posted by businesses with less than 300 employees in 2014 (Figure 1.7). In terms of vacancies that went unfilled according to the Occupational Labour Force Survey at Establishments data of the MOEL in the first semester of 2017, 67% of the unfilled vacancies were low-skilled and most of the unfilled low-skilled jobs (93%) were among SMEs.

Figure 1.7. The number of vacancies are rising, especially in less skilled occupations

Inflow of newly registered vacancies and skill level 1 & 2-1 unfilled vacancies, 2004-17

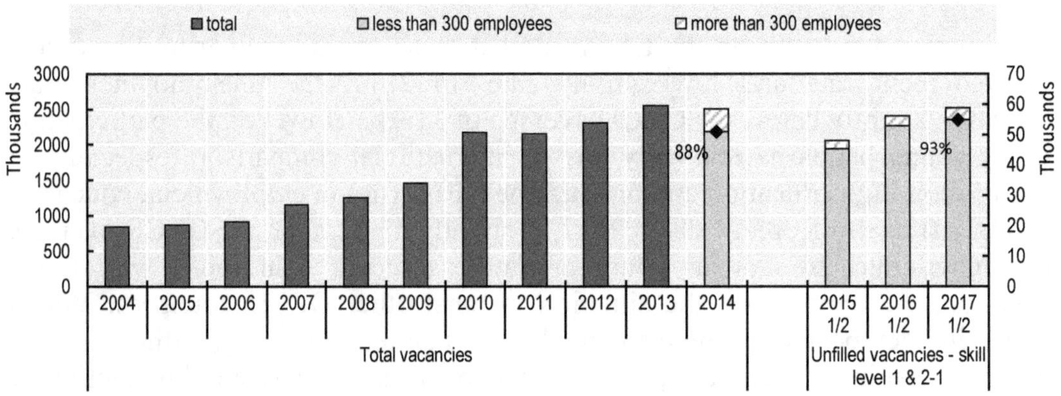

Note: 1) The share of vacancies in SMEs in 2014 comes from "March 2015 Employment Issue" of KEIS. 2) The skill level classification employed in the Occupational Labour Force Survey at Establishments classifies the skill level by five categories with regards to work experience, educational attainment and certificates: skill level 1 refers to an occupation with no requirement for experience, diploma, and certificate; skill level 2-1 refers to an occupation that requires one to two years of experience or technician certificate or educational attainment of high school graduate or less.

Source: Worknet, Occupational Labour Force Survey at Establishments, Ministry of Employment and Labour, 2004-17.

Labour shortages have been an issue in Korea since the early 1990s, especially in low-skilled manufacturing jobs, where shortage indices have been higher than for skilled workers (Park, 2002[5]). In the mid-2000s, shortage rates were twice as high for low-skilled jobs as for higher-skilled jobs (Lee and Park, 2008[6]). Since the crisis of the late 2000s the number of job vacancies has been increasing, even as it has become easier to fill positions (Figure 1.8). Vacancies in SMEs reached almost 700 000 in the first quarter of 2017, although only one in eight went unfilled.

Examining vacancies, labour shortages in Korea appear concentrated in a few sectors and a few occupations. The Occupational Labour Force Survey at Establishments (2017) indicates the difficulties by sectors. In spite of employers' recruitment efforts, a number of occupation types were difficult to fill. In the second half of 2017, 11.7% of overall vacant positions could not be filled. The share of vacancies which could not be filled was much higher in driving and delivery (34.6%), food processing (22.2%), and materials, chemicals, textile and clothing (24.4%). When looking at unfilled vacancies by skill level, the number of unfilled positions was concentrated in low skill positions, level 1 and level 2-1 in particular.

Figure 1.8. The share of vacancies which can't be filled has been declining

Number recruited and hired, and share of vacancies unfilled, 2009-17, in thousands

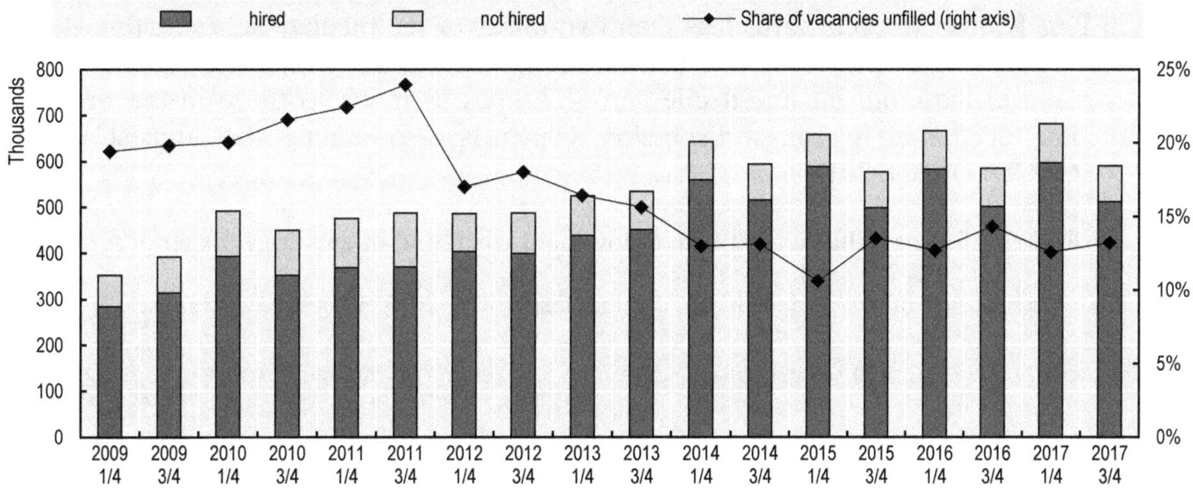

Note: Establishments with five or more employees are included in the panel. The reference period is.1.1-3.31 for first quarter and 1.7-30.9 for the third quarter each year.
Source: Occupational Labour Force Survey at Establishments.

There are still many low-quality jobs

Low quality jobs – low wages, poor employment prospects, and poor working conditions – are widespread in Korea, especially in small and microenterprises. Employment in SMEs is associated in Korea with lower wages than in large companies. Hourly wages in companies with 10-29 employees are half those in large enterprises; in firms with fewer than five employees, wages are only one-third that level. Overall, turnover in Korea is higher than in any other OECD country. In 2015, 30.9% of employees in Korea were in their jobs for shorter than one year – compared with an OECD average of 17.6% (OECD, 2018[7]). This is highest in the smallest firms - 50.7% workers in enterprises with fewer than five employees have job tenure of less than one year.

Many workers in SMEs earn minimum wage, and the minimum wage is low. The statutory Minimum Wage (MW) as of January 2017 was KRW 16.2 million per year for a full-time worker, around 42% of the median wage, putting Korea's minimum wage in the lower third of OECD countries which have a statutory MW. Around 15% of all workers in Korea (17.4% in 2017) earn MW – this is much higher a share than in most other OECD countries where typically only around 5% or less earn the minimum wage.

The changing educational composition of the working age population has not meant the disappearance of low-productivity, low-wage jobs. Further, the minimum wage is not enough to keep families out of poverty, especially for single-income households. The minimum wage is planned to increase gradually by about 30% from 2018 to 2020; however, the increase may not necessarily raise real earnings in the absence of enforcement. Further, it will not affect the wage of the self-employed.

In addition to MW employment, there are many other low-paid jobs. Almost one in four Korean workers earns less than two-thirds of the median earnings; this is one of the highest rates of low-paid work in the OECD (Figure 1.8). Further, workers in the ninth income decile earn 4.7 times as much as those in the first income decile, an earnings dispersion which is also among the highest in the OECD (OECD, 2018[7]).

Figure 1.9. Korea has a high rate of low-paid work and of earnings dispersion

The incidence of low-paid work[a] and earnings dispersion[b], 2015 or latest year available[c].

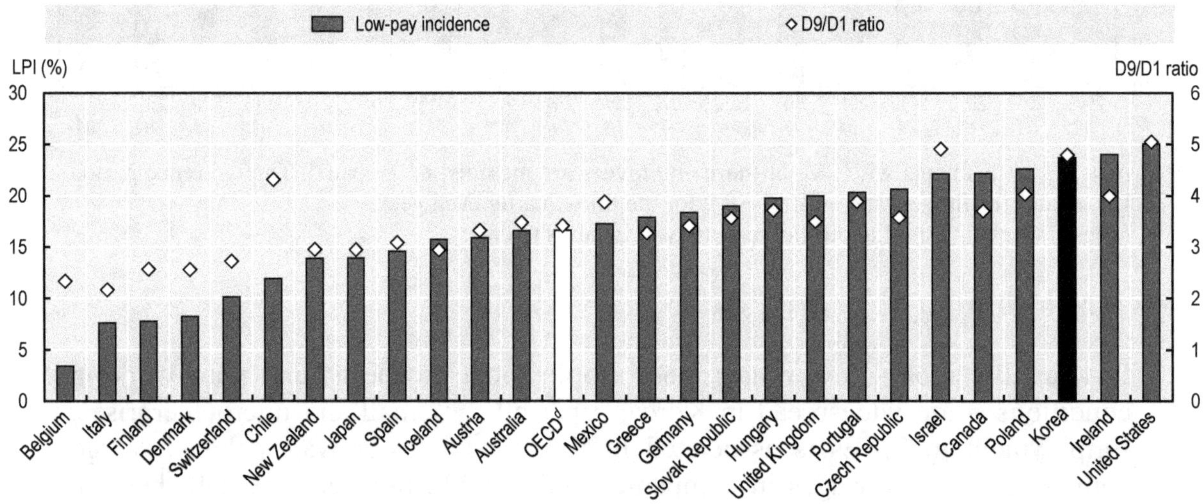

Note: a) The incidence of low pay refers to the share of workers earning less than two-thirds of median earnings. b) Earnings dispersion is measured by the ratio of 9th to 1st deciles limits of earnings. c) Data refer to 2011 for Israel; to 2012 for Spain; and to 2014 for Australia, Belgium, Germany, Greece, Iceland, Italy, Japan, Korea, New Zealand, Poland, Portugal and Switzerland. d) Unweighted average of the 26 countries shown above.
Source: *OECD Earnings Distribution Database*, www.oecd.org/employment/emp/employmentdatabase-earningsandwages.htm.

In summary, Korea's labour force is undergoing a profound transition, already well-advanced, towards a much higher-educated working-age population. This is especially true for youth cohorts, which are progressively smaller. There are fewer and fewer young people with lower educational qualifications. Young people with higher education tend to invest in further qualifications in an attempt to enter the regular labour market, rather than accept non-regular employment or low-quality jobs. The labour supply of less educated is aging and will soon start to diminish rapidly. At present, there are many poorly paid jobs, filled by workers with skill profiles which are becoming increasingly scarce. The difficulty in filling jobs which pay poorly and which do not require high levels of education points to the challenge in how Korea will meet the labour needs in these jobs. The jobs themselves are low-productivity, suggesting that without productivity gains, it will be difficult to increase wages substantially. For some jobs, it may be possible to increase productivity and wages, attracting Korean workers. For other jobs, in SMEs in the manufacturing sector where margins and capital investment are low, the absence of low-cost labour may force production cuts, or a loss of competitiveness compared to competitors in other countries. Even beyond manufacturing – in agriculture and services – the same question appears. It is in this context that labour migration has begun to play an important role.

References

Lee, K. and S. Park (2008), "Employment Structure and Effects of the Foreign Workforce", *KLI Monthly Labor Review*, Vol. September, https://www.kli.re.kr/kli_eng/selectBbsNttView.do?key=220&bbsNo=31&nttNo=100745&searchY=&searchCtgry=&searchCnd=all&searchKrwd=&pageIndex=7&integrDeptCode= (accessed on 13 November 2017). [6]

Ministry of Education (2017), *Educational Statistics Analaysis (교육통계 분석자료집) 2017*, KEDI, Seoul. [2]

OECD (2018), *Towards Better Social and Employment Security in Korea*, Connecting People with Jobs, OECD Publishing, Paris, https://dx.doi.org/10.1787/9789264288256-en. [7]

OECD (2018), *Working Better with Age: Korea*, Ageing and Employment Policies, OECD Publishing, Paris, https://dx.doi.org/10.1787/9789264208261-en. [4]

OECD (2013), *OECD Skills Outlook 2013: First Results from the Survey of Adult Skills*, OECD Publishing, Paris, http://dx.doi.org/10.1787/9789264204256-en. [3]

Park, M. et al. (2015), *100세 사회 고용. 일자리 분야 전망 및 대응방안 (100 year old social employment – Occupational prospects and countermeasures, KEIS)*, http://keis.or.kr/user/extra/main/2102/publication/publicationList/jsp/LayOutPage.do?categoryIdx=131&publdx=1648&onlyList=N. [1]

Park, W. (2002), "The Unwilling Hosts: State, Society and the Control of Guest Workers in South Korea", *Asia Pacific Business Review*, Vol. 8/4, pp. 67-94, http://dx.doi.org/10.1080/713999161. [5]

Chapter 2. Evolution and Characteristics of Labour Migration to Korea

This chapter covers the recent history of migration to Korea and the development of overall migration policy in the country. It notes the transition to a net immigration country in the 2000s. It discusses the rising share of foreigners in the total resident population, compares it to trends in other OECD countries and examines the categories under which foreigners are resident in Korea. The chapter examines the age, education and employment characteristics of the foreign population in Korea, by gender, relative to that of the Korean population and in international comparison. The chapter examines the contribution of foreigners to employment in different sectors of the Korean economy, assessing the role of foreigners in the composition of change in the labour force over the past decade as compared to other OECD countries. The chapter then discusses the main institutional actors and recent economic migration policy milestones in Korea. The chapter concludes with an overview of the visa system and of inflows by visa category.

The statistical data for Israel are supplied by and under the responsibility of the relevant Israeli authorities. The use of such data by the OECD is without prejudice to the status of the Golan Heights, East Jerusalem and Israeli settlements in the West Bank under the terms of international law.

Korea has become a net immigration country

Korea was for many years a country of emigration. In the first half of the 20th century, prior to the Second World War, more than 4 million Koreans migrated to Japan and China, according to the National Archives of Korea. Following the War, migration opportunities were more limited, and it was not until the late 1960s that Koreans started to emigrate in large numbers. However, emigration ran at high levels in the 1970s and 1980s, especially to North America. Over these two decades, the United States admitted 613 000 Korean permanent residents, and Canada admitted about 70 000.

In addition to this emigration – which was supported by the government at the time – Korean companies contracted labour abroad, imposing conditions and currency controls to keep earnings in Korea. In the 1960s, Korea dispatched about 8 000 miners and 10 000 nurses to Germany. Another large outflow of labour migration was deployment of construction workers to Middle Eastern countries in the 1970s. The Korean government deliberately encouraged overseas employment, but required that some part of the migrants' wages be paid in Korea in order to finance domestic economic growth (Park, 1991[1]).

Migration to Korea only began in the late 1980s. When the Korean War ended in ceasefire in 1953, Korea was one of the poorest and least developed countries, and faced the challenge of building industries and stabilise its system; in the decades which followed, few foreigners had occasion to come to Korea. Entry was strictly controlled by the government, primarily for security reasons. Immigration began to occur in significant numbers when full employment was reached in the late 1980s. Labour shortages began to be felt in SMEs, especially for the most taxing jobs in so-called 3D (difficult, dirty, and dangerous) industries: dyeing, plating, heat-treatment, casting and tempering, machinery, footwear, glass, leather, electricity, electronics factories, and construction (Seol and Han, 2004[2]). The number of foreigners gradually increased, mainly due to growing inflows from China of Chinese and of ethnic Koreans – descendants of those who left in the early 20th century – and in the number of trainees entering from other Asian countries. The normalisation of diplomatic relations with China in 1992 contributed to the inflow (Oh et al., 2012[3]). Still, it was not until the 2000s that immigration flows exceeded the number of Koreans migrating overseas. Since 2005, net migration to Korea has been positive.

The increase in the foreign population between 2000 and 2015 was about 400%, by far the largest increase among OECD countries (Figure 2.1, Panel A). It rose from 0.5% of the population in 2000 to 2.3% of the population in 2015. This excludes temporary residents (those with permits for less than 90 days) and undocumented foreigners.

Figure 2.1. Korea has a fast-growing but relatively small foreign-born population

Panel A. The change in the foreign population 2000-2015 and the share of total population in 2015.

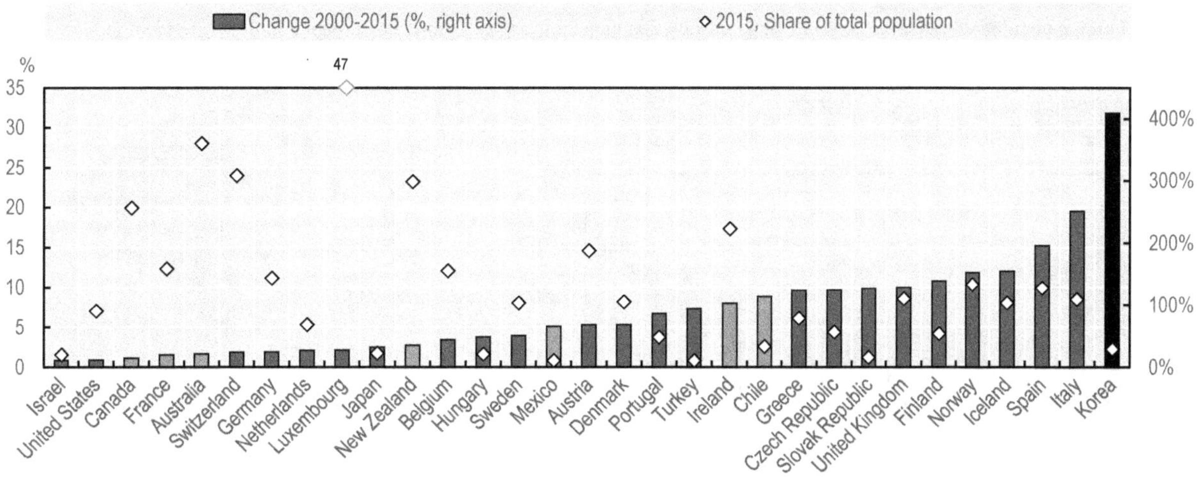

Panel B. The foreign population as a percentage of the total population, 2000 and 2015.

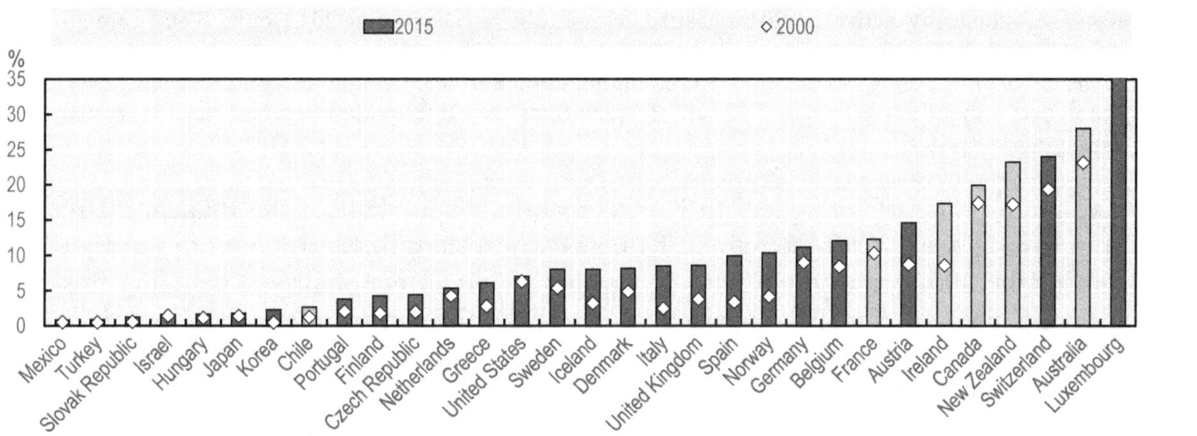

Note: Data refer to 2000 or the closest available year, and to 2015 or the most recent available year. For countries shown in grey (Chile, France, Ireland, Canada, New Zealand and Australia), the data refer to the foreign-born population rather than the foreign population. Israel: foreigners are legally resident foreign workers and asylum seekers, see (OECD, 2010[4]).
Source: OECD International Migration Database.

The foreign population in Korea, as a share of the active population age 15 and above, rose from 3.1% in 2013 to 3.7% in 2016 (Figure 2.2, Panel A.). Legal long-term foreign residents rose from 2.2% of the total Korean population to 3% of the total population over the same time period, excluding temporarily present foreigners and illegal overstayers, who together add an additional 1% to the share.

Figure 2.2. The foreign population in Korea is a growing share of the active population

Panel A. Foreign population in Korea, 2004-2016, thousands, economically active and inactive population and as a share of total population, 2012-2016

Panel B. Foreign population resident in Korea, 2016, by category.

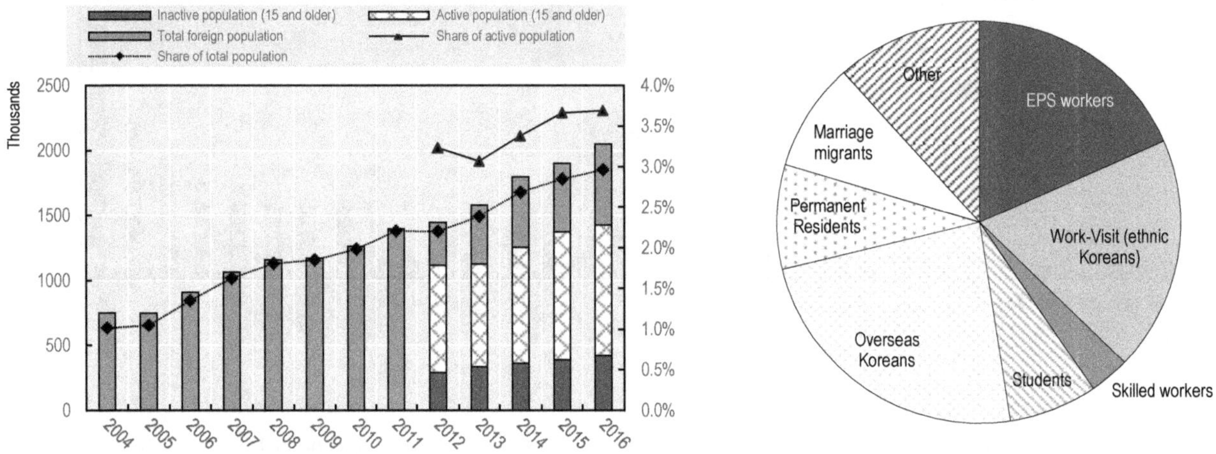

Note: Economically active population aged 15 and above. Data from 2012 only. Total foreign population includes short-term stays and overstayers.
Source: Panel A. Foreign Population, Korea Immigration Service. Economically active population: Foreigners Labour Force Survey, 2013-16, Korean Statistical Information Service. Panel B. Korea Immigration Service

The main group of foreigners in Korea, accounting for half of the total in 2016, comprises Korean-Chinese, ethnic Koreans whose families left Korea in the first half of the 20th century and who do not hold Korean nationality. Excluding this group, Chinese nationals comprised 14.3% of the foreign population, followed by Vietnamese (9.4%). In addition to labour migration, one factor in the growth of migration over the course of the past two decades, was the sudden and sharp increase in marriage migration. Marriage migration to Korea has largely involved women from China and Southeast Asia marrying Korean men, who are often low-educated and resident in rural areas. Many of these marriages were arranged or brokered (Lee, 2008[5]). The share of marriages with a foreigner rose from less than 2% in 1990 to 3.5% in 2000, then to 13.5% in the peak year of 2005, when about one in three marriages involving a rural man was brokered with a foreigner. Marriages with foreigners have since fallen to about 7% of the total in 2015 (OECD, 2017[6]). This group of migrants accounted for about 15% of all foreign residents in 2010 and has continued to grow, although less rapidly than other groups. By 2016, two categories composed almost entirely of Korean Chinese accounted for 43% of all foreigners in Korea: a Work-Visit (19%) and a long-term stay visa for overseas Koreans (24%). Temporary guestworkers comprised 18% of foreign residents. Permanent migrants who are neither ethnic Koreans nor family members of Koreans accounted for 8%; this includes major investors and family of other foreigners. Skilled workers comprised about 3.2% of foreign residents, although some skilled workers have obtained long-term stay permits and are classified as permanent migrants.

Overall, about half of the resident foreign population held temporary-type permits, some of which are indefinitely renewable, while half held long-term stay permits.

The foreign population has different characteristics from the Korean population. Notably, it is younger: 31% of foreign residents are between 25 and 34 years old. Further, the educational attainment of the foreign population is far below that of the Korean population (Figure 2.3). Among OECD countries, Korea is one of the countries where the gap between the share of highly educated among native and foreign-born is greatest. This gap is even greater when considering that the younger Korean population in particular has a very high educational attainment.

Figure 2.3. There is a wide gap between the education of natives and foreigners

Shares of the highly educated among native- and foreign-born 15-64 year-olds who are not in education, 2017.

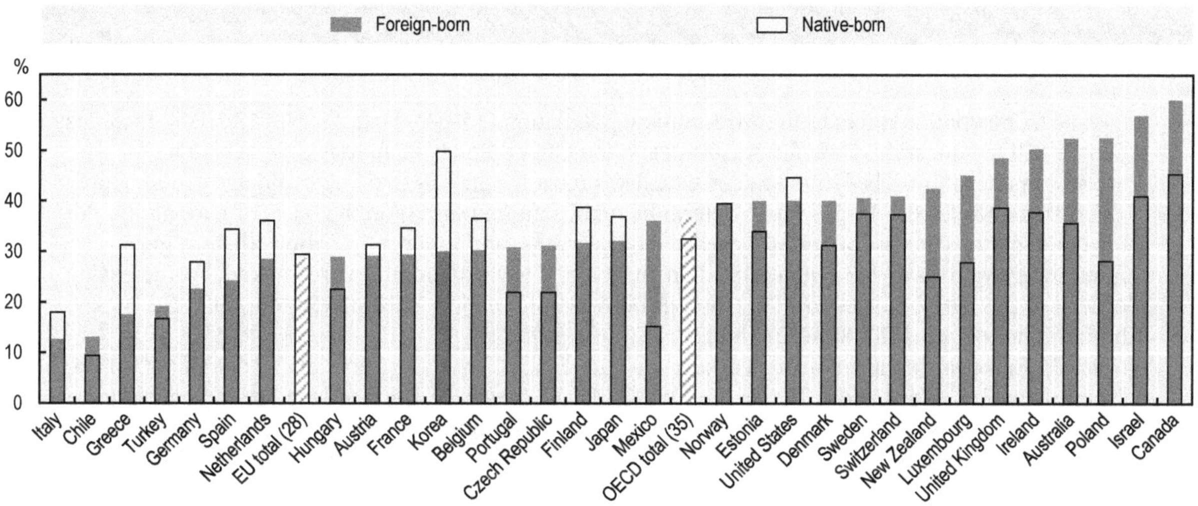

Note: For Korea, data covers foreigners and immigrants who have been naturalised in the past 5 years.

Source: European countries and Turkey: Labour Force Surveys (Eurostat); Australia, Canada, Israel, New Zealand: Labour Force surveys; Chile: Encuesta de Caracterización Socioeconómica Nacional (CASEN); Mexico: Encuesta Nacional de Ocupación y Empleo (ENOE); United States: Current Population Surveys. Korea: Survey on Immigrant's Living Conditions and Labour Force 2017 and Economically Active Population Survey of Korean nationals (EAPS) 2017, provided by MRTC.

In 2017, the employment rate of foreigners in Korea, 71% is, despite the lower educational attainment, slightly higher than the Korean average (68%). The employment rate of foreigners in Korea is also above that of the foreign-born in most OECD European countries and comparable to the rate in the United States (Figure 2.4). This relatively high rate partly reflects the younger age of the foreign population and the fact that it is skewed towards men, who have a higher employment rate (the foreign population above age 15 is 55.3% male). However, it also reflects the fact that employment and economic opportunity are the main channels through which foreigners come to Korea.

Figure 2.4. Foreigners in Korea have a higher employment rate than nationals

Employment rate by place of birth, 2017.

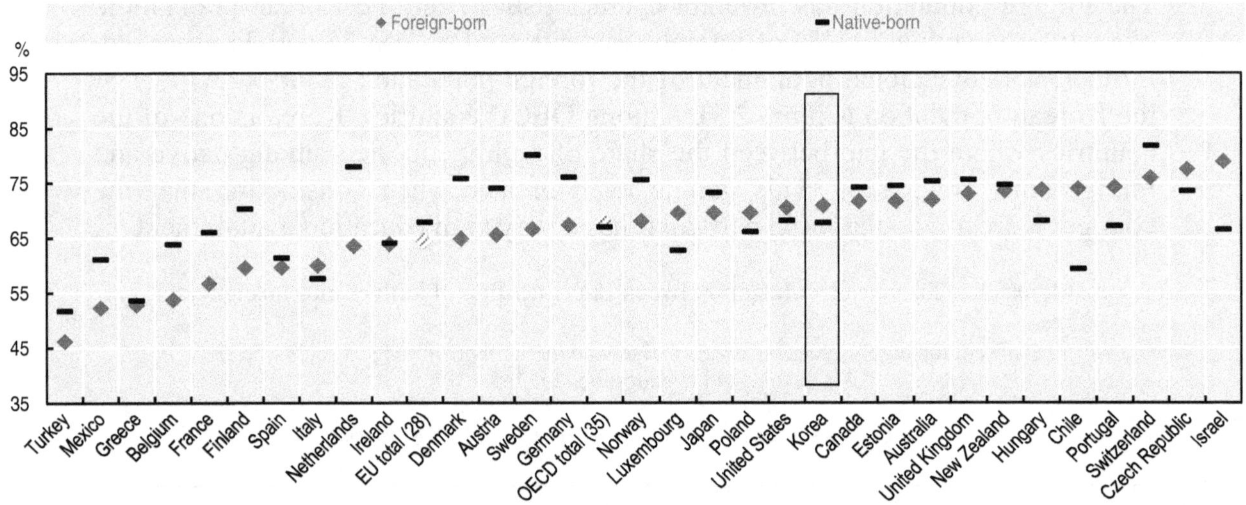

Note: The population refers to the working-age population (15-64). Data for New Zealand includes people still in education. Data for Australia and the United States include people aged over 24 who are still in education. The United States calculates rates for the 16- to 64 year-old age group. Korea calculates rates for the 15-59. Japan determine who is an immigrant on the basis of nationality, not on the basis of country of birth. Korea includes in the immigrant population all foreigners and immigrants who have been naturalised in the past 5 years. Countries are ranked by increasing order of the 2017 values of the foreign-born employment. Information on data for Israel: http://dx.doi.org/10.1787/888932315602.

Source: European countries and Turkey: Labour Force Surveys (Eurostat); Australia, Canada, Israel, New Zealand: Labour Force surveys; Chile: Encuesta de Caracterización Socioeconómica Nacional (CASEN); Mexico: Encuesta Nacional de Ocupación y Empleo (ENOE); United States: Current Population Surveys. Korea: Survey on Immigrant's Living Conditions and Labour Force 2017 and Economically Active Population Survey of Korean nationals (EAPS) 2017, provided by MRTC.

Relative to other OECD countries, the foreign population in Korea is predominantly male (Figure 2.5). Men comprise 55.3% of the foreign population age 15 and above, while the average across OECD countries is closer to 50%. The employment rate of male foreigners is 81%, which is the comparable to the United Kingdom and the United States, and much higher than in most Western European countries. The employment rate of female foreigners, however, is just 51%, similar to the United States and many European countries.

Figure 2.5. Korea has a high share of men among foreigners, and low employment among foreign women

Foreign residents by gender and employment, age 15-64, 2015.

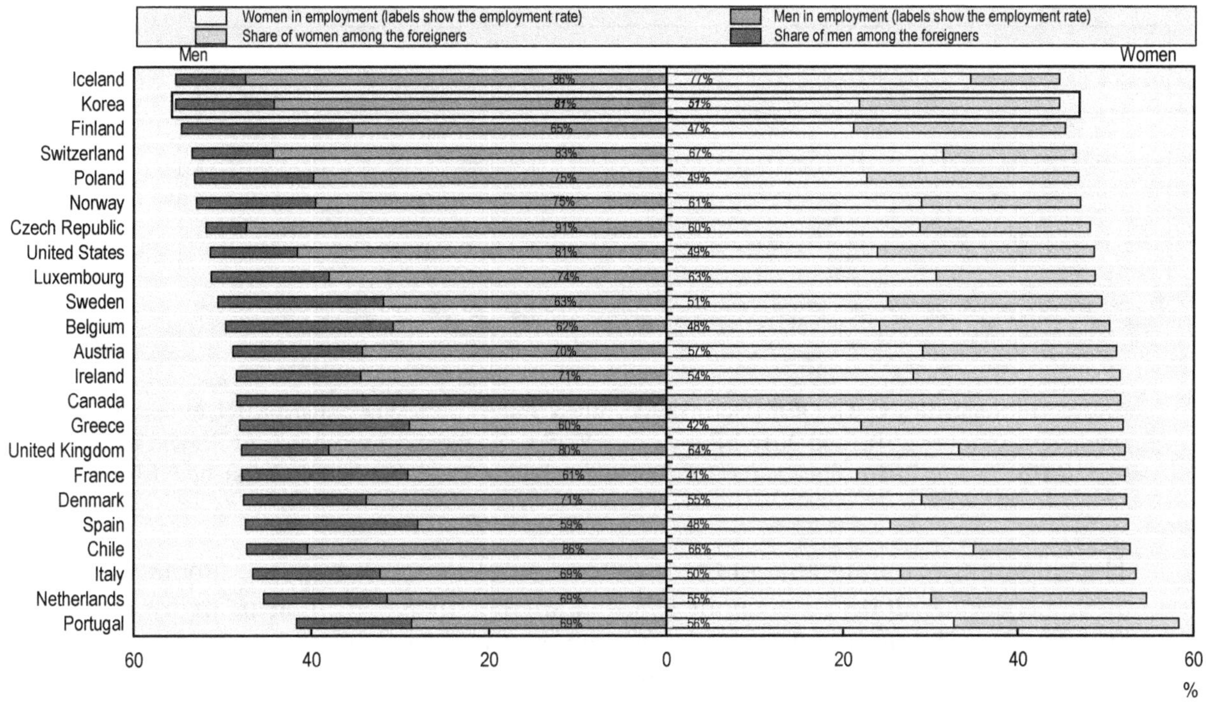

Note: For Korea, age 15+, 2016.
Source: European labour force surveys, CPS for United States, FLFS for Korea.

The share of foreigners in employment in Korea more than doubled over the past decade, increasing from 1.6% in 2005 to 3.6% in 2016. In relative terms, this was the largest increase in the foreign share of employment in any OECD country (Figure 2.6). Korea still has a lower share of immigrants in employment than the share in most OECD countries, however. Korea was not alone in seeing an increase in the foreign share of employment over the decade: almost all OECD countries have seen a growing share of employment comprising foreigners. The increase is particularly notable in some Western and Southern European countries: it more than doubled in Denmark, Norway and Finland, and grew by 70-80% in the United Kingdom, Czech Republic, Ireland and Italy. In contrast, some major immigrant destinations such as France and Spain saw very little change over the decade.

Figure 2.6. The share of foreigners in employment has increased sharply over the decade

Share of foreign in total employment, 2005 and 2015 or latest year.

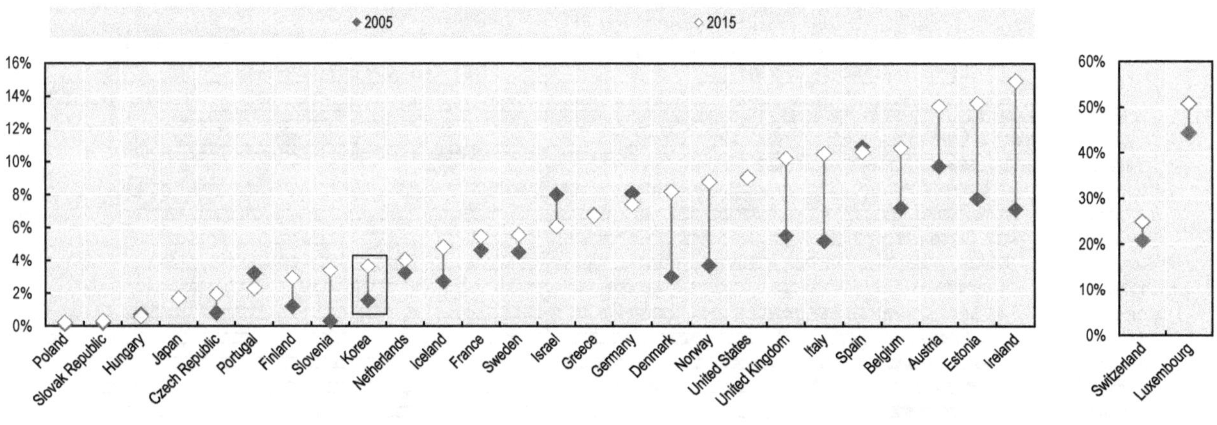

Source: Europe: LFS or GSOEP (Germany); United States: CPS. For Japan, MHLW survey of employers, October 2016, and 2016 LFS. Korea, 2005 KIS Statistical yearbook, FLFS and EAPS, May 2016. Israel, PIBA figures for foreigners (including cross-border workers) and LFS for nationals, 2016.

The role of new immigrants in the composition of the change in the labour force over the decade 2005-15 – about 9% - is smaller in Korea than in many other OECD countries (Figure 2.7). The total labour force increased significantly over the decade, by about 12%. Change in the labour force is driven by retirement of older workers, entry from inactivity and exit to inactivity by prime-age workers, young workers entering the labour force, and new migrants. The loss to retirement over the decade 2005-2015 in Korea was among the lowest in the OECD, although this is expected to increase in the following decade 2015-25. Overall, 14% of new entries comprised new immigrants, 79% were young workers, and 7% were prime-age workers. The importance of new immigrants in the composition of labour force change was particularly strong in the manufacturing sector, where overall labour force growth of 10% was among the highest in the OECD (Figure 2.A.1). The population employed in low-skill occupations also increased over the decade, in all likelihood due to new immigrants (Figure 2.A.2).

Figure 2.7. New immigrants are driving labour force growth in many OECD countries including Korea

Composition of the change in the labour force, by demographic group, 2005-15.

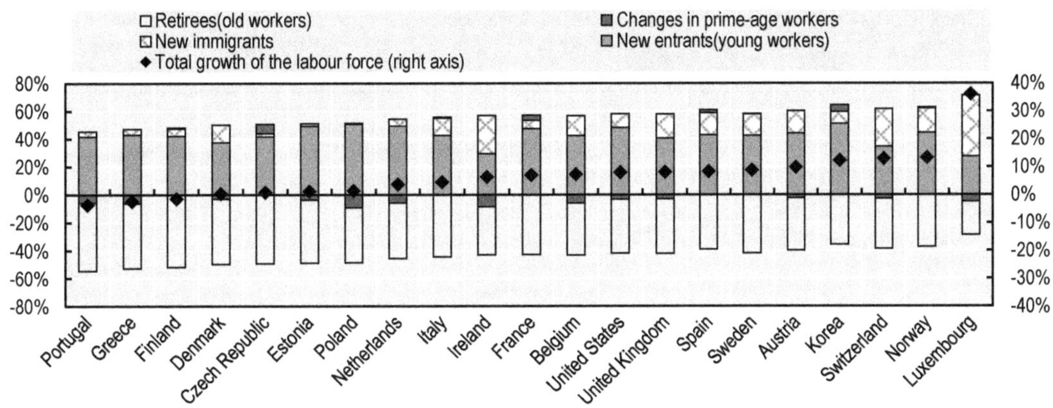

Source: Europe: LFS; United States: ACS; Korea: LFS, FLFS

Driving employment of foreigners appears to be a group of firms which relies on recruiting foreign workers, a fraction of total employers which has not varied over recent years. The bi-annual survey of establishments, which covers firms with at least five employees, indicates that since 2008 about 10% of firms have turned to foreign workers to meet vacancies (Figure 2.8). While other responses to labour shortages in firms have varied over time – notably, firm willingness to increase wages, and a lower reliance on temporary and dispatched workers – the share seeking foreign workers has remained stable. This figure of 10% of firms is much higher than the share of foreign workers in employment of firms over five employees.

One aspect which is particularly noteworthy is that while other firm strategies for dealing with labour shortage have changed significantly over the past decade, recruitment of foreign workers has seen little variation. For example, in July 2011, the 40-hour statutory work week was extended to firms with 5-19 employees (firms with four or fewer employees are exempt from statutory limits on work hours). This affected the ability of these firms to use overtime to meet labour demand, evident in the corresponding drop in Figure 2.8. Training and use of dispatched workers are also variable, as are wage increases. The stability of the share recurring to foreign workers suggests that there is a demand-side limit to the use of foreign workers to fill vacancies, or a supply-side constraint on the type of firms which are eligible to consider employment of foreign workers.

Figure 2.8 The share of firms recurring to foreign workers has remained stable

Firms' responses to need to fill vacancies, 2008-16, share of firms employing each response

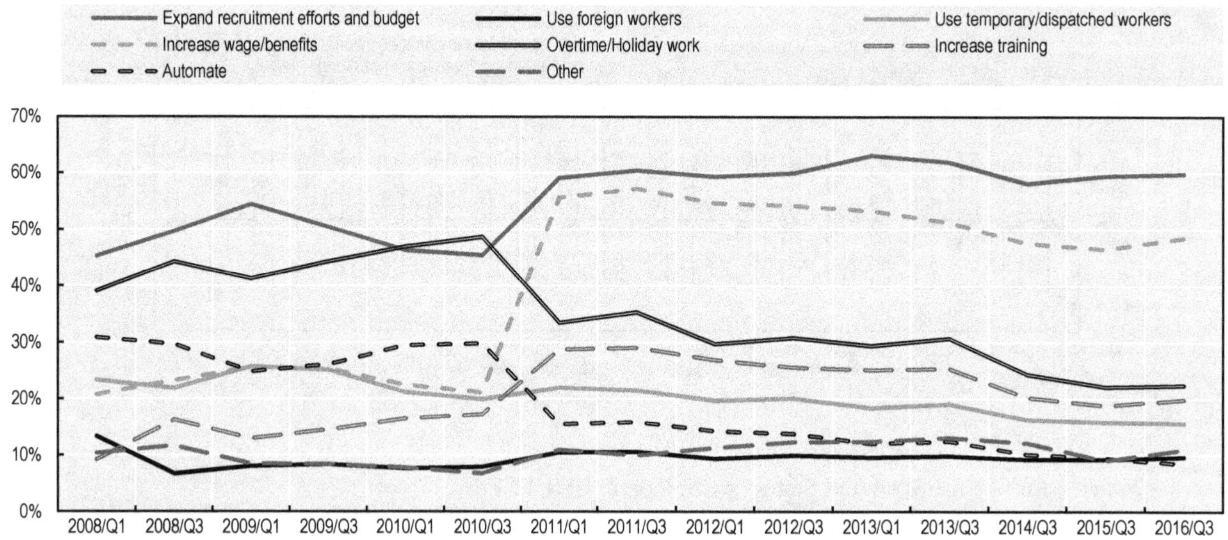

Note: Excludes firms which did not take action following unfilled vacancies.
Source: Occupational Labour Force Survey at Establishments.

Box 2.1. Data sources on migration in Korea

The Population Census and Labour Force Survey of the Statistics Korea

The analyses on the context for labour migration in Korea mainly use the Population Census and the Economically Active Population Survey (EAPS), which are particularly useful to capture long-term dynamic changes of demographic structure and economic activity by virtue of their long history. Korean statistics system follows the citizenship classification not the place of birth in investigating the nativity information of individuals. The annual population census records nationality at birth and current nationality, not the place of birth. Aggregate statistics on foreign population by age, sex, nationality and the year of entry is publicly available. The EAPS is a monthly survey targeting residents aged 15 years or older in Korea. This survey includes foreigners in its sample from 2009 in the light of the increasing foreign population and the statistics disseminated through the survey represents the overall economic activity of the nationals and foreigners.

By the early 2010s, as the number of foreign residents in Korea surpassed one million, the inadequacy of survey instruments to capture these new residents was apparent. To improve coverage, the first Foreign Labour Force Survey was conducted in 2012. This annual survey, based on a sample drawn from residence permit holders, was conducted until 2016. In 2017, it was replaced by a more ambitious Survey on Immigrant's Living Conditions and Labour Force. The SILCLF introduced two major improvements. First, the revision increased comparability with statistics from other OECD countries by including in the sample citizens naturalised within the preceding five years, and identifying the current and at-birth nationality of parents. Second, the SILCLF added biennial questionnaires on social participation, health and living condition, as well as a triennial permit-specific module, covering non-professional workers and students in 2017, ethnic Koreans in 2018, and permanent residents in 2019.

Administrative data sources on immigration

In Korea, administrative data is another major source on migration and every entry and exit is recorded owing to its geographical characteristics equivalent to a remote island (double-card system). The Korea Immigration Service under the Ministry of Justice, which administers the entire procedure of permit issuance and immigration, publishes statistics on administrative data on visa applications, nationality acquisition, stock and inflow of foreign residents by age, sex, nationality, sojourn status, and duration of stay since 1960. Another administrative dataset, the Status of Foreign Residents in Local Governments, from the Ministry of Security and Public Administration, disseminated from 2006, is one of the few sources that provide information on naturalised citizens in Korea. This source includes population by previous nationality before naturalisation and the date of naturalisation as well as the population of minor children of foreign residents at the local municipality level.

Sources on Employment Permit System and sector data

Data for the Employment Permit System is managed by the Ministry of Employment and Labour which is in charge of the policy planning and implementation. The ministry's affiliated organisations, the regional employment centres and the Human Resources Development Service of Korea (HRD Korea) collect data and report it to the Korea Employment Information Service (KEIS). EPS raw data - the details of E-9 and H-2 workers' economic activity - is used in policy making of non-professional foreign manpower such as allocating monthly permit quotas by industry. Limited information on the number of businesses and foreign workers by nationality and industry under the EPS is available through the Employment Trend report of the Employment Permit System. On the other hand, the Survey on the Status of the Ppuri (Root) Industry of the Ministry of Trade, Industry and Energy allows firm-level analysis in this subset of the manufacturing sector, where foreign manpower comprises mainly E-9, H-2 and E-7 holders. The survey is the only publicly available source, as far, on the turn-over rate, tenure, language skill of foreign workers by firm-level as well as the transition of E-9 workers to E-7 status. Lastly, an annual Survey on Establishment of Small and Medium Enterprises by the Small & Medium Business Administration entails information on manpower shortages, difficulties in recruiting and employer efforts to retain workers of SMEs in the manufacturing, service and construction sector, from 2008.Additional surveys on EPS employers and workers are conducted by research institutions and business associations, such as KLI, KBiz, KOSBI, on different topics as necessary, though these are generally one-time and feature a small sample size.

Sources on education and mixed-background households

Lastly, the analyses on international students and professors were possible with data from the Korean Educational Statistics Service (KESS). In addition, although not used in the review, there is an abundance of surveys targeting "mixed households" and their children (families which consist of at least one Korean national), including the Survey on the Actual Conditions of Multicultural Families, the Multicultural Youth Panel Survey, and the National Multicultural Acceptance Survey. Aggregate statistics are accessible from the Korean Statistical Information Service (KOSIS).

The Basic Plans on Migration and co-ordinated migration policy

Korea's modern labour policy migration co-ordination dates to the 2007 Act on the Treatment of Foreigners in Korea, the first attempt to bring immigration policy under a single co-ordinating platform. Since then, immigration policy co-ordination has occurred under the Immigration Policy Commission, established under the Prime Minister. The lead ministry (assistant administrator) is the Ministry of Justice.[1] This Commission produces the Basic Plan for Immigration Policy every five years, which covers border control management, nationality, and social integration. The Plan is re-formulated every five years with the consultation of heads of relevant national-level administrative bodies.

In 2008, the Ministry of Justice introduced the First Basic Plan for Immigration Policy approved by the Immigration Policy Commission. The first plan aimed to control systematically and centralise the immigration policy as well as to set a long term plan and prospects based on multiculturalism and global competitiveness.

The first plan proclaimed an "open-door" policy to reinforce global competitiveness by attracting a more highly-skilled foreign work force, accepting low-skilled labour only where necessary, and giving incentives to overseas Koreans in terms of easy entry and employment. Second, it pursued a "multicultural society where other cultures and race are well received and can co-exist". This was to prepare a highly diversified society and to protect human rights of foreign residents. In addition, it emphasized the importance of order and law regarding immigration. Measures against illegal employment of foreigners and border control were toughened. It also planned to strictly monitor the length of stay, employment of migrant workers and any crimes committed by foreigners.[2]

The Second Basic Plan for Immigration Policy for 2013-17 ("Vibrant Korea growing with immigrants") encompassed similar issues as the first plan (border control, immigration, nationality, and social integration). Based on multiculturalism, it reinforced the previous policies. The Plan focused on improving infrastructure for foreigners, attracting more high-skilled workers and students, providing public services for foreigners to help adapt to Korean society, defending human rights of foreign nationals and migrant workers and offering skill development in sending countries. It again emphasized stricter border security, control of information on foreign residents and sanctions for illegal employment aimed at both workers and their employers.

The managed labour migration components in the Second Basic Plan fell primarily under the first of the five overall objectives, "openness". This pillar was meant to support economic stimulus and attract human resources, specifically under four sub-objectives: i. to increase the number of visitors, ii. to attract "in-demand [foreign] human resources", iii. to attract foreign students, and iv. to bring investment for "balanced regional development".

The Second Plan largely maintained the dichotomy between non-professional and professional workers, even as it recognised that resident foreigners could be divided into highly-skilled, "partially-skilled" and unskilled. The plan maintained the principle that the number of unskilled workers granted work permits should remain subject to a limit (without specifying that limit), and that recruitment among SMEs should be allowed "to a reasonable extent". At the same time, the Second Plan, unlike its predecessor, made explicit the need for a bridge for unskilled workers to acquire skills to pass from the unskilled category to higher-skill categories. The Plan called for programmes to develop the language, social and vocational skills of high-potential unskilled foreign workers.

The Third Basic Plan for Immigration Policy was published in February 2018. It advances many of the same objectives as previous plans. Several key points in the first of five pillars have direct implications for immigration policy in the next five years: to strengthen support for and attract talents; to secure growth engines and invite foreign workers; to increase economic stimulation through tourism and investors; to establish an immigrant inflow system with a converging perspective; and to reorganise residence and nationality system and prepare for immigrant population increase. The Basic Plan for 2018-22 acknowledges the growing role of the foreign workforce and the increasing share of immigrants in the Korean population. At the same time, it does not signal any major policy shift regarding temporary labour migration, although it reflects policy objectives to reduce the proportion of low-skilled workers, and attract higher-wage, higher skill migrants.

The plan does not set numerical targets for migration, although these may be established in individual action plans by different ministries to achieve objectives agreed under the Basic Plan. The Basic Plan rather guides policy development in the domains it covers, identifying issues which have emerged in the implementation of the preceding plans. Key policy decisions, such as the ceilings on the stock of ethnic Korean work-visitors, the annual admission quotas for the EPS E-9 programme, the duration of stay of workers and the lists of eligible and non-eligible occupations, are decided through consultations rather than fixed in the Basic Plan. Decision making on such key policy choices occurs through different political mechanisms in other OECD countries, according to their objectives (Box 2.2).

Box 2.2. Migration planning and "Foreign workforce" management policy structures

The objectives of migration policy vary among OECD countries. Most countries do not have an explicit demographic objective of maintaining a working age population, although Australia, Canada and New Zealand plan admission volumes on an annual or triennial basis with demographic considerations in mind (OECD, 2014[7]) These countries select candidates for their economic migration programmes based on different criteria, and set levels for programme management and to regulate the impact on residents of inflows. Humanitarian resettlement programmes are also set, in these and other OECD countries, according to decisions on annual processing and integration capacity, in line with general policy objectives and funding allocations. Family migration channels are sometimes also capped, although certain categories such as spouses of nationals are exempt (OECD, 2017[8]). Permanent migration levels under planned targets and caps may shift according to economic circumstances, as was seen during the downturn of the late 2000s (OECD, 2009[9]). Countries with ageing populations and forecast rapid changes in the dependency ratio have not turned to migration as an explicit strategy to counteract this trend, as the inflows necessary to change the dependency ratio are in most cases much higher than current flows.

Labour migration management, with the exception of the planning used in the countries above, has been focused on demand-driven migration and deciding which mechanisms to use to weigh employer interest in recruiting foreign workers from abroad against other policy priorities, such as protecting resident workers, upskilling the working age population, maintaining social cohesion, etc. The bodies determining foreign workforce policy are usually not separate from the general labour policy bodies. While some decisions on foreign worker numbers and sectors are taken through the political process – which may lead to fixing entries in legislation, as in the United States H-1B and H-2B programme – the process usually involves a phase of empirical data analysis and a consultation with social partners and other stakeholders to reach a compromise solution.

The labour migration framework in Korea

The modern migration framework brings together a series of disparate visas and permits which have developed over the past three decades.

Korea has a complex visa framework for migration management comprising more than 170 separate sub-categories. The overall framework, introduced in 1993, divides visas into visa classes from A to G; the classes of relevance for labour migration include C (short-term visas), D (research and study), E (employment), H (overseas Koreans visiting) and F (long-term and permanent residence). Within each class of visa, there are categories (e.g., "E-9: non-professional employment") and sub-categories (e.g., "E-7-4: skilled worker through the points-system"). The conditions for admission and employment vary according to the permit sub-category (Table 2.1).

With the exception of a few categories, initial admission of economic migrants is dependent on sponsorship by their employer (i.e., a valid employment contract). For most categories, there is a possibility of changing status to long-term stay (F visas), although residence duration and criteria vary among categories. Korea has a number of long term stay categories (F-1 to F-4) which grant varying degrees of rights.

Permanent residence (F-5) – unconditional stay and right to reside and work in any occupation, comparable to long-term permanent residence in European OECD countries and to permanent migration in the United States and "settlement" OECD countries (Canada, Australia, and New Zealand) – can be acquired after five years of residence, although there are some pathways which require only a shorter period.

Table 2.1. The visa framework for labour migrants is complex

Permit categories related to labour migration, 2017.

Major Category	Category	Target Group	Conditions for entry/employment
Short-term employment	C-4	Short (up to 90 days) visit for employment	Employer-sponsored
"Professional Employment"	E-1	Highly Qualified Employment	Employer-sponsored
	E-2	Teachers and professors	Employer-sponsored
	E-3	Researcher	Employer-sponsored
	E-4	Technical Instructor / Technician	Employer-sponsored
	E-5	Professional	Employer-sponsored
	E-6	Entertainer, Athlete	Employer-sponsored
	E-7	Skilled employment (list of occupations)	Employer-sponsored
	E-7-4	Points-based skilled E-9 visa holders	Employer-sponsored
"Non-Professional Employment"	E-9	Temporary workers under EPS	Employer-sponsored
	E-10	Maritime workers/ship crew	Employer-sponsored
	H-2	Overseas Koreans "visiting employment"	Labour market access
Study and Research	D-1	Culture/Art	Institutional sponsorship
	D-2	International Students	Institutional sponsorship
	D-3	Training	Institutional sponsorship
	D-4	Language and non-degree education	Institutional sponsorship
	D-5	Journalist	Institutional sponsorship
	D-6	Religious Worker	No labour market access
	D-7	Intra-company transfers	Employer-sponsored
	D-8-1	Skilled employees of a FDI company	Employer-sponsored
	D-8-3	Required employment for a FDI company	Employer-sponsored
	D-9	Trade Management	Employer-sponsored
	D-10-1	Job-Search Permit	Seek E-1 to E-7 job
Investors and entrepreneurs	D-10-2	Start-up entrepreneur	Employer-sponsored
	D-8-2	Tech venture investor	Employer-sponsored
	D-8-4	Tech investor/entrepreneur	Employer-sponsored
	D-9-4	Owner of foreign investment firm	Employer-sponsored
	F-2-8	Real-estate investor	Labour market access
	F-5-5	High-investment investor	Labour market access
Long-term stay	F-1	Family members of F-2 and F-4 visa holders	No labour market access
	F-1-2X	Domestic employees of certain foreigners	Employer-sponsored
	F-2	Family reunification, other forms of residence	Labour market access
	F-2-6	E-9/H-2 meeting skill and income requirements	Labour market access
	F-2-7	Points-Based Residence	Labour market access
	F-3	Spouse/child of D-1 to 10 (but not D-3) and E-1 to 7	No labour market access
	F-4	Overseas Koreans	Occupation restrictions
	F-5	Permanent residence (5 year requirement)	Labour market access
Permanent Residence	F-6	Spouse/Child of Korean national	Labour market access

Note: Not all visa sub-categories are shown, not all details of each visa are provided.
Source: Ministry of Justice.

As a result of the many long-term stay categories, the pathway from temporary residence to permanent residence involves multiple possibilities, more than in most OECD countries, and appears more complex. OECD countries can be distinguished into those which grant immediate permanent residence to selected economic migrants (the United States and settlement countries) and those in Europe which grant initial temporary permits, allowing permanent residence after a certain number of years (generally four or five). In the United States and settlement countries, the clear trend in recent years has been towards two-step migration, with labour migrants first arriving as temporary workers and transitioning to permanent residence. This is now the majority of cases of permanent residence even in settlement countries. Also prevalent in labour migration channels is three-step migration, where students become temporary workers and then permanent migrants (OECD, 2014[10]).

Korea, however, has a permit system where pathways from temporary to permanent stay have multiplied, with conditions attached to each sub-category. Temporary skilled workers with an E-7 visa, for example, may qualify for an F-2 long-term stay visa; if they do not, they may wait five years before applying for an F-5 permanent residence visa. Many long-term stay visas require the recipient to remain in the same job, so cannot be compared with long-term residence or permanent status in other OECD countries. Depending on the field of employment and characteristics of the employer, graduating international students may receive an E-2, E-3 or E-7 visa, or certain long-term stay visas depending on the field (e.g., overseas Korean may receive an F-4-21 visa for teachers, and F-4-18 for professors), or qualify immediately under a points-system for an F-2-7 visa, which allows an F-5 visa after three years instead of five. The maximum duration of permit issuance related to individual visas varies as well, so that some E-7 permits may be issued for up to two years and others up to three.

Regarding the rights of family members, residence rights and labour market access depend on the sponsor visa. Students (D visas) and workers (E-1 to E-7 visa holders) may bring family, but their family members do not have work rights. F-2 and F-4 long-term stayers may also bring family, but the employment access of their family members varies. Most family members on F visas do not have labour market access without qualifying for another visa category independently. In other OECD countries, the conditions for family reunification and the employment access of family members are specific to each permit. The wide range in conditions for eligibility for different permits, and the varying rights of these permits, reduces the transparency of the Korean labour migration system relative to other OECD countries.

Inflows by main categories

There are two main categories of temporary labour migration to Korea: non-professional and professional. Prior to 1990, there were almost no labour migrants in Korea. There has been a steady increase in the inflow of temporary foreign non-professional workers – first as trainees and later under the two main categories of temporary non-professional work permits. This group now is split into foreign workers admitted under bilateral agreements (the Employment Permit System, or EPS) and ethnic Koreans admitted on a Working Visit permit (H-2 visa). By 2004, non-professional labour migrants comprised around 2% of total employment of the medium-educated, and by 2009 more than 3.5%. This excludes those who obtained permanent residence status, a growing group. In 2016, overseas Koreans holding permanent residence accounted for the single largest category of foreign residents, about one-quarter, of which about 65% were in the economically active population.

Figure 2.9. A sharp increase in the number of temporary foreign workers in the late 2000s

Non-Professional Temporary Foreign Workers, stock and share of low-educated employment, 1990-2016.

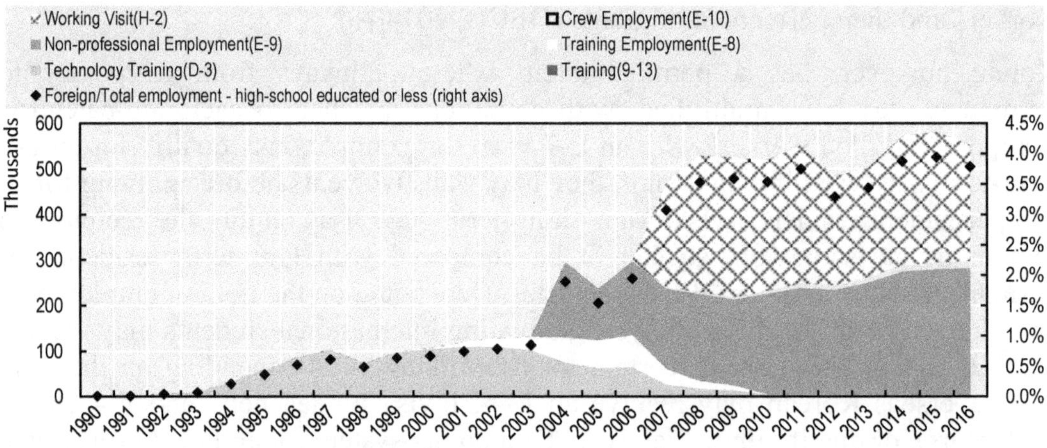

Note: 1) Total employment is taken from the number of employment of the EAPS for lower education levels. 2) Status classification is completely revised in 1993, so values before 1993 are linked with relevant status after revision. Employment Status 9-11 pre-1993 is considered professional.

Source: Korea Immigration Service Statistics Yearbook.

In addition to non-professional workers, there is a smaller but also growing number of professional labour migrants. Prior to 1993, all these workers fell under a single category. Since then, there are separate classifications for different professional activities. The largest group has historically been language instructors; their number peaked in 2010 at 23.3 thousand, but has since fallen as Korean youth cohorts shrink and the demand for native English speakers has declined in response to changes in university admission requirements. The group which has grown the most is that of Special Occupations (E-7), a catch-all category for different skilled occupations ranging from specialty chefs to skilled tradespeople. Nonetheless, labour migrants account for a marginal share of total employment in professional occupations in Korea.

Figure 2.10. Higher-skilled labour migration has been much less significant

Professional Temporary Foreign Workers, stock and share of high-educated employment, 1990-2016.

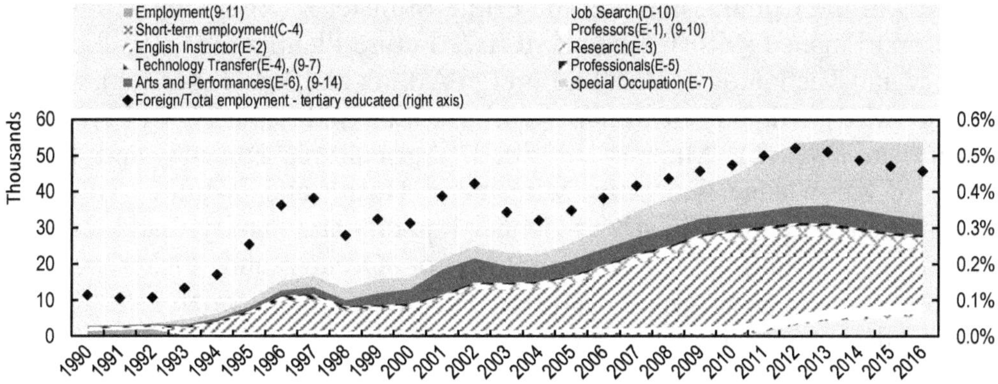

Note: 1) Total employment is taken from the number of employment of the EAPS. 2) Status classification is completely revised in 1993, so values before 1993 are linked with relevant status after revision.

Source: Korea Immigration Service Statistics Yearbook.

Notes

[1] Members of the Commission are: the Prime Minister's Office, the Ministries of Strategy and Finance (MSF), Science, ICT & Future Planning (MSIF), Education & Science and Technology (MEST), Foreign Affairs and Trade (MFAT), Ministry of Justice (MoJ), Ministry of Public Administration and Security, Culture, Sports and Tourism (MCST), Ministry of Food, Agriculture, Forestry and Fishery, Ministry of Knowledge Economy, Ministry of Health and Welfare, Ministry of Employment and Labor, Ministry of Gender Equality and Family, Land, Transport and Maritime Affairs (MLTM), Ministry of Oceans and Fisheries, Korea Communications Commission, National Police Agency, Small and Medium Business Administration, and the Korea Coast Guard.

[2] Budget lines associated with the Basic Plan have been significant: the first Basic Plan in 2009 led to a budget of about USD 555 million, mostly for social integration (55.6%). The Commission reported in 2013 that about twice as much was effectively spent on related projects between 2009 and 2012.

References

Lee, H. (2008), "International marriage and the state in South Korea: focusing on governmental policy", *Citizenship Studies*, Vol. 12/1, pp. 107-123, http://dx.doi.org/10.1080/13621020701794240. [5]

OECD (2017), "A portrait of family migration in OECD countries", in *International Migration Outlook 2017*, OECD Publishing, Paris, http://dx.doi.org/10.1787/migr_outlook-2017-6-en. [6]

OECD (2017), "A portrait of family migration in OECD countries", in *International Migration Outlook 2017*, OECD Publishing, Paris, http://dx.doi.org/10.1787/migr_outlook-2017-6-en. [8]

OECD (2014), "Managing labour migration: Smart policies to support economic growth", in *International Migration Outlook 2014*, OECD Publishing, Paris, http://dx.doi.org/10.1787/migr_outlook-2014-6-en. [7]

OECD (2014), "Managing labour migration: Smart policies to support economic growth", in *International Migration Outlook 2014*, OECD Publishing, Paris, http://dx.doi.org/10.1787/migr_outlook-2014-6-en. [10]

OECD (2010), "Better Managing Labour Migration", in *OECD Reviews of Labour Market and Social Policies: Israel*, OECD Publishing, Paris, http://dx.doi.org/10.1787/9789264079267-8-en. [4]

OECD (2009), "International Migration and the Economic Crisis: Understanding the Links and Shaping Policy Responses", in *International Migration Outlook 2009*, OECD Publishing, Paris, http://dx.doi.org/10.1787/migr_outlook-2009-3-en. [9]

Oh, J. et al. (2012), "Migration Profile of the Republic of Korea", *Research Report Series*, No. 2011-01, IOM Migration Research and Training Centre, Seoul, http://iom-mrtc.org/eng/business/business02.php?admin_mode=read&no=119&make=&search=&s_url= (accessed on 18 October 2017). [3]

Park, Y. (1991), *Foreign Labor in Korea: Issues and Policy Options.* [1]

Seol, D. and G. Han (2004), "Foreign Migrant Workers and Social Discrimination in Korea", *Harvard Asia Quarterly*, Vol. 8/1, pp. 45-50. [2]

Annex 2.A. Supplementary figures

Annex Figure 2.A.1. Composition of the change in employment by industry sector, by demographic group, 2005-15

Panel A. Manufacturing and mining sector.

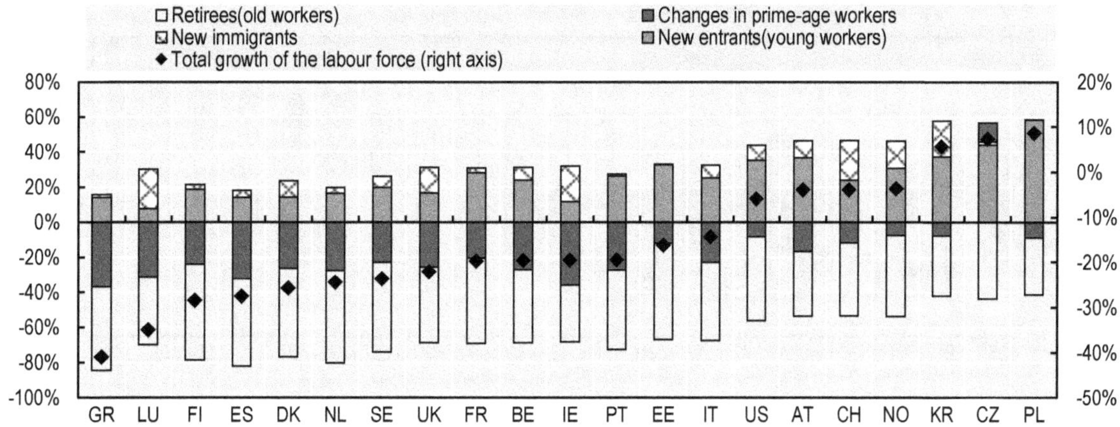

Panel B. Construction sector.

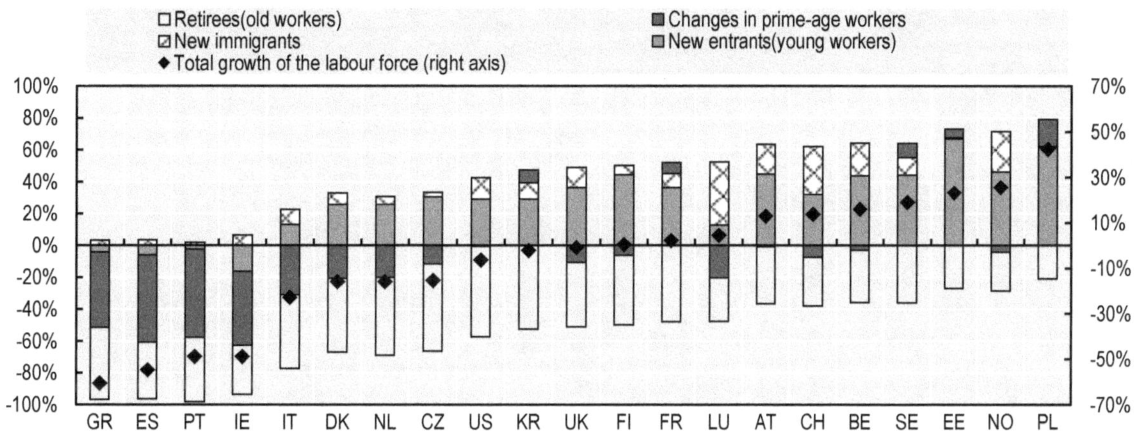

Panel C. Agriculture, forestry and fishing sector

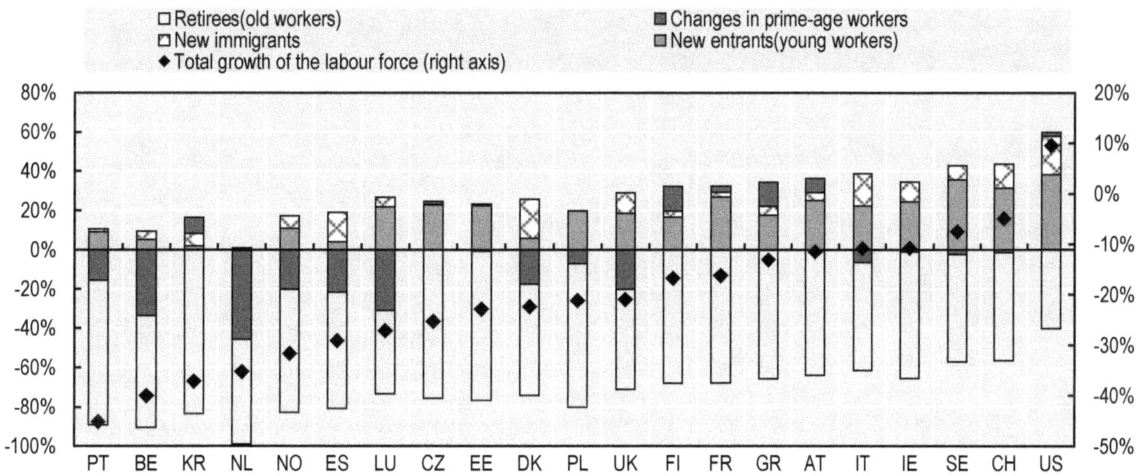

Source: Europe: LFS; United States: ACS; Korea: Ministry of Employment and Labor, LFS, FLFS.

Annex Figure 2.A.2. Composition of the change in low-skill occupation, by demographic group, 2005-15

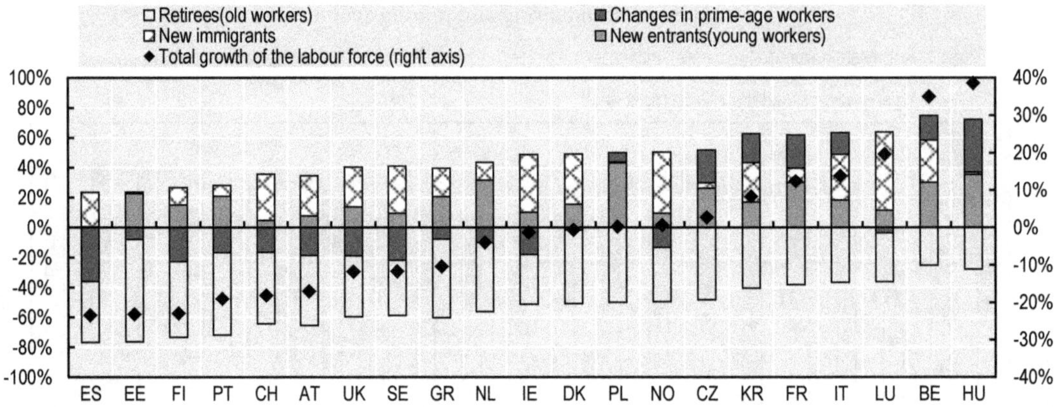

Source: Europe: LFS; United States: ACS; Korea: Ministry of Employment and Labor, LFS, FLFS.

Chapter 3. Low-skilled labour migration in Korea

This chapter discusses the low-skilled labour migration framework in Korea, whether current policy can meet future needs and safeguard local workers and programme participants. The chapter traces the evolution of the Employment Permit System and options for the future. The different features of the EPS are described and compared with prevailing practice in other OECD countries, highlighting unique features such as a points system for authorising employers to recruit foreign workers and ongoing state management. The programme for ethnic Koreans, which accounts for a large share of foreign workers, is also analysed. The chapter examines whether constraints on mobility suppress wage growth for workers. Compliance measures to reduce overstay and abusive practices by employers are reviewed, including incentives for return and facilitations for mobility and status change. The chapter then concludes with a discussion for the more efficient operation of the system.

The statistical data for Israel are supplied by and under the responsibility of the relevant Israeli authorities. The use of such data by the OECD is without prejudice to the status of the Golan Heights, East Jerusalem and Israeli settlements in the West Bank under the terms of international law.

The development of a low-skilled foreign worker programme from trainees to the EPS

Foreign workers started to appear in Korea in the late 1980s. As the immigration flow grew during the 1980s, the Korean government decided to simplify entry and departure formalities. In addition to simplifications in the administrative process, the government made efforts to join the globalising world and attract more foreign companies and investors to Korea. Visitor numbers also increased following the Asian Games in 1986 and the Olympic Games in 1988. Along with the increased inflow of temporary visitors, concern grew over the need for appropriate measures to prevent foreigners from overstaying their visa. Many of the foreign residents did not leave at the end of their stay, finding illegal employment opportunities.

In 1991, the first regulated system for low-skilled workers was created, under the form of an Industrial Technical Training visa. The programme, the Overseas Investment Firm Industrial Trainee System (ITS) was nominally intended to admit foreigners to work in Korean forms in order to acquire skills they could then bring back to their home countries. ITS was originally oriented towards firms with factories abroad: the system allowed those companies to bring workers from potential market countries to Korea to educate them as trainees and send them back to their countries to work for the same firm. In this, it mirrored the Industrial Training visa introduced in Japan in the 1960s. As in Japan, however, it was used largely as a means to fill demand for low-skilled labour. ITS was expanded in 1993 to allow all SMEs to request "trainees" (again mirroring a similar extension in Japan in 1990). Following this decision, the numbers of so-called "trainees" in manufacturing rose sharply. ITS was based on a ceiling of workers; in April 1993, this was set at 10 000 foreign "trainees" to designated 3D industries every year. A few months later, an additional 20 000 trainees were added to the programme. The total number of trainees reached about 90 000 in 1997. The ITS ceiling reached 145 000 in 2002.

Trainees were not covered by labour law and were particularly vulnerable to illegal employment practices. Further, high fees imposed in the recruitment process in origin countries meant that trainees were often indebted and under pressure to accept illegal employment practices and to violate their visa conditions. Overstay was thus high among ITS visa-holders: the rate of unregistered workers reached almost 64% of the total foreign workers during the late 1990s. In 2000, ITS was modified to allow participants who completed two years of traineeship to undergo a skills test (including a language test) and work for one more year under labour law (similar reforms had been implemented in Japan). The number of trainees approached 98 000 in 1999, while the number of foreign workers in violation of their visa rose to 135 000 (OECD, 2001[1]).

The channels opened in the 1990s also led to a growing foreign population. By the end of 1997, the number of foreign nationals staying more than 90 days (and registered as required under the Emigration and Immigration Act) was 177 000, still less than 0.5% of the total Korean population. During the Asian financial crisis of 1998 the number fell by 16% but increased by 28% in 1999 alone, to just over 189 000. Indeed, by 2001, foreign workers of various status, including irregular workers, accounted for just over 1% of the total workforce. They were composed principally of Chinese, Taipei Chinese, Japanese, Filipino and Vietnamese nationals (OECD, 2001[1]).

Many of the workers under ITS were ethnic Koreans from China; as they spoke Korean, they were able to find work not only in the manufacturing sector but also in the service sector, even if the latter was not authorised under ITS or other visa programmes. Recognising this state of affairs, Korea introduced the Employment Management System (EMS) in 2002, which authorised ethnic Korean Chinese to work in additional sectors, subject to registration, a short training course and sector restrictions.

The limits of ITS were clear to the government: trainees were taking on debts to pay rents to unscrupulous middlemen, were vulnerable to exploitation in the workplace, had a high rate of violation of visa conditions and overstay, and often worked in sectors for which they were not authorised. Korea decided in 2003 to phase out the programme. At that point, there were 103 000 legally resident trainees, as well as numerous overstayers. The 2003 Act on the Employment of Foreign Workers took effect with the introduction of the Employment Permit System (EPS) in mid-2004. EPS recognised foreign workers as workers. ITS was phased out by 2007, with all workers shifted into the EPS for the remaining duration of their ITS stay. The introduction of EPS also included a regularisation for overstayers, who were allowed to shift into EPS. In 2002, prior to EPS, undocumented workers accounted for 80% of the total; this was brought sharply down in 2005 through the opportunities to acquire an initial extension of stay under EPS.

Non-professional employment visas under the EPS, the E-9 visas, began to be issued in 2005. The objective of EPS was, and remains, to address the labour shortage in low-skilled occupations in firms with certain characteristics (initially, sector and size, as well as level of demand), while maintaining the temporary status of workers and protecting their rights prior to, and during, the employment period. Recruitment occurred through bilateral agreements and with employers offered a roster of potential candidates, reducing recruitment fees substantially. EPS will be described in more detail in the next section. When first introduced, the E-9 visa had a duration of three years maximum. This was extended to four years ten months when the first workers reached the end of their term in 2008; when the new limit was first reached in 2010, provisions were introduced to allow some workers to be admitted for a second employment period after a return to their home country.

Initally, EPS subsumed the Employment Management System (EMS). While EMS was originally only for ethnic Chinese with family ties, it was transformed in 2007 into a Visit Work Visa (the H-2 visa), available to ethnic Koreans from China, Russia, Mongolia and Uzbekistan, regardless of whether they had family ties in Korea. The H-2 visa was capped at 303 000 residents, and had the mixed policy objective of re-establishing ties with Koreans overseas, and supplying labour to sectors of the Korean economy which were clamouring for additional workers. The H-2 visa rapidly reached its ceiling. H-2 visa holders were originally subject to some training requirements and reporting requirements, but these have been gradually lifted. Further, in 2010, the important decision was taken to allow status change from H-2 to a permanent residence status (F-4), an option which was immediately utilised by many H-2 visa holders. The number of F-4 holders rose from 51 000 in 2009 to 129 000 in 2010 alone, and continued to rise sharply in the following years. By 2016, the total number of F-4 visa holders had reached 373 000.

Box 3.1. Key actors in Korean labour migration policy

A number of actors play a key role in managing labour migration in Korea.

The Ministry of Employment and Labour (MoEL) has a focus on addressing labour shortage faced by SMEs and preventing irregular and overstaying migrant workers. MoEL conducts surveys to analyse the reasons why Koreans avoid such jobs and employers' preferred solutions to the shortage. The MoEL adopted the EPS and signed MOUs with the partner countries to import workers. MoEL is involved in the selection process and job referral.

The MoEL delegates specific tasks to Human Resource Development (HRD) Korea, which is an affiliated agency of the Ministry. HRD branches exist in each partner country to manage local tasks of the EPS. They guide applicants and operate the EPS-TOPIK language exam. HRD also provides pre-departure and post-arrival training sessions to selected EPS job seekers and support services during their employment in Korea. HRD also provides training to ethnic Koreans under the H-2 Work Visit permit.

The MoEL is also responsible for commissioning research regarding foreign manpower policy. Research may cover labour shortages, conditions and status of foreign workers, employer satisfaction, adaptation of foreign workers, and other issues related to recruitment of foreign workers. MoEL may also commission public agencies to conduct research on these topics.

The Korea Employment Information Service (KEIS) is responsible for supporting people to find jobs, improving their skills, conducting relevant research and operating employment information systems including the job matching portal Work-Net and the HRD-Net training portal. KEIS offers policy recommendation along with the labour market forecasts. KEIS conducts labour market testing and ranking of employers wishing to hire foreign workers under EPS.

The Ministry of Justice (MoJ) enforces the immigration policy and foreign workers policy. The MoJ and MoEL are jointly responsible for the EPS and programme for overseas Koreans. Under the MoJ, the Korea Immigration Service (KIS) is responsibility for controlling the formalities of entries and departures, issuing visas and work permits for migrant workers and keeping records on their length of stay, overstays, status changes and re-entries. The MoJ inspects worksites to evaluate the implementation of foreign worker regulations.

EPS: A general framework for low skilled labour migration

The main programme for temporary low-skilled work in Korea is the Employment Permit System (EPS). EPS is the largest temporary foreign worker programme operating on a bilateral basis among OECD countries, and has become a model of reference for practices in this field. This section examines the structure of the EPS.

In 2003, the Ministry of Employment and Labour announced a plan to introduce an "employment permit system" for temporary foreign workers under which they are granted greater labour rights than previously, and legal protection equivalent to their Korean peers. The EPS framework for labour migration was laid out in 2004. Under the Act on the Employment of Foreign Workers, the EPS was the first official provision for temporary labour migration, offering low-skilled foreign workers two types of visas. Initially, the nonprofessional Employment Visa (E-9) was offered; the Working visit Visa (H-2) was created in 2007. While foreign workers already accounted for about 2% of total civilian employment, EPS was designed specifically to ease labour shortage in SMEs while tackling the shortcomings of the previous systems. It allowed employers, in manufacturing, agriculture, livestock, fishery and construction industries, to request temporary foreign workers, who would be selected, trained and brought through a government-to-government bilateral programme.

The EPS matches employers in Korea with workers in origin countries (Figure 3.1). Candidates age 18 to 39 take a basic Korean language exam, the Test of Proficiency in Korean for EPS (EPS-TOPIK), developed specifically for the programme. Those who pass are admitted to a pool for consideration by the home country agency, which reviews their qualifications. EPS-TOPIK test does not guarantee the employment in Korea. After passing EPS-TOPIK a medical exam is conducted to screen for officially designated communicable diseases. After the language test, candidates have two years to apply. The sending agency keeps the application in the pool for one year, sending information to (the "roster") to HRD Korea. HRD Korea translates the job applications and checks and approves the qualification of job applicants. HRD Korea and the Job Centre manage the roster.

On the Korean side, HRD Korea and the Job Centre manage Korean small and medium sized enterprises which want to hire foreign workers due to labour shortage. To hire foreign workers enterprise must request and receive permission. Prior to asking for foreign workers, the companies have obligation to make efforts to hire native workers for certain periods – normally over 14 days or seven days with announcement through the mass media such as the advertisement on newspaper or broadcast – as a labour market test to ensure that local workers are not adversely affected. If recruitment is unsuccessful, it has three months to submit an application to the Job Centre. KEIS ranks employers on a number of different criteria and assigns employment permits to firms. For each permit, the Job Centre identifies and sends three possible candidates. The separate pools eliminate opportunities for rent-taking in the recruitment procedure: no actor in the process can guarantee to the candidate that selection will occur.

Employers choose workers from this list of candidates. A Standard Labour Contract is drawn up respecting the conditions specified in the original Employment Permit application form the employer had previously submitted. The contract specifies working conditions including wage, working hours, holidays and workplace, etc. HRD Korea receives and forwards the Standard Labour Contract to the sending agency in the origin country (through an online system). The sending agency provides the contract information to the candidates and ascertains whether they want to sign the labour contract with the firm offering employment. If candidates agree to job offer and the Standard Labour Contract, the sending agency reconfirms its conditions and sends it back to HRD Korea electronically. Candidates are allowed to reject a proposed contract only once; a second refusal to accept a job offer excludes them from the active roster for a full year. If the candidate accepts the contract, both sides sign. Any problems which emerge in this phase, such as discrepancy of conditions in the contract between the employer and foreign worker or misinformation about foreign workers, are addressed by HRD Korea, which can verify and modify the conditions or the information.

EPS is a temporary programme; originally, the maximum duration of stay was limited to three years. An extension in 2010 brought this to four years and ten months. The E-9 visa granted to participants does not allow them to bring family members to Korea. In its original implementation, it was not intended to allow status change to residence permits allowing indefinite stay.

In terms of treatment of workers under Korean labour and social security law, EPS grants equal conditions to Korean nationals. Under the EPS scheme, migrant workers are guaranteed the same basic labour rights as Korean nationals, with the exception of job mobility, and are eligible for the same social insurance benefits and labour rights as domestic workers, although not the same health insurance scheme. Like other foreign nationals, they are not eligible for social support such as Basic Livelihood Security (BLS) or the Earned Income Tax Credit (EITC). They are covered by four different types of insurance: Departure Guarantee Insurance, national health insurance, return cost insurance, wage payment guarantee insurance and national pension.

EPS has evolved considerably since its inception to incorporate new developments in labour migration management policy and to react to programme evaluation as well as changing profiles of demand in Korea.

Figure 3.1. EPS selection winnows down the pool of candidates and employers

Simplified flowchart of candidate and employer steps in EPS.

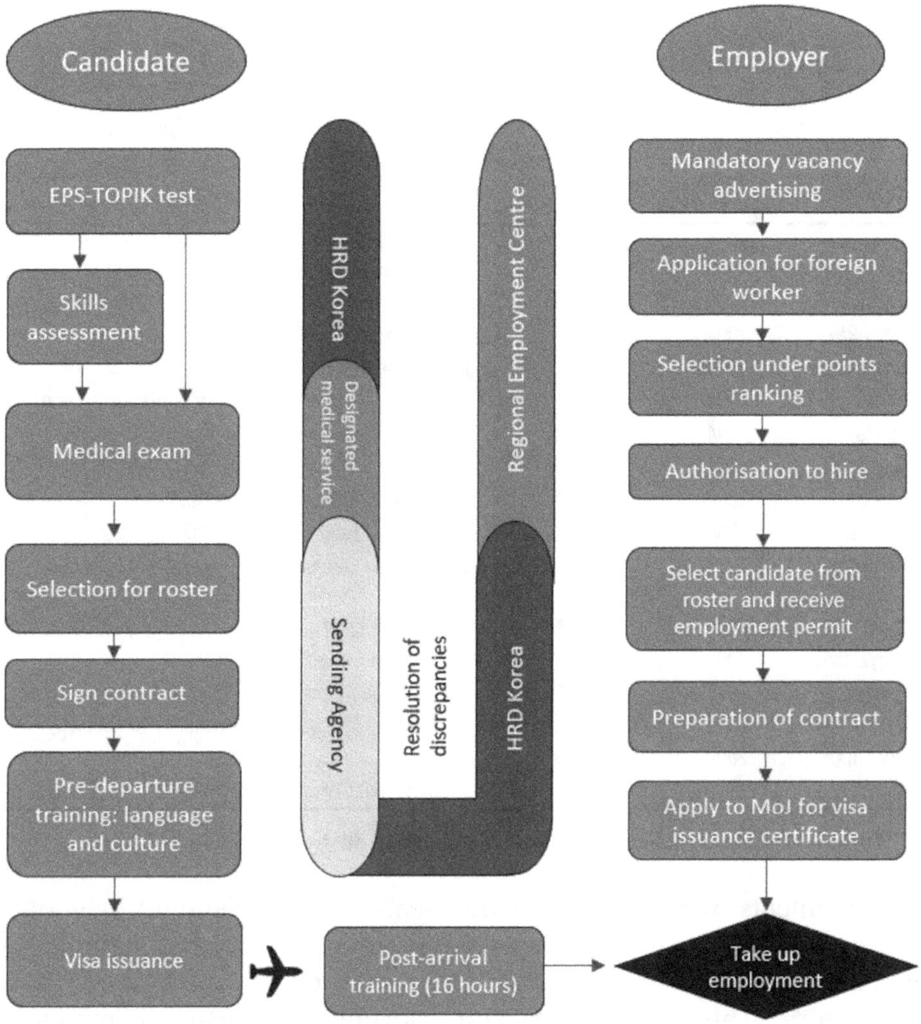

Source: OECD Secretariat based on HRD Korea.

Bilateral agreements

The recruitment process for the E-9 visa starts with the Ministry of Employment and Labour signing Memoranda of Understanding (MOUs) with governments of sending countries. Since the EPS was launched, the government has signed the MOUs with 16 partner countries to import workers (Table 3.1). The partner countries are Bangladesh, Cambodia, China, East Timor, Indonesia, Kyrgyzstan, Mongolia, Myanmar, Nepal, Pakistan, Sri Lanka, Thailand, the Philippines, Uzbekistan and Vietnam, and PDR Laos. The government bodies in these countries are directly involved and responsible for the selection and admission process of the foreign workers to guarantee transparency and fairness.

The largest supplier of labour force to Korea since the programme began until 2018 is Viet Nam, followed by Thailand and Indonesia. In terms of the number of active participants, in 2016 Viet Nam was the first, with 14.5% of all permit holders, followed by Cambodia (13.5%), Indonesia (11.5%) and Nepal (10.6%).

Table 3.1. EPS is based on a growing number of bilateral agreements

Countries with which Korea has bilateral agreements (MoUs) for labour migration under the EPS.

Country	Year of agreement	Share of total present, 2016	Sending agency
Indonesia	2004	11.5	National Board for the Placement and Protection of Indonesian Overseas Workers
Mongolia	2004	3.5	The Labor and Social Welfare Service Office
Sri Lanka	2004	8.6	Sri Lanka Bureau of Foreign Employment
Thailand	2004	9.1	Department Of Employment
Philippines	2004	9.4	Phillippine Overseas Employment Administration
Viet Nam	2004	14.5	Center for Overseas Labour
Cambodia	2006	13.5	Manpower Training and Overseas Sending Board
Pakistan	2006	1.4	Overseas Employment Corporation
Uzbekistan	2006	5.6	Agency for foreign Labor Migration Affairs
Bangladesh	2007	3.7	Bangladesh Overseas Employment and Service Limited
China	2007	1.4	Investment Promotion Agency, Ministry of Commerce
Kyrgyzstan	2007	0.4	Information Consulting Center
Myanmar	2007	7.1	Shwe Inn Wa Services Agency Co., Ltd
Nepal	2007	10.6	Department Of Labor Employment Promotion
East Timor	2008	0.6	Overseas Employment Office
Laos	2017	0	Employment Service Center

Source: Ministry of Employment and Labour, Ministry of Justice, HRD Korea.

While the contents of the bilateral agreements are confidentially negotiated and not disclosed, there is no indefinite commitment to receive nationals of the participating countries, nor is there a fixed annual quota on admissions from any partner country. This gives Korea some leverage to ensure compliance with programme regulations, quality control and to react to spikes in overstay by workers from individual partner countries. Since the introduction of EPS, recruitment has been suspended from certain countries due to concern over illegal overstay among nationals from these countries. This was the case for Viet Nam in 2013, for example. Since origin countries consider the possibility to deploy workers to Korea as very desirable, recruitment suspensions have led origin countries to strengthen integrity measures in order to restore the bilateral recruitment mechanism. Measures taken by origin countries to improve compliance have included, for example, suspending access to EPS in regions where high overstay rates have been noted. Measures taken by Korea have included disqualifying relatives of overstayers from eligibility for EPS.

Most EPS partner countries deploy temporary workers to a wide range of destinations in the Gulf Countries and among Southeast Asian developed economies, with flows to Korea comprising only a small share of total deployment

(OECD/ADBI/ILO, 2018[2]). In 2015, Korea was the destination for fewer than 2% of workers deployed from Nepal, and 10% of workers deployed by Viet Nam. Yet wages are much higher in Korea than in other destinations, and fair recruitment means that workers pay much lower fees for recruitment and are able to remit a larger share of their earnings to their families, making EPS one of the most attractive programmes for partner countries and workers.[1]

Box 3.2. An origin country perspective: EPS in Nepal

As one of the partner countries, Nepal sends a labour force with rather high education within the country to Korea. Labour migration occurred even in the 1980s, when Nepali workers used brokers to receive a short-term trainee visa through an invitation letter from a Korean SME, remaining to work in agriculture, livestock and manufacturing. The brokerage system was expensive – accessible only to wealthier Nepalis – and illegal. The trainee programme reduced costs, but the insecure working status as trainees often led to illegal employment. In fact, protest by Nepali interns in 1995 over abuse of human and labour rights in workplaces under the trainee programme drew government attention to the issue.

When the EPS was adopted, Nepali job seekers flocked to Korean language institutions to prepare for the TOPIK. 31 000 sat for the exam in 2008, and 36 000 in 2010. However, interest in the programme has fluctuated due to the difficulties in passing the exam, changes in the recruitment quota and financial barriers. The pass rate was 21.7% in 2008 and 11.5% in 2010. Nonetheless, TOPIK participants and EPS applicants remain high, and 4 000 to 6 000 Nepali workers arrive annually in Korea.

The HRD Korea local branch is in charge of all practical affairs in Nepal including registration, execution and grading of TOPIK, selecting top scored applicants, conducting skills test and a medical check-up. It also works in close collaboration with sending agencies, other institutions and NGOs promoting Korean language education. Another governmental body, KOICA, contributes indirectly by sending high-skilled Korean officers to national universities in Nepal to teach various areas of expertise including Korean language and culture. All these efforts add up to attract more applicants to the EPS.

The exam remains a barrier. Attaining a score above 80 on the EPS-TOPIK requires a strong commitment to studying Korean and often taking Korean language courses in on of the expensive private language institutions which have cropped up since EPS was introduced. Migrant workers selected through EPS still belong mostly to relatively wealthy families and have higher education.

The government hopes to increase the placement quota for Nepali workers gradually. It hopes to influence the preference of employers for Nepali workers and counteract previous negative perception due to their visible participation in protests. As the reputation of previous workers by nationality indeed affects the recruitment quotas in the future, HRD Korea in Nepal works to inform potential workers about their impact on the future inflow of Nepali workers to Korea.

Annual quotas by sector

The Foreign Workforce Policy Committee (FWPC) under the Prime Minister's office, an interministerial working group, determines the inflows of low-skilled foreign workers, including the ceiling on the total number, industry of employment and countries of origin every year.[2] Before the FWPC is held, the Foreign Workforce Employment Committee in the Ministry of Employment and Labour previews the agenda brought to the FWPC. A "Working Committee for Policy on Foreign Human Resources" under the FWPC meets prior to the FWPC. The "Working Committee" comprises up to 25 representatives of social partners (employees and employers), public interest members such as NGOs, and high-level government officials responsible for foreign worker issues. It is chaired by the Vice Minister of Employment and Labor. This "Committee" functions as a consultation mechanism in determining policy, including quotas. Following input from this committee, the FWPC examines demand from employers and considers the need to protect resident workers, as well as the overstay rate of foreign workers of sending countries. In general, the quota is set after subtracting the number of returning workers and adding the estimated number of additional manpower in need. The FWPC also decides the permitted work sectors which can hire foreign workers with an E-9 visa. The main sector which receives employment permits is manufacturing (Figure 3.2).

Figure 3.2. Annual quotas have largely favoured the manufacturing sector

Annual admission quotas for E-9 visas programme, 2004-18.

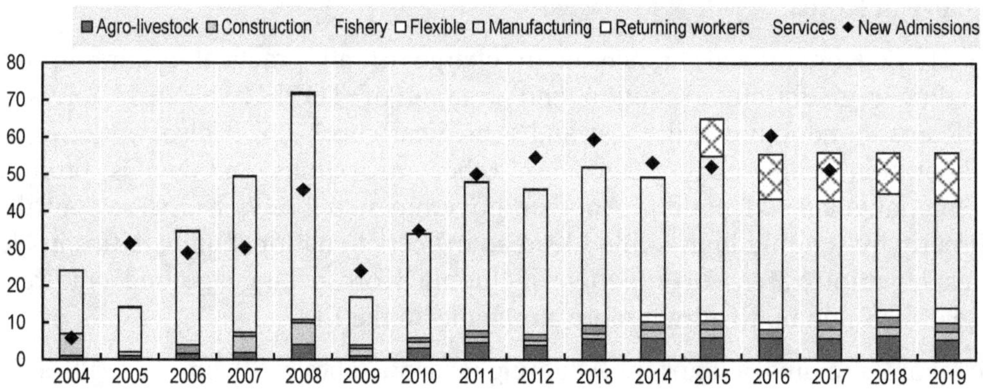

Note: Returning workers have been admitted since 2012 with sector assignment. "Flexible" workers may be allocated to sectors during the year depending on demand.
Source: Ministry of Employment and Labour.

The quotas have varied from year to year, with a sharp cutback in 2009 with the global financial crisis and the drop in employment. Since 2011, admission numbers have been fairly stable. Since 2011, returning workers under the two provisions for returns have been included in the quota, with a certain set-aside based on the expected number of returns under the "diligent worker" provision, and with a ceiling placed on re-admission based on the advanced Korean language test. Since 2014, a small part of the annual quota has been kept in reserve to allocate to sectors where demand is particularly acute during the year.

Demand has historically been higher than the quotas, so that not all employers receive work permits. In the agricultural sector, for example, applications stood at 26 000 in 2014 and rose to 29 500 in 2016, compared with about 6 000 permits authorised under the quota.

Box 3.3. Quotas and caps in labour migration programmes

Many OECD countries use quotas and caps as a management tool for labour migration programmes. Methodologies for setting quotas vary, as do their policy objectives. The overall objective of placing a ceiling on entries within temporary labour programmes is to restrict entries below demand of employers, in order to protect the resident labour market from negative effects if not distortion. As a consequence of their objectives, the form taken by quotas and caps varies. They can be general (e.g., Hungary, Estonia), for temporary renewable skilled worker programmes (e.g., United Kingdom, the United States), for temporary unskilled programmes (e.g., Italy, Israel, the United States) and for seasonal programmes (e.g., Italy, Spain, New Zealand, United States).

Korea is unusual among OECD countries for setting sector-specific quotas for the manufacturing industry. While caps on seasonal agricultural workers are in place in a number of countries, most temporary programmes for lower-skilled workers are labour-market tested rather than capped.

Ceilings may also be applied to youth mobility programmes such as working holiday makers, and to pilot programmes during the testing phase. Countries with permanent economic admission programmes (e.g., Australia, Canada, New Zealand, the United States) also set caps. In the case of permanent migration, caps may also be meant to limit the effect on labour markets, but may also relate to processing capacity or broader objectives of supplying labour force, as well as ensuring that no occupation dominates entries. From the late 2000s until the mid-2010s, Canada set occupation-specific quotas within its Federal Skilled Worker permanent migration stream to ensure that certain occupations did not dominate inflows. Australia similarly applies an annual occupational ceiling to applications its SkillSelect permanent migration stream.

Some quotas are set relative to total employment. In Estonia, the inflow quota, from which there are numerous exemptions, is set relative to total population, and has stood at 0.1% since 2007. Between 1990 and 2013, foreign employment in Austria was capped relative to total employment, with the ceiling first set at 10% of total employment, and later lowered with the expansion of exemptions (OECD, 2014[3]).The quota was of the stock of work permits – similar to the stock quota used for H-2 in Korea –

and when reached, no new permits would be issued.

While the form of the EPS quota for E-9 and H-2 workers is unlike that in other OECD countries, the process for assessing the level is similar. Empirical data on vacancies and labour supply are taken into account, and stakeholder consultation plays a major role in negotiation, leading to a compromise.

When temporary labour migration programmes have quotas, these are generally set through bargaining between interest groups, with employers usually pushing for higher allocations. Empirical analysis generally provides the background for discussion, with final allocation based on negotiation (Chaloff, 2014[4]). In some cases, expert bodies or planning commissions are created to determine quotas. Italy's 1998 labour migration law foresaw a triennial planning document, based on empirical analysis, to establish entry quotas.

The TOPIK language test

The second screening criteria for foreign candidates is the Test of Proficiency in Korean (TOPIK) for the EPS. TOPIK is a standardised Korean language test, based on levels of proficiency, developed by the National Institute for International Education (NIIED) in 1997 as the benchmark assessment of language skills. When a language test was added to the EPS system in 2005, the basic existing TOPIK level was not appropriate for the non-professional jobs targeted under EPS, requiring the development of a new test. The EPS-TOPIK evaluates Korean language proficiency and understanding of Korean culture. The questions consist of 25 listening questions and 25 reading comprehension questions. They evaluate basic understanding of the Korean society as well as ability to communicate job responsibilities and industrial safety.

The TOPIK result is the basic threshold for eligibility for EPS; applicants must score at least 80 points out of 200. Among the applicants meeting the threshold, the Human Resources Development Service of Korea (HRD Korea) selects the top scoring.

HRD Korea is in charge of all the practical affairs including implementation and registration of TOPIK. The local branches of HRD Korea in partner countries collaborate with public organisations (sending agencies) to operate the examination. The sending agencies publicise the upcoming test on their websites and in local newspapers. Applicants selected through a pre-registration screening process can register for TOPIK online or in person at designated sites; the registration fee is about 24 USD. The test consists of listening and reading parts in the form of multiple choice questions. In preparation for the exam, HRD Korea provides open question books to the applicants explaining about EPS and showing the sample questions of the test. The book and audio files are available on the EPS-TOPIK website. However a large number of applicants take Korean language classes in private institutions. From 2007 to 2017, more than 1.7 million applicants took EPS-TOPIK in the sending countries, far more than were admitted to EPS. Most applicants to the test are men; the pass rate in 2017 was 24.3% (Table 3.1). The pass rate varies between countries and has been higher in the past (32.5% in 2013, for example) but has never exceeded 50%.

Table 3.2. A large number of candidates have taken the EPS-TOPIK

Number of EPS-TOPIK applicants, 2011-17, and pass rate in 2017

Year	Total	Gender		Age		
		Male	Female	Below 20	21-29 years	Over 30
2011	298895	259479	41261	10230	203725	84940
2012	166082	138147	27935	12429	89505	64148
2013	221871	195580	26291	18312	125137	78422
2014	235589	202910	32679	2924	23651	16239
2015	237232	204093	33139	3394	34250	22268
2016	293584	245377	48207	3524	38388	25175
2017	284820	237594	47226	3775	44998	20560
Pass rate in 2017	24.3%	24.7%	22.5%	18.8%	24.7%	24.8%

Source: Ministry of Employment and Labour.

The TOPIK result is valid for two years. Passing applicants submit their EPS job application and other required documents to sending agencies as long as the TOPIK result is valid.

Korea is unusual in requiring that candidates for migration submit to a language test. Most OECD countries do not require low-skilled temporary workers to pass a language test. Given that the employment period is for several years, and that workers will be placed in small firms where they will not be able to work without speaking Korean, the test is essential for the success of the programme.

For applicants, the investment in the language test is significant in terms of time, and sometimes in terms of financial expenditures. The TOPIK is also indirectly a screening for the ability of candidates to work with modern technology, since test preparation requires not only basic literacy but also competences in using computers and on-line testing applications. The shift to computer-based testing also ensures that the candidates who pass the test are able to interact with modern user interfaces.

The willingness of candidates to invest in studying for the TOPIK, in light of the low pass rate and the fact that even successful candidates are not assured a place in the EPS, indicates the high value of the programme for workers in origin countries.

The points system for selecting EPS workers

A further innovation in the recruitment system was the introduction of a points system for selection of EPS workers. In the first years of the EPS, selection on the basis of TOPIK scores and qualification on the basis of physical strength was considered sufficient. However, in the pool of TOPIK test participants, some candidates had specific and relevant experience in the fields for which they were applying - especially manufacturing and agriculture - which were not taken into considered. Even if they passed the TOPIK, low scores excluded them from consideration. The points system was introduced in 2014 to allow prior professional experience to be taken into account. For all candidates who pass the TOPIK, and who have specific skills, it is possible to undergo the skills test. Points are given for skill level, work experience, training, qualifications and job capacity. Candidates who only take the Korean language test may score up to 200 points. Candidates who pass the test and take the additional skills test may score up to 100 points for Korean language, 100 for skill levels and 100 for work experience, training and qualifications. The roster takes the top scoring candidates. The system has proven very popular: in 2016, 90% of applicants took the additional skills test (Park and Kim, 2016[5]). As a result, the roster now includes candidates with lower Korean language skills but with specific experience or qualifications. The EPS workers entering from 2017 are therefore better qualified than those who came under the pre-points system.

Building the Candidate Pool and selecting candidates

In origin countries, the basic eligibility requirement is age, between 18 and 39 years of age. The age requirement is, in Korea as well as in other countries, one of the paradoxes of labour migration: countries with age-discrimination legislation for employment of resident workers apply discriminatory policy to the selection of labour migrants. Age is sometimes a factor in ranking and selection of applicants for permanent economic migration (OECD, 2014[6]). The logic for permanent migrants is based on the lifetime contributions expected from immigrants. Temporary workers whose stay is linked to their employment are less often subject to age requirements. For example, there is no age requirement for temporary seasonal workers in Canada or New Zealand.

The sending agencies translate, check and approve the job applications. The government bodies in the sending countries compose a roster with about 2.5 times the applicants of the designated national quota, based on the profiles and TOPIK scores, and provide the rosters to HRD Korea. This allows the Korean authorities to choose candidates based on their characteristics, and prevents anyone in the sending country from determining who will be chosen. As a result, EPS represented a sharp decrease in recruitment costs, which have generally fallen below 1 000 USD, excluding the time spent preparing for the TOPIK exam. Recruitment costs for workers under EPS are very low (Box 3.4).

Box 3.4. Recruitment costs under EPS

EPS was introduced in part to eliminate the high fees paid to intermediaries under other channels used by labour migrants to come to Korea. For example, workers spent more than 3 000 USD in recruitment fees alone to come under the ITS programme which preceded EPS (Kyung, 2013[7]). A survey conducted in 2014 of 119 newly-arrived workers under EPS from three countries (Thailand, Viet Nam and Indonesia) identified the main costs they underwent - an average of USD 1 385 (Abella and Martin, 2014[8]). The average cost of preparing for the language exam was about USD 250. The necessary skills and medical tests under EPS cost less than USD 100.

Candidates are drawn from the roster by the HRD Korea based on the preferences of employers in different sectors, by gender, nationality and age. This means that not everyone on the roster can make it to the pool. In practice, younger male workers of certain nationalities have higher chances to be chosen as candidates.

According to a 2014 MOEL survey of employers, the leading category of preference was nationality (39%), followed by skill (17.4%), gender (11.9%), Korean language level (9.9%), age (8.3%) and physical condition (7.8%). It may be that the selection process addresses the latter three characteristics effectively, by excluding workers with poor physical condition, age above 40 and no language ability, allowing employers to focus their preferences on characteristics not filtered by EPS selection in 2014.

The selection has favoured young candidates (Figure 3.3). Among the candidates who are admitted to the roster for selection, firms tend to pick a younger population of workers. The age limit for admission is 40 years, but 2% are over 40 due to being re-employed after an initial spell.

E-9 participants are fairly well-educated, given that the programme is for non-professional work. In 2013, an analysis showed that 20% of those selected and admitted to Korea had tertiary level education, 60% at least secondary, and only 20% less than secondary. This higher education level has important implications for their eventual prospects to remain in Korea, since the limited bridges to other visa categories depend in some part on their education level.

Applicants to EPS are mostly men, but selection leads to a smaller share of women among those admitted to Korea. In 2013, 11.8% of test-takers were women, and 11.9% of passers were women. 16.4% of those admitted to the roster were women. Fewer than 10% of those admitted were women in 2013, and by 2016, only 8.6% of the E-9 visa holders in 2016 were women, however.

Figure 3.3. Most EPS workers are very young

Age distribution of primary applicants for EPS, 2005-09 and 2010-15, new permit recipients in 2015, and employment in Korea.

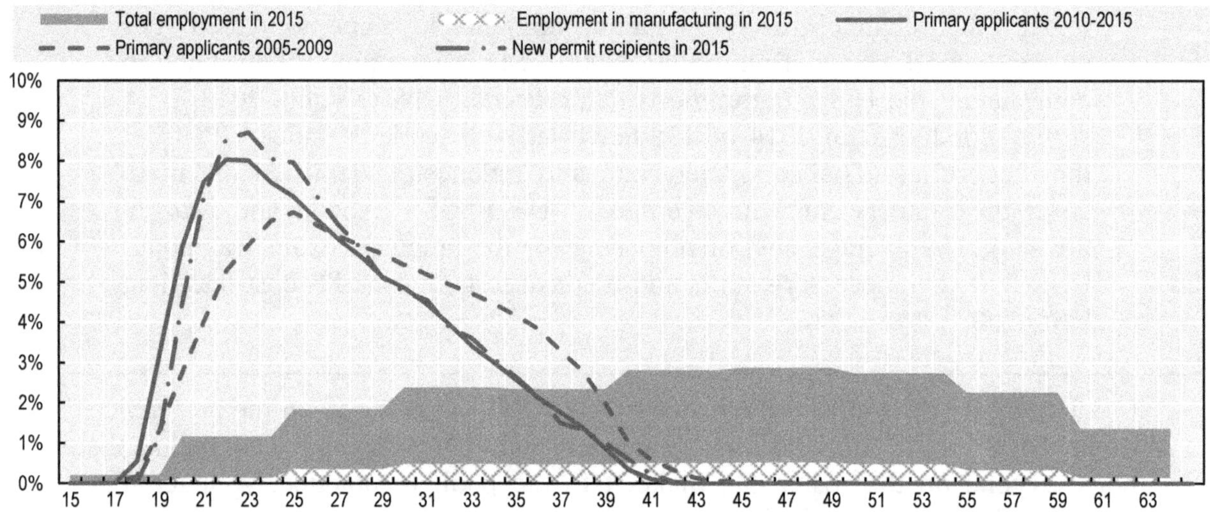

Note: Primary applicants are EPS-TOPIK passing candidates (not re-entering workers).
Source: Ministry of Employment and Labour, Korean Statistical Information Service.

The labour market test

In Korea, there are two steps for employers who wish to hire workers under EPS: first, submit to a labour market test; second, compete for the limited number of employment permits offered under the annual quotas.

Employment Permits are issued pursuant to a labour market test, which takes the form of a mandatory publication of the vacancy at the public employment centre (Job Centre). When EPS was first set up in 2004, the minimum duration of the listing was set at 30 days. In 2005, this was reduced for certain sectors (identified by the Ministry of Employment) to just seven days listing, or three days if the listing was also posted in newspapers and television). Employers can begin the process by applying for the Employment Permit at Job Centres only after having failed to find a Korean for the job. From 2010, the general requirement was reduced to 14 days. For active media advertisements (TV, magazine or newspaper) for seven days, the Job Centres are likely to authorise the request to hire foreign workers. Job Centres may send local candidates for consideration by the employer. If employers twice refuse to hire candidates the Job Centre deems suitable, the Job Centre may reject the employer's request for an employment permit for a foreign worker. In practice, the labour market test is nominal, with very few cases of rejection of applications due to failure to hire locally.

In comparison with other OECD countries, the EPS labour market test is relatively short in duration (Figure 3.4), although the requirement to hire workers referred by the Job Centres is on the stricter side of labour market tests. This discretionary mechanism depends on the jobseekers enrolled with the Job Centre and the willingness of caseworkers to consider jobseekers suitable for the jobs advertised.

Caseworkers can insist on sending older workers, or workers of a different gender than those preferred by employers, for example. In practice, however, the increasingly segmented labour market for foreign workers is reflected in the predominance of vacancy listings at Job Centres for foreign workers.

Figure 3.4. Korea's advertising requirement is within the range of most OECD countries

Duration of the advertising period in the labour market test for temporary non-skilled labour migration permits, 2017.

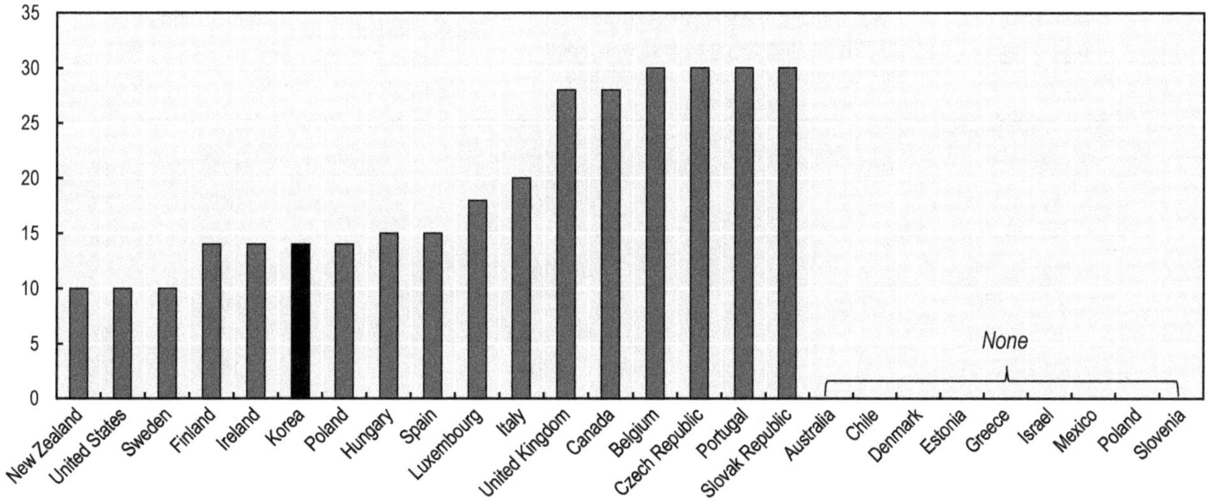

Note: Where countries have varying durations for different visa/permits, the lower end of the range is used. For instance Germany takes up to 14 days for seasonal work, Spanish Seasonal Work takes 25 days and Finland 2-4 weeks for low-skill work. In some instances, numbers denote the average days used in practice as in New Zealand. Australia, and Denmark have no fixed duration. Estonia, Greece, Israel, and Mexico have no LMT.
Source: OECD Secretariat.

Employers are able to file on-line. At first, prospective employers were required to visit government-designated employment support centres to request state permission to employ foreign workers under EPS. However, starting in 2009, employers have been able to use an online registration system.

Firm-level limits to the number of workers

A firm-level limit applies to employment of E-9 workers (Table 3.3). Businesses were originally limited to 20% of their workforce being comprised of E-9 workers; this was raised to 30% for businesses with fewer than 10 employees, and a bonus E-9 worker was allocated to firms with fewer than 50 employees in "root industries"[3]. At present, small firms in particular are authorised to have high shares of E-9 workers. Notably, in the manufacturing sector, the limit has increased in firms with 50 employees or less since the introduction of EPS. Firms with six to ten employees and firms with 31 to 50 employees were originally allowed to recruit maximum five and ten E-9 workers respectively; however, the firms now can employ additional two E-9 workers. The threshold leads to some anomalies, such as firms with 11 employees authorised to have 90% of their employees on E-9 permits, while firms with 10 may only hire five E-9. For small firms wishing to increase their E-9 workforce, it may be worthwhile to expand employment of other workers when applying to EPS, in order to qualify for a higher allotment.

Table 3.3. Smaller firms may employer a larger share of E-9 workers

Firm size and maximum number of E-9 employees in manufacturing, 2018

Number of employees		Number of E-9 employees allowed (+20% in 6 manufacturing sectors with labour shortage including "root industries" and provincial firms)	Annual limit of new permit issuance	Maximum firm-level share of E-9 workers	
From...	to...			From...	to...
1	5	5	3	500%	100%
6	10	7		117%	70%
11	30	10	4	91%	33%
31	50	12		39%	24%
51	100	15	5	29%	15%
101	150	20		20%	13%
151	200	25		17%	13%
201	300	30	6	15%	10%
301	-	40		13%	-

Note: Total employees refers to the number of national employees enrolled in national employment insurance.
Source: Ministry of Employment and Labour.

Foreign workers employed under other permit categories (e.g., H-2, E-7 or F-4) do not count against the E-9 firm limit, so that a firm can employ as many foreign workers as it wishes, as long as the E-9 visa-holders do not exceed the statutory limit. Layoffs of employees which occur after the E-9 worker is authorised are not necessarily reported to HRD Korea, so the share of E-9 workers may exceed the limit due to layoff of other workers, and not be detected until subsequent applications for E-9 workers.

Points-based system for employers

Since 2012, employers must not only labour-market test vacancies but also score on a points-based workforce allocation system in order to obtain employment permits. Previously, employers were served in a first come, first served order, with employers physically queueing outside of government offices. Under the points-based system, all applications are scored, and the top-ranking are issued permits until the quota is exhausted. Further, since permits are issued during the course of the year, employers with higher scores receive permits earlier, while those with lower scores may have to wait longer. The points-based system includes a number of limits which were already present in the distribution of employment permits.

The initial application is filed with an employment centre, which checks if it meets the basic eligibility (labour market test, sector restrictions, firm size, etc.).

The employment centre sends approved requests to the KEIS, which scores the application and awards employment permits three times a year. KEIS informs the employment centres, which then notifies employers by text message that they have been awarded employment permits.

The points system comprises three elements: basic requirements, bonus points, and penalty points (Table 3.1).

Table 3.4. The points system for attributing EPS workers to employers

	Items included	Points
Basic Items (100 points total)	• the ratio of foreign workers employed to the number permitted	22.4-30
	• ratio of foreign workers whose re-employment contracts have expired / total number of foreign employees	22.4-30
	• the number of new foreign workers requested	19-20 points
	• the number of people (natives) hired from employment centres during the labour market test	14-20 points
Bonus Points	• full enrolment/payment of return cost insurance and accident insurance of all foreign employees	1
	• establishment and operation of quality dormitories*	3
	• employers' completion of training for workers*	2
	• no workplace accidents for five consecutive years	1
Penalties	• violated any law according to the enterprise guidance and inspection results of the previous year	-0.1 to -0.3
	• failure to pay for departure guarantee insurance on time	-0.5 to -2 per worker, up to 5
	• EPS workers have left due to: (non-cumulative)	
	o Sexual violence	-5
	o Verbal / physical abuse, sexual harassment	-3
	o violation of working conditions	-3
	• Death of a foreign worker in the previous two years	-2

Note: * Points attributed for manufacturing sector are lower, 0.5 for housing and 0.2 for training. Points are attributed for two years maximum.
Source: Ministry of Employment and Labour.

Basic items in the points system provide a minimum of 77.8 out of 100; bonus points for good practices in programme bring up to 7 (2.7 for manufacturing) points, making the effective range from 77.8 to 107 (102.7 for manufacturing).

Penalties are imposed for violating the regulations of labour law and EPS regulations, for a workplace fatality of a foreign worker, and for causing the departure of an EPS worker due to violence, abuse, harassment or failure to pay wages or other violations of workplace regulations. The maximum penalty is 12.3 points. Employers with many penalties for having lost workers due to abuse may still rank high enough to receive workers if their labour shortages are acute and they score high enough on the basic characteristics of labour demand.[4]

The attribution of points has changed since the system was first introduced in 2012. The most significant changes occurred in 2014. The number of points for hiring Korean workers was increased sharply; originally there had been little difference between firms hiring no Koreans (18 points) and those hiring six or more (20 points). This changed to 14 points for no hiring and 20 points for those hiring three or more Korean workers. Another change was to offer more points to firms requesting a large number of foreign workers; this was taken as a sign of labour needs, rather than of dependency on foreign workers. Bonus points for quality housing and for offering workplace training were increased for all sectors but manufacturing, to provide agricultural workplaces especially an incentive to improve working conditions.

Penalties for mistreatment and abuse of workers were increased, although employers who have committed such abuses are still allowed to recruit foreign workers if they score high enough.

The introduction of these changes led to the exclusion of many employers in 2014, and to the first time in which the quota was not entirely used due to insufficient eligibility of firms for employment permits.

Box 3.5. Penalties for abusive employers in foreign worker programmes

Most migration management systems have provisions to exclude employers who have abused the conditions of issuance of permits – i.e., have violated migration regulations – from participating in the programme. However, many temporary foreign worker programmes do not have specific provisions for sanctioning abusive employers, beyond the standard civil and criminal penalties for violation of labour law. The possibility of banning, blacklisting or excluding the employer from future recruitment, or withdrawing authorisation for other foreign workers employed by the same employer, is not always among the sanctions possible for cases of physical or sexual abuse and harassment.

The 2014 EU Directive on Seasonal Workers requires Member State to "provide for sanctions against employers who have not fulfilled their obligations under this Directive, including the exclusion of employers who are in serious breach of their obligations under this Directive from employing seasonal workers".

In Israel, provisions were introduced in 2017 to allow the Ministry of Interior not to grant a permit - or renew a permit - for a permit holder to employ a foreign worker if the employer was convicted of serious offenses against a foreign worker. The Ministry also has discretion to refuse renewal, for up to 18 months, when the employer is suspected of serious offences. Prior to this, no explicit reference to recruitment bans was included.

Canada includes, among possible sanctions for non-compliance with the regulations of the temporary foreign worker programme, a recruitment ban of one to five years. Among the possible grounds for exclusion is failure to ensure that the workplace is free of abuse, including physical, sexual, psychological and financial abuse. This extends, in principle, the liability of the employer to behaviour by other employees at the worksite. In the cases where a ban has been applied, it has generally been for two years.

Similarly, in the United States, violations investigated and confirmed by the Wage and Hour Division (WHD) following complaints from temporary workers regarding may lead WHD to initiate debarment proceedings, which may result in an employer exclusion for one to five years. In the H-2B programme, which does not allow employer change, employers are liable for return costs if the worker leaves for reasons of constructive dismissal, including harassment of different types.

Employer selection of candidates

Employers who have been approved following a labour market test and have been assigned an employment permit are contacted by the Job Centres. Job Centres provide employers a list of qualified candidates; Job Centres give up to three opportunities to employers to choose among EPS candidates. After receiving the list, the employers review the applicants and select based on the provided information on their eligibility and competence of candidates. Once the decision is made, the employer provides an employment contract to the selected applicant. The work contract must contain working conditions including salary, working hours, workplace and holidays. At the final stage, the employers apply for Certificate for Confirmation of Visa Issuance to the Ministry of Justice. When this certificate is sent to the origin countries, the selected applicants receive a working visa at the Korean Embassy. The duration from the start of the process to the arrival of the worker is about four months; given the size of SMEs, variations in labour demand are often related to a sudden contract, requiring workers quickly.

Arrival in Korea and placement in the firm

Workers receive some additional training in the origin country prior to departure: 38 hours of Korean language and seven hours of Korean culture.

Small groups of EPS workers arrive throughout the year. As soon as the workers arrive in Korea, they are met at the airport (flights generally arrive in the early morning). They participate in employment training sessions prior to employment, for three days, including language, the EPS, labour law and relevant information for daily life and for compliance with the obligations of EPS. The technical content of the training courses is determined by the federations of employers. There is also a health examination prior to placement in the firm. At the end of this three-day training, employers pick up the workers.

Many employees live in company dormitories. In 2015, more than 90% of workers had housing provided by their employer; of these, two-thirds of employers paid their housing costs entirely (Seol and Ko, 2015[9]).[5] The need to provide separate dormitories for men and women is one explanation for the employer preference for male workers. Employers of one or two workers may rent private accommodation for their workers. The rent paid by workers for employer-provided housing is not regulated by EPS and is subject to private contractual agreement between workers and employers.

During the stay in Korea

All workers arrive with an initial three-year contract. Three months after arrival, there is a follow-up by telephone to check on the adaptation of the worker. In some cases, there are issues which emerge in the workplace: employers may find that the work doesn't have the physical strength expected, and employees, many of whom are highly educated in their home country, may have difficulty adjusting to the low-skill job. These issues are mediated by local HRD offices. Workers or employers may request additional training during the stay in Korea, which is provided by the local HRD office; these trainings are paid for by public funds directly to training agencies. Courses are generally short, and held on weekends; this is also a means to keep workers engaged when they are not busy at work. HRD checks with firms twice a year.

To serve foreign workers, the Ministry of Employment and Labour has established nine regional Support Centers for Foreign Workers. These are funded by the government and operated by NGOs.[6] The centre offers in-person and telephone support in multiple languages, primarily to E-9 and H-2 workers. Centres offer courses, including Korean language classes and certification. They also organise cultural and sport activities, and in some centres, a medical clinic. HRD Korea also maintains a call centre which serves employers and operates offices around Korea, as well as a pool of interpreters.

After three years in Korea, employers decide whether they wish to extend the contract of the worker for an additional 22 months.

The preparation for return is built into the system. Workers are contacted by direct mail three months prior to return (six months prior to 2018). Two months prior to departure, HRD contacts the worker to provide information on how to recover contributions and benefits, and to propose pre-return and post-return training, the latter supported by HRD in the home country. Contacts with Korean firms in the home country are also provided. Text messages are sent in the months before return. Prior to 2018, visits and consultations were conducted six months prior to return to propose services. From 2018, contacts are made two weeks before return with workers.

The entire process of EPS is funded by the Korean government with almost no costs borne by employers. Employers of foreign workers pay only for the pre-employment training expenses.[7] There are some private agencies assisting companies with the procedures related to requesting foreign workers, and some training provided by employers is only partially reimbursed by HRD Korea, but these expenses are not substantial.

The insurance system for foreign workers

All workers in Korea are guaranteed basic labour right and are eligible for the same social insurance benefits and labour rights. Non-professional foreign workers (E-9 and H-2) are covered by four major social insurances within the same scheme with Korean workers: Industrial Accident Compensation Insurance, National Health Insurance (NHI), National Pension and Employment Insurance. Among them, all foreign workers and employers who employ them are subject to compulsory subscription to the first two insurances.

Industrial Accident Compensation Insurance applies to all business places that employ workers regardless of their nationality. The premium rate is decided annually at the end of the year, according to occupation category; the employer pays the entire premium. The Korea Workers' Compensation and Welfare Service is in charge of overall management, application of insurance and collecting premiums. Foreign workers' health-related risk is also subject to NHI, which covers the whole Korean population. Eligibility for workplace insurance is under the EPS, once employers submit qualification report of employees to the NHI within 14 days of employees' taking up duty. Both employer and employee pay a premium corresponding to 3.035% (total 6.07% in 2015) of monthly salary. Neither E-9 nor H-2 workers are covered by health insurance when they are between jobs.

In agriculture and fisheries, individual employers are not required to pay health insurance or workplace injury insurance; in small enterprises, there is no disability insurance. Workers employed by individuals or small firms rather than pay the full contributions themselves generally choose not to pay into these schemes and are not covered.

Regarding the national pension scheme, the principle of reciprocity applies: foreign workers' pension right in Korea would be guaranteed only if the same rule applies to Koreans who reside in their origin country. According to the bilateral social security agreement with sending countries of the EPS, E-9 and H-2 visa holders from eight countries out of 15 countries (China, Kyrgyzstan, Thailand, Mongolia, Uzbekistan, Philippine, Sri Lanka, Indonesia) are eligible for the National Pension benefit. Subscription is obligatory only for foreign workers from those countries and both employee and employer pay a contribution (4.5% of the average amount of monthly income). On the other hand, the principle of reciprocity does not apply regarding the lump sum refund, i.e. National Pension contributions allow cashing out when the foreign workers return to their country, even if the same regulation would not apply to a Korean.

Lastly, foreign workers under the EPS may voluntarily join the Employment Insurance in Korea; insured foreign workers receive unemployment benefits equal to those of native workers. An insurance contract is established by the employer applying to the regional employment centre if the employee wishes to be insured. The premium rate is 0.45% and 0.7% of monthly wage for each employee and employer. The Korea Workers' Compensation and Welfare Service administers the Employment Insurance as well as Industrial Accident Compensation Insurance. Foreign workers and their employers who are covered by such an insurance policy are subject to each regulation.

The Act on Foreign Workers' Employment regulates mandatory subscription of foreign workers and their employers to four supplementary insurances, based on employment management and protection of the EPS workers: Departure Guarantee Insurance and Trust, Return Cost Insurance and Trust, Guarantee Insurance against Overdue Wages, and Injury Insurance.

First, the Departure Guarantee Insurance aims to have employer compensate superannuation to foreign employees who work more than one year in the same workplace. Subscription is the obligation of every workplace with more than one regular employee; however, employer of H-2 holders in the construction sector is exempt from this plan. As a premium, employees pay 8.3% of regular monthly wage on work permit contract every month and the foreign worker could receive it by reporting departure date to employment centre and applying to insurance company. The amount of insurance money substitutes for statutory superannuation by Guarantee of Workers' Retirement Benefits Act. However, if the quantity of departure guarantee insurance does not satisfy that of Retirement Benefits Act, the employer should pay the difference to the foreign employee. Departure Guarantee Insurance accrues to the worker, but is forfeited to the employer in two cases: if the employee stays less than 12 months with the employer, or if the worker leaves the employer without justification. This is an unusual arrangement, not employed elsewhere in temporary labour migration programmes, in which the worker must compensate the employer if the contract is broken through no fault of the employer. The amount of the insurance, 8.3% of salary, is not a substantial amount at the beginning of an employment spell but adds up to one month salary at the end of a year, providing a strong disincentive for workers to leave their employer once they have spent some time at the workplace.

EPS requires foreign workers to pay return cost as soon as they arrive in Korea. EPS workers establish an insurance contract through the employment training centre and must pay the premium within the prescribed period. The premium varies according to origin countries, between KRW 400 000 and 600 000, and can be paid in up to three instalments within 80 days from the date of entry into force of the contract. Foreign workers face 800 000 KRW of penalty if they do not subscribe to the plan. The insurance guarantees that workers have the means to pay for their ticket home at the end of their employment.

In the case of accident injury or illness other than occupation accidents, foreign workers have an obligation to be insured to casualty insurance as well. Foreign workers subscribe to the plan through the employment training centre and pay premium immediately in cash. The amount of premium varies according to age and health condition of employees; indicatively, it is about KRW 9 100 per year for 30-year old men.

Lastly, foreign workers under the EPS are protected from unpaid wage through employer-paid Guarantee Insurance. Employers of a workplace with less than 300 regular employees or where the Wage Claim Guarantee Act is not applied are required to subscribe to this guarantee insurance[8], which covers up to KRW two million of unpaid wage. The employer pays KRW 16 000 per year and per foreign employee to the insurance company. The foreign worker could make a claim on a wage to the insurer, in the case the employer delayed payment of wages. The employer could be charged of less than KRW five million of penalty if they do not follow the policy.

Departure guarantee insurance is returned to the worker within 14 days of departure. Starting in 2013, insurance benefits have been paid at Incheon International Airport, so that insurance benefits can be paid – without commission – upon leaving Korea.

Unemployment insurance is not compulsory for foreign workers (E-9 and H-2), although it is possible to sign up on a voluntary basis. Very few, if any, EPS workers pay into the UI system.

Working Visit Permit (H-2) for ethnic Koreans

The H-2 visa, offered since 2007, is a special employment permit for ethnic Koreans whose ancestors emigrated or were deported to foreign countries during the difficult times in modern Korean history prior to 1945. Most of these emigrants are in China, with some in Russia, Mongolia and several former republics of the USSR. The H-2 visa was introduced to replace the Special Case Employment Permit System, itself put in place in the early 2000s to regulate the employment of ethnic Koreans, who were allowed employment in a number of authorised occupations. This occupation list has changed over time and now comprises about 80 occupations (Annex Table 3.A.1). A list of 38 "positive" sectors (including construction) is included in the Emigration and Immigration Act as of 2018. Prior to the introduction of the Special Case EPS, there was no specific programme for ethnic Koreans, who used other available channels to come to Korea. This was in contrast to Japan, where ethnic Japanese from South America were admitted as labourers starting in 1989 (Skrentny et al., 2007[10]). Korea is not the only country to create a privileged channel for persons of national descent in its migration system (Box 3.6).

Ethnic Koreans who wish to work in Korea may apply for an H-2 visa at Korean embassy in their home countries. Ethnic Koreans can receive the visa as long as the total number of permit-holders does not exceed a ceiling; this ceiling has been set at 303 000 since programme introduction; the ceiling was set through consultations between the Ministry of Justice and the Ministry of Employment and Labour without a fixed reference to the labour market, and has not been adjusted since then. Upon receiving a visa and entering Korea, , visa holders must receive three days of training at a HRD Korea centre prior to employment. The training consists of education on Korean language and culture and relevant instructions on the EPS elements applicable to them (insurance) and on Korean labour law. Regardless of the employment status, job seekers with H-2 visa must file an application for foreigner registration within 90 days from entry. They need to notify employment or change in workplace within 14 days of its occurrence.

Box 3.6. Co-ethnic migration programmes in OECD countries

Many OECD countries harbour the goal of embracing far-flung national communities and/or their descendants (OECD, 2014[6]). Measures to include co-ethnic communities from outside national boundaries can also affect labour migration policies, with preference given to co-ethnic communities. Finland has long offered preferential treatment to foreign nationals of Finnish extraction wishing to immigrate. Italy's labour immigration legislation incorporates a quota of South Americans of Italian origin. Germany grants favourable migration conditions to ethnic Germans living in East European countries, who comprised a large share of immigrants in the 1990s. Greece admitted a large number of Pontian Greeks in the 1990s. In the 1990s, Japan opened up recruitment in less-skilled occupations for South Americans of Japanese descent. Israel proactively encourages Jews abroad to migrate to Israel, where, in the absence of a permanent labour migration stream, recruitment efforts focus on candidates who meet this ethnic preference. Public support in destination countries for such programmes has traditionally been strong and draws on solidarity or a sense of belonging. Challenges to labour market integration have arisen primarily where language skills have been limited.

Under this ethnic-priority scheme, the H-2 visa allows the permit holders to stay and seek jobs freely in Korea. Unlike the E-9 visa, it allows access to jobs in the service and construction sectors, which are otherwise closed to most non-professional foreign workers.

The general presumption of the H-2 programme is that the participants speak Korean, although this is not always the case (especially for participants from CIS countries). At first, H-2 recipients were subject to language requirements if they did not have relatives in Korea, unless they were employed in special employment. Until 2011, overseas Korean guest workers from China without relations in Korea, selected through a visa issuance electronic lottery, had to pass the Test of Proficiency for Business in Korea (B-TOPIK), which is monitored by the Korea Institute for Curriculum and Evaluation. However, in 2011, those eligible were selected through an electronic lottery out of all those that passed the existing tests and since 2012, eligibility has been decided through an electronic lottery only, without any tests. The language requirement has thus effectively expired.

The H-2 visa guarantees three years of stay and can be extended up to four years and 10 months in case an employer wishes to extend the employment of the migrant worker. Extensions must be requested prior to the expiration of the initial permit.

The stock of ethnic Koreans under H-2 visas has not changed drastically, and has stayed largely below the government quota of 303 000. The number of participants in the guest worker programme started off at 226 700 in 2007, and although it peaked at 306 300 in 2009, it declined to 240 200 in 2013 and to 255 000 in 2016. Since there are a number of options for extension of stay and changes of status, the H-2 visa has not been associated with a high illegal overstay rate. The number of persons overstaying their H-2 visa stood at 6 300 in 2013, 2.6% of the total; this fell below 1% in 2016. An amnesty offered in 2016 allowed H-2 visa holders to exit Korea voluntarily and return with an F-4 visa.

The employment rate of H-2 visa holders has been high, about 80% from 2012-16 according to the Foreigners Labour Force Survey. Despite the fact that H-2 workers are able to work in any sector, many (33%) were still working in manufacturing in 2016 (Figure 3.5). Employment was also highly concentrated in wholesale, accommodations and food service (30%), and the construction sector (19%).

Figure 3.5. Most Working Visit (H-2) holders are in manufacturing, construction and hospitality

Sectors of employment for H-2 foreign workers, 2016.

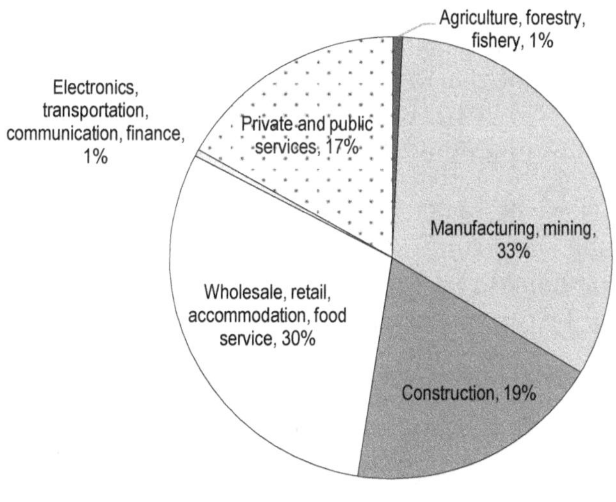

Source: 2016 Foreign Labour Force Survey.

The construction sector, which has been mostly off-limits to E-9 workers due to a very small quota under EPS, relies more heavily than other sectors on H-2 workers. A large number of ethnic Koreans in the initial period worked in construction. When the H-2 visa was introduced, it was accompanied by sector limits (Annex Table 3.A.2). During the economic downturn in 2008-2009, concern over the impact of H-2 workers on construction wages led the government to exclude them from the construction sector. H-2 employment in the construction sector is now contingent on receiving a special authorisation, under the Construction Industry Employment Registration System introduced in 2009. Employment requires a Certificate of Construction Industry Employment

Confirmation, issued after employment registration and training. The number of certificates issued is capped; the cap has varied between 55 000 and 60 000 since 2010, although the number can be adjusted during the year.

Also in 2009, incentives were offered to H-2 workers to find employment in SMEs in the manufacturing sector. The incentives proposed included shortening the length of stay required for permanent residency from 10 to five years and favourable treatment when inviting family members to Korea. In addition, in 2009 only, an entry quota was set for H-2 workers, at 17 000 new entries.

Relative to the E-9 visa, for which 92% of permit-holders are men, the H-2 visa is more gender-balanced, with 43% of H-2 holders being women. This also affects the sectors in which they are employed, with many working in hospitality services and domestic work. The fact that they speak Korean also facilitates their employment by families in childcare and eldercare.

H-2 visa holders have average incomes which are comparable to the incomes of Korean nationals with the same characteristics, suggesting that in the labour market they are able to compete.

The H-2 visa, originally developed to provide a specific status for ethnic Koreans abroad, has not only been loosened in terms of eligibility but has also become a major pathway to permanent residence. The F-4 visa for overseas Koreans was originally destined to ethnic Koreans from developed countries such as the United States, and was not issued to Chinese Koreans. This restriction was struck down in 2003. Starting in 2010, three separate grounds were offered for H-2 visa holders to acquire an F-4 permanent resident permit:

- First, H-2 visa holders who worked in the same work place in manufacturing in rural areas (population centres with less than 200 000 inhabitants) and agriculture for at least two years were allowed to adjust status. Two years as a baby-sitter also qualified (F-4-24).
- Second, persons over the age of 60 are eligible for status change (F-4-25).
- Third, since the F-4 visa is not meant for low-skilled employment, ethnic Koreans who acquire a professional certification are allowed to change status (F-4-27).

Professional certification has been the main channel of status change. Since most ethnic Koreans on H-2 visas have lower education levels – about 7% hold tertiary or post-secondary vocational qualifications – the F-4 provision has created a market for professional certification with the sole scope of status change. Private training academies have seized on the market and offer certification courses in a number of occupations, such as hairdressing or certain semi-skilled trades. The list of eligible occupations has been revised by the Ministry of Justice in response to oversubscription by H-2 visa holders. Nonetheless, the number of F-4 permanent residence holders has risen, with 50 000 new F-4 visas issue in 2016 alone (Figure 3.6). About one-third of the new F-4 visa holders in 2015 were changing status from H-2 directly, while others were returning to Korea after a spell in their home country.

Although the F-4 visa is a permanent-type residence visa, restrictions on employment apply. F-4 visa holders are not allowed to be employed as elementary labourers, certain service jobs (such as retail sales) to protect the domestic labour market and to comply with public interest (see Annex Table 3.A.1). The list of non-eligible occupations is drawn up by the Ministry of Justice. The number of occupations on the list have varied since the restrictions have been in place. In 2003 all employment in elementary labour (as well as in potentially problematic occupations related to gambling and nightlife) was prohibited. In 2009 the list specified 62 occupations and in 2010 it decreased to 58, and further decreased to 53 occupations in 2015. According to the current list, from 2015, the number of prohibited occupations to F-4 holders included 41 elementary simple labour (the least skilled), and 12 occupations in service and sales that are deemed to be against the public interest and domestic employment order; employment restriction in gambling and nightlife remain. The violation of this restriction could lead to a refusal of visa renewal and F-4 holders' expulsion, as well as penalties for employers. F-4 visa holders are eligible for F-5 permanent residence which lifts all restrictions on employment after five years residence; they may also receive the F-2 99 which also lifts restrictions.

Figure 3.6. The stock of overseas Korean permanent residents is rising due to status change from H-2 visas

Panel A. Stock of F-4 visa holders and new H-2 and F-4 visa issuances.
Panel B. Status change from H-2, 2015.

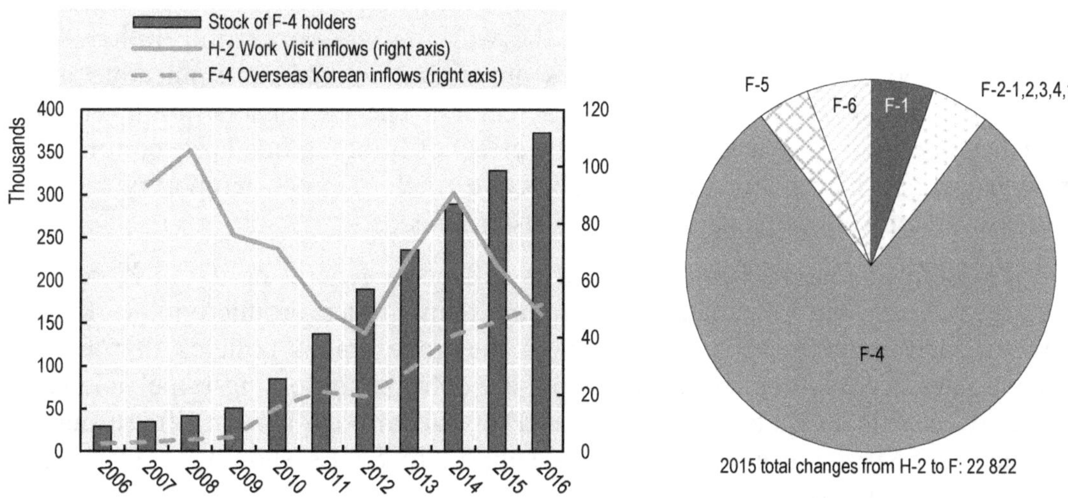

Source: International Migration Statistics of Statistics Korea for inflows, Korea Immigration Service for stock.

The rising number of F-4 visa holders will have important consequences for the labour market for foreigners. The employment rate of F-4 visa holders has remained at about 60% since 2012, even as the number increases, despite the fact that F-4 visa holders are 52% women. Unlike the H-2 permit, there are no restrictions on total duration of stay, and F-4 visa holders may eventually request Korean nationality. The E-9 visa has more restrictions than either visa for ethnic Koreans, but also provides a legal framework for redressing cases of illegal employment practices. Ethnic Koreans are more exposed to the same low-quality employment as their Korean peers.

The potential scope of the H-2 and F-4 visas are limited only by the number of ethnic Koreans living in China, estimated at most at about three million (Skrentny et al., 2007[10]). This group cannot be relied upon as an inexhaustible pool of workers on which Korea can draw. Already almost half of the ethnic Koreans in Korea are over the age of 50, with low educational attainment and facing the same challenges in the labour market as older Korean workers. Less than 30% of H-2 visa holders are under age 40. The ethnic Korean population in China is aging along with the rest of the Chinese population, educational attainment of the youth is increasing in line with trends in China, and improved economic conditions in the regions where ethnic Koreans live have reduced the incentive to migrate to Korea to take up lesser skilled employment.

Designing a low-skilled labour migration system for the future

As described in the previous section, Korea's low-skilled labour migration programme comprises two main pillars. One, EPS, is focused on specific sectors, with temporary stay. The other grants broader labour market access and facilitated access to permanent residence. Together, these programmes are contributing to meet labour demand in less qualified positions.

Korea's migration policy does not aim to counteract or correct the negative demographic trend affecting the size of the working age population; rather, the temporary labour migration programmes are meant to address immediate and structural demand for labour in specific sectors. The expansion of the ethnic Korean Work Visit programme has had the effect of bringing in a large contingent of permanent residents, but the main objective of the Korean temporary labour migration framework remains meeting short-term needs.

The provision of foreign workers to SMEs reflects a general policy in Korea to promote the survival of small firms, rather than higher productivity (OECD, 2016[11]), and may be considered one of the government policies that boost survival rates of low–productivity firms but are detrimental to long-run efficiency. To the extent that access to non-professional foreign workers is a specific resource provided to SMEs, the generosity of its support to SMEs should be examined carefully (OECD, 2016[11]).

In light of the policy objectives in Korea – to support immediate and structural labour needs in small firms, while limiting potential adverse fiscal and labour market impact on residents – this section examines how other OECD countries have designed labour migration systems.

Framework for managing low-skilled labour migration in other OECD countries

The central objective of labour migration management in OECD countries is to "help meet those labour market needs which cannot be satisfied through tapping domestic labour supply in a reasonable time frame, without adversely affecting the domestic labour market"; (OECD, 2011[12]). The framework should include the following elements (OECD, 2009[13]):

- A means to identify unmet labour needs;
- Work permits in numbers commensurate with the extent of labour needs;
- Means for matching immigrant workers to jobs, either overseas or in-country;
- Efficient permit processing and delivery procedures;
- Means for employers to verify the status of potential employees;
- Effective border control and workplace enforcement procedures

Putting the framework in place requires a definition of "needs", "reasonable time" and of "adverse effects", three parameters for which there is no absolute measure. The policy settings in OECD countries reflect the range of interpretation of needs, timeframes and adverse effects. In particular, the latter often involves a trade-off between groups which may benefit from labour migration and those which may not.

Lower skilled jobs are seen in most OECD countries as relatively simpler to supply from resident labour due to the low barriers to uptake, and the risk of adverse effects of labour migration to these jobs as higher, due to potential complementarity with residents with low education. For this reason, most OECD countries have subjected labour migration for low-skill jobs – and by low-educated foreigners – to stricter control than migration for higher-skill occupations. Many have limited provisions for low-skilled migration in labour migration channels allowing indefinite stay (OECD, 2014[6]). Indeed, a skill threshold is one of the main constraints on labour migration channels in many countries (OECD/EU, 2016[14]). However, there are a number of OECD countries which do not apply a skill threshold to their labour migration schemes, but use a combination of salary thresholds, labour market tests, and/or numerical limits to govern labour migration (Table 3.5).

Table 3.5. Channels for low skilled labour migration in selected OECD countries

	Countries	Characteristics
No skill threshold applied in general labour migration channel	Chile, Czech Republic, Estonia, Finland, France, Greece, Hungary, Italy, Norway, Spain, Sweden, Poland, Portugal	Labour market test (except Chile, Sweden), numerical limits in some countries
Specific channel for lower-skilled occupations, potential permanent stay	Austria, Belgium, Canada, Germany, Ireland (pilot 2018), Netherlands, United States	Labour market test applied, numerical limits may also apply (United States, Ireland), or may be limited to bilateral partners (Germany)
Time-limited channel only for labour migration in lower-skilled occupations	Israel, Japan, Korea Also in parallel in United States, Canada	Labour market test (Korea, United States, Canada), numerical limits
Seasonal worker programme only	Australia, Denmark, New Zealand	
No programme	Switzerland, United Kingdom	

Note: Excludes free movement.
Source: OECD Secretariat.

Although the main labour migration channel allowing potentially indefinite stay may be closed to migrants in low-skilled occupation, most OECD countries have some form of temporary or short-term channel open for less skilled labour migrants. Only a few OECD countries, as noted, exclusively have programmes offering limited-term stay to low-skill labour migrants.

Part of ensuring that there is no adverse effect on the local labour market is to ensure that the cost of foreign workers is at least as high as that of local workers. The labour market test usually takes into account the wage level offered to the foreign worker, benchmarked against a minimum, prevailing or collectively-agreed wage. Following admission, measures must be in place to ensure that the real cost of foreign workers does not fall below that of local workers. When foreign workers, who are already vulnerable due to lack of familiarity with the language and/or legal system of the country of employment, are further made more vulnerable due to their inability to change jobs or sectors, or dependence on their employers for housing, there is a risk of exploitation at a cost lower than that of local workers. To counteract that risk, compliance mechanisms include education and information, inspections (physical and virtual), and financial monitoring measures such as mandatory payments into local bank accounts.

Other measures can also be used to increase the cost of employment of foreign workers. One such measure is to impose and employment levy, or tax (Box 3.10). The idea of levies is one which has been discussed in Korea, and appears as a policy measure to explore in the Third Basic Plan, as a potential measure to "protect national jobs". Levies have been discussed for some time, with the Foreign Manpower Committee raising this possibility for the first time in 2010, and again in 2012 and 2014, deciding each time not to impose one (KOSBI, 2016[15]). Unsurprisingly, employers have opposed levies, on the grounds that resident labour is not available (Noh, 2015[16]).

The 2016 Economic Plan of the Ministry of Strategy and Finance included the introduction of levies, but the proposal was also withdrawn. One proposal for levies was to limit application to firms which have employed many foreign workers for a long period, e.g., firms with more than 10 EPS workers employed for more than five years (Seol et al., 2015[17]). The objective of such a targeted levy would be to signal to employers that meeting firm-level long-term and structural labour needs is not the objective of the EPS. This signalling effect could be achieved through reducing the firm-level quotas for "dependent" employers (see Box 3.3). Whether this signal is necessary depends on whether EPS is seen as meeting temporary or structural needs.

Is the demand temporary or structural?

One of the key questions driving migration policy design is whether need for labour is structural or temporary. When demand is structural, and there is little complementarity with locally available labour, it is difficult to argue for a temporary labour migration programme if workers are likely to be in demand and remain employable indefinitely. Previous OECD recommendations have noted that temporary labour migration for permanent labour needs is a contradiction (OECD, 2009[13]).

In the Korean case, there is a clear demand, but whether it is truly structural is not evident. At present, demand exceeds supply of foreign workers. While vacancy listings at the PES (Worknet) are not mandatory in general for employers, and do not represent the bulk of all job vacancies, they are a requisite for any employer wishing to hire a foreign worker through EPS. Consequently, vacancy figures reveal both total and foreign vacancies registered through the employment centre by employers. PES in data in Korea, as in other OECD countries where PES listings are obligatory for labour market tests, overrepresent demand for foreigners. However, they do reflect the occupations for which employers wish to hire foreigners and which are covered by the EPS. Vacancy data suggest that there are some occupations for which employers hope to fill a large share of vacancies with foreign workers (Figure 3.7). This is true for agriculture forestry and fisheries (68.4% of vacancies are for foreign workers), but also for manufacturing and construction occupations. Management, accounting, and office work is the most demanded sector in absolute terms; however, few employers opened their vacancy for foreigners– perhaps because the employer or sector was not eligible for the EPS.

Figure 3.7. Vacancies for which employers seek foreign workers are concentrated in a few sectors

Vacancies by sector and share of demand for foreign workers in 2013.

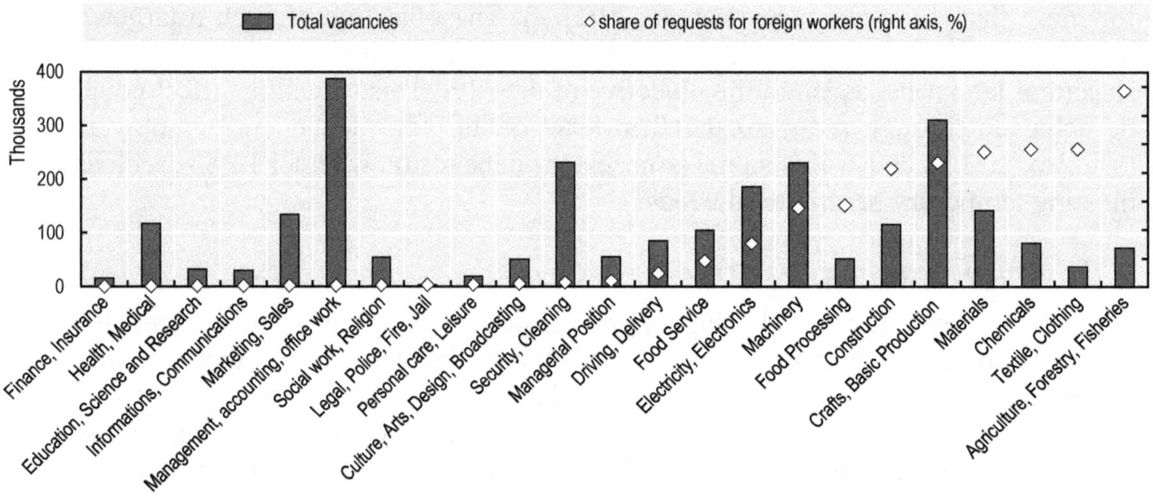

Source: Worknet.

Overall, demand is very high for foreign workers. In 2013, there were almost half a million vacancies on Worknet where employers sought foreigners. Of these vacancies, most were for jobs with low qualifications and where the salary was between KRW 1 and 1.5 million per month, or between USD 900 and 1 335 (Figure 3.8).

Figure 3.8. Vacancies for foreign workers are for low-skilled, low wage jobs

Panel A. Education requirements for jobs for foreigners. Panel B. Monthly salary (KRW 1000) offered. 2010-13.

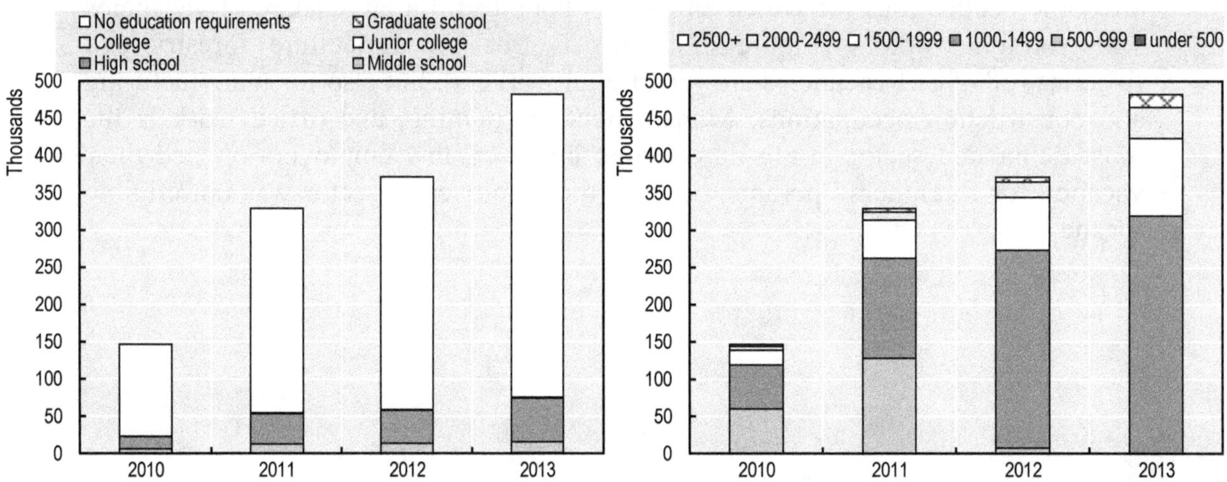

Source: Worknet.

Further, smaller firms are the ones which mostly try to recruit foreign workers (Figure 3.9). This is in line with programme design and with the strong labour demand among low-productivity SMEs. The growing number of requests from 2010 to 2013 involved firms of all sizes, but it was the smallest firms where demand grew more quickly at first. The bulk of demand in 2013 was in firms under 30 employees.

Figure 3.9. Foreign workers are mostly recruited by SMEs and micro-enterprises

Requests for foreign workers, 2010-13, by firm size.

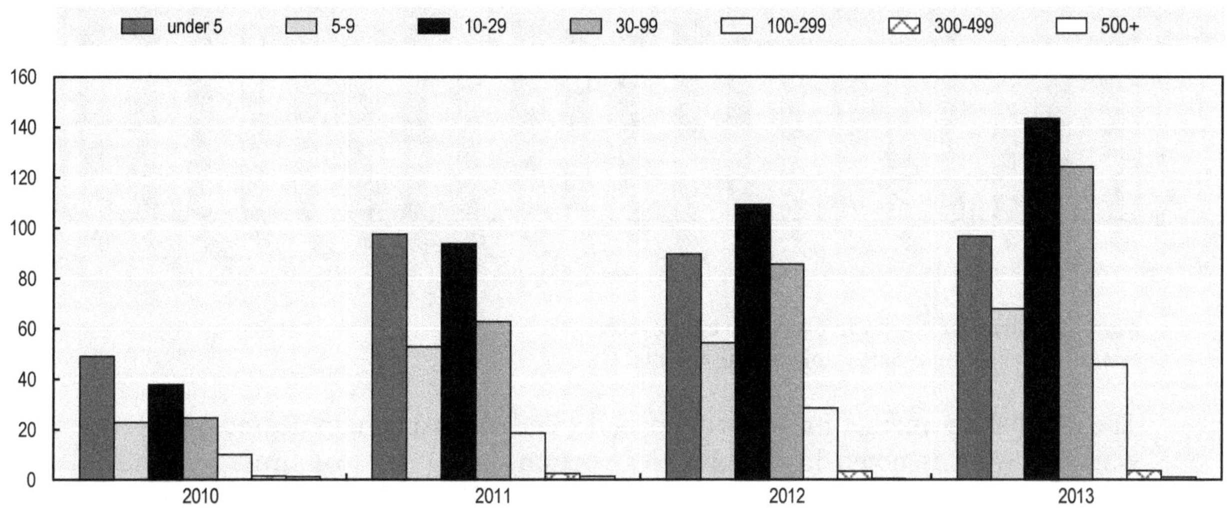

Source: Worknet.

Demand for foreigners exceeds the ability of firms to find available foreign workers. Between one in ten and one in three positions for foreigners went unfilled between 2008 and 2017 (Figure 3.10).

Figure 3.10. Part of the demand for foreign workers goes unfilled

Bi-annual demand for foreign workers, positions filled and unfilled and share of total vacancies 2008-14.

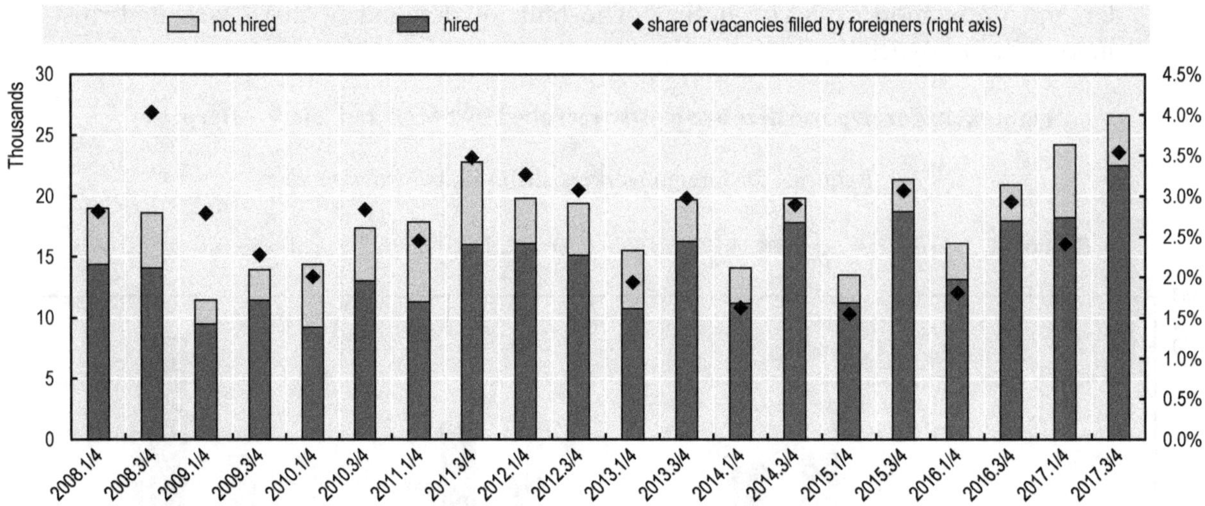

Note: Establishments with five or more employees.
Source: Occupational Survey of Establishments.

The dual labour market in Korea appears dependent to a certain degree on foreign workers. As was noted in the previous section, about 10% of firms respond to labour shortage by calling on foreign workers. These firms are offering low-quality employment, yet due to the restrictions on importing foreign workers, are unable to fill all the positions they would otherwise wish to fill.

Employers claim that the reason they hire foreign workers is that they are unable to recruit Korean workers (Figure 3.11). This is cited as a much more important reason than the long working hours. Low wages are more of an obstacle to hiring Korean workers in greater Seoul than in the rest of the country. When it comes to reasons why firms have difficulty replacing foreign workers with Korean workers, wages are again cited as a problem, especially in greater Seoul, but other factors - long working hours, a harsh working environment - are also cited.

Figure 3.11. Employers of foreign workers say that Korean workers are hard to find

Panel A. Reasons for hiring foreign workers, by region. Panel B. Reasons why it is difficult to replace foreign workers with Korean workers. 2015

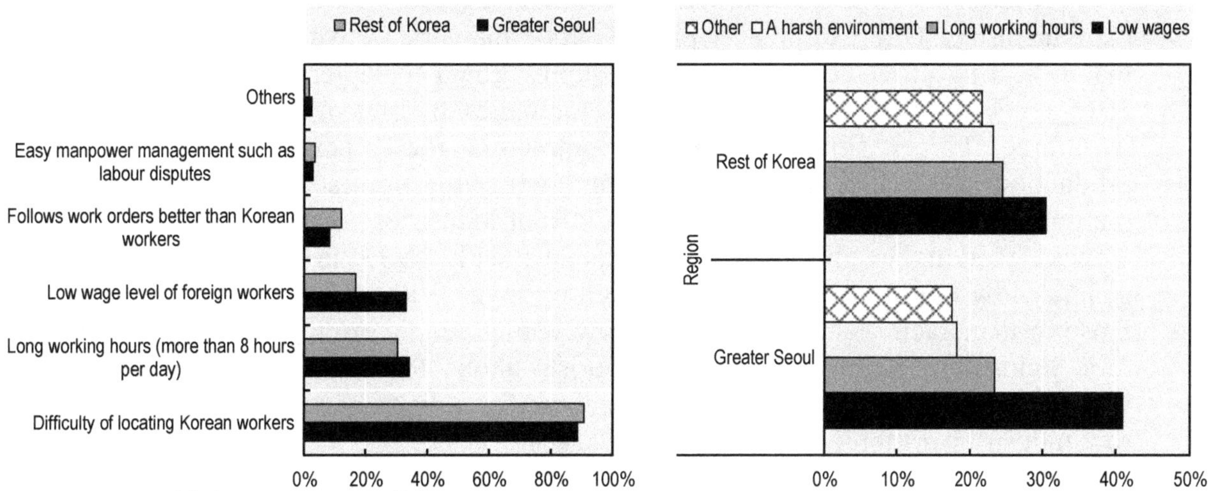

Note: Multiple responses possible.
Source: KOSBI survey cited in (Noh, 2015[16]).

In the manufacturing industry, the increase in the foreign share of employment has been noteworthy across the OECD in recent years (Figure 3.12). The share of employment in Korea, close to 10%, is among the higher levels in the OECD, but almost all OECD countries have seen a sharp increase in the foreign worker share of manufacturing employment. The example of root industries in Korea (Box 3.7) provides an illustration of the drivers of foreign employment in manufacturing.

Figure 3.12. The increase in foreign employment in the manufacturing sector is common

Share of foreign in total employment in manufacturing, 2005 and 2015 or latest year

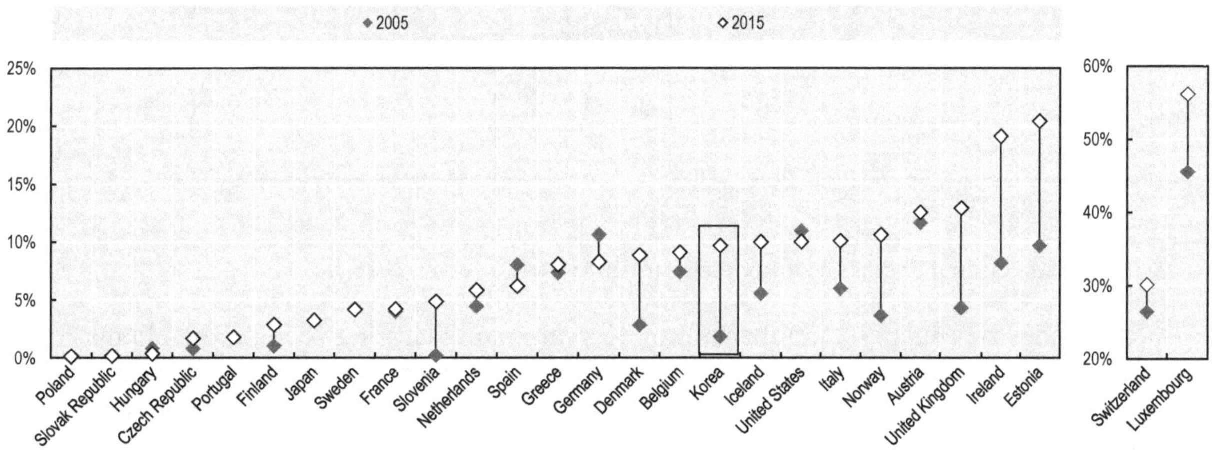

Note: .Fforeign employment in Korea in 2005 is from the 2005 KIS Statistical yearbook, based on the Industrial Training and the Employment Permit visa.
Source: Europe: LFS or GSOEP (Germany); United States: CPS. For Japan, MHLW survey of employers, October 2016, and 2016 LFS. Korea, FLFS and EAPS, May 2016. Israel, PIBA figures for foreigners and LFS for nationals, 2016.

Box 3.7. "Root Industries" and reliance on foreign workers

Non-professional foreign workers in Korea are concentrated in SMEs in manufacturing. One example is that of "root industries", which conduct basic manufacturing processes as part of the supply chain to larger firms (Lee et al., 2016[18]). These comprise about 450 000 employees, or 14% of the manufacturing workforce. Larger firms rely on subcontractors for important parts of the production process. Competition among SMEs for contracts is intense and margins are low; the industrial processes in root industries – casting, heating, etc. – make working conditions difficult, and, as with SMEs in manufacturing in general, low wages also contribute to high turnover. Vacancy rates are similar to those in manufacturing in general, but few young people are in the workforce in root industries. Foreign workers comprise about 9% of the root industry workforce; since most are young, they account for a disproportionate share of the root industry workforce (Figure 3.13, Panel B).

Figure 3.13. Root industries have an aging workforce and rely on foreign workers

Panel A. Root industry employment, 2013-16, by nationality Panel B. Root industry employment, 2016, by nationality and age

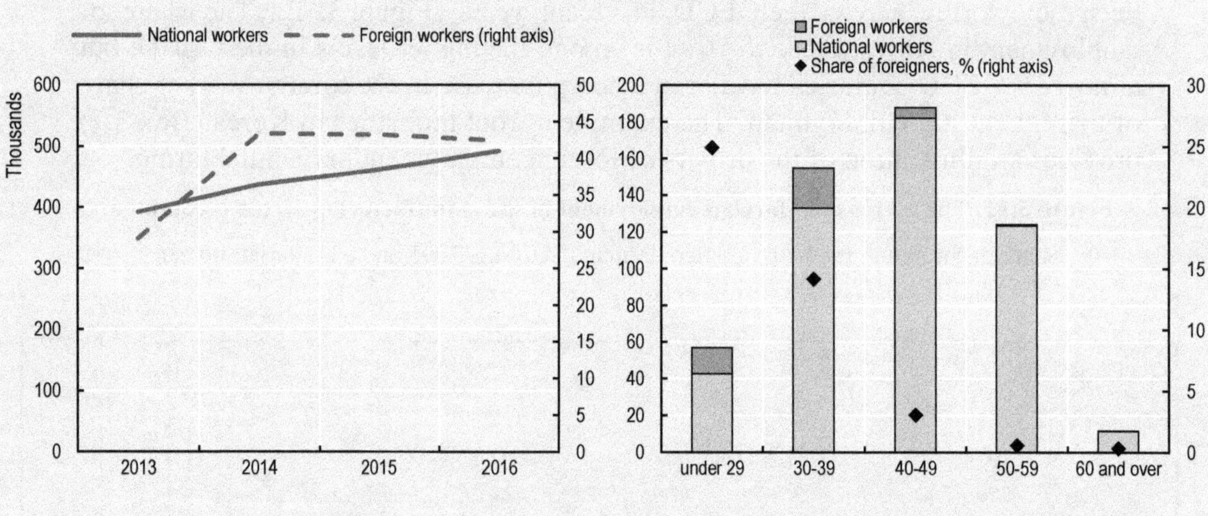

Source: Survey on the situation of Root Industry 2015-16 (Lee et al., 2016[18]).

Root industries supply a number of key Korean manufacturing sectors; the clients of these SMEs are primarily in the automotive and machine-tooling sectors, which require proximity of suppliers. The root industry benefits from favourable provisions in its access to workers under EPS.

In agriculture, the reliance on foreign workers in OECD countries varies, although it has been increasing (Figure 3.14). In Korea the share of foreign workers in agriculture is about 3.5%, while the United States and Spain have much higher shares. Further, these figures are based on labour force surveys, which largely exclude the seasonal workers who play an important part in agricultural employment in many OECD countries; they number as many as half a million in Poland, for example, and several hundred thousand in Germany. The structural reliance on temporary foreign workers in agriculture is a common feature of the sector across OECD countries.

Figure 3.14. A few OECD countries rely heavily on foreign workers in agriculture

Share of foreign workers in total employment in agriculture, 2005 and 2015 or latest year.

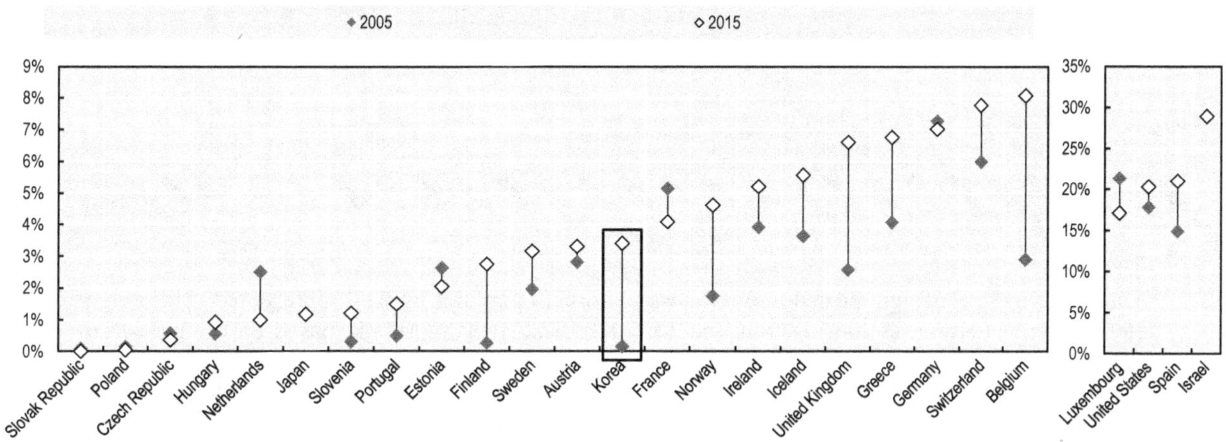

Note: 1) Due to LFS design, seasonal workers may not be well represented. 2) Foreign employment in Korea in 2005 is from the 2005 KIS Statistical yearbook, based on the Industrial Training and the Employment Permit visa.

Source: Europe: LFS or GSOEP (Germany); United States: CPS. For Japan, MHLW survey of employers, October 2016, and 2016 LFS. Korea, FLFS and EAPS, May 2016. Israel, PIBA figures for foreigners and LFS for nationals, 2016.

The construction sector is a different situation (Figure 3.15). While in Korea the share of employment, 4.6%, is higher than foreigners' share in overall employment, it is still less than the role of foreigners in most other OECD countries, where large changes have been seen in the past decade. However, the share of foreign workers in construction declined sharply in the European countries hardest hit by the crisis of the late 2000s and the end of the construction boom: Portugal, Spain and Greece. In most other countries it increased.

Figure 3.15. Foreign workers in construction in Korea are a low share in international comparison

Share of foreign in total employment in construction, 2005 and 2015 or latest year.

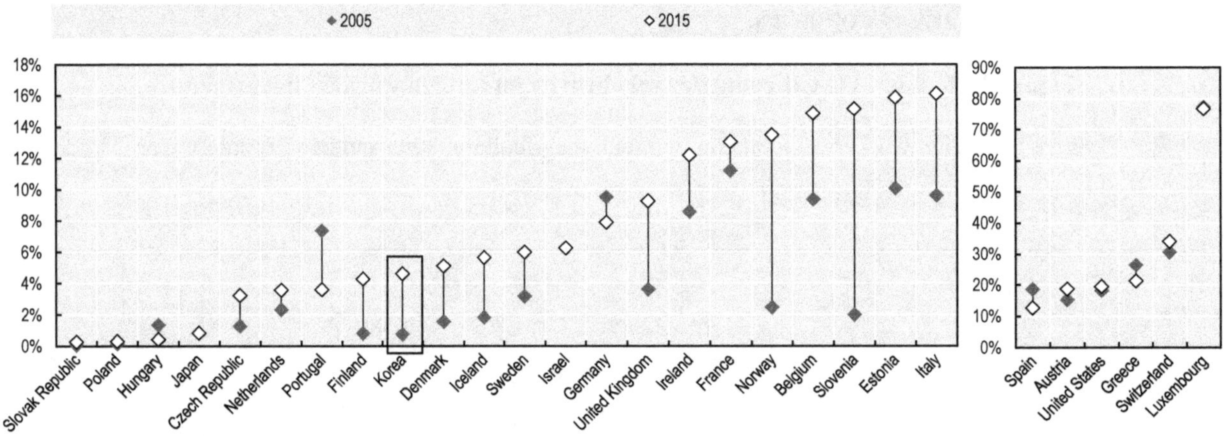

Note: Due to LFS design, posted and temporary workers may not be well represented. 2) Foreign employment in Korea in 2005 is from the 2005 KIS Statistical yearbook, based on the Industrial Training and the Employment Permit visa.

Source: Europe: LFS or GSOEP (Germany); United States: CPS. For Japan, MHLW survey of employers, October 2016, and 2016 LFS. Korea, FLFS and EAPS, May 2016. Israel, PIBA figures for foreigners and LFS for nationals, 2016.

Box 3.8. Efforts to bring resident workers into sectors of employment of foreign workers

When occupations are especially reliant on foreign workers, especially temporary labour migrants, there may be a risk that the occupation ceases to be attractive for resident workers, either because it is stigmatised – i.e., loss of prestige due to association with low-status foreign workers (Zimring, 2004[19]) – or because networks leading to employment become weaker for natives. Some OECD countries have tried to attract resident workers into these occupations through subsidies and training initiatives.

To attract resident workers back into employment in sectors where employers recruit from abroad, subsidised training and employment programmes may be proposed. In Israel, a number of programmes since 2010 have attempted this approach in different sectors. In the agricultural sector, a programme begun in 2010 offered employers about USD 200 per person and per month for new workers who come into the sector for employment at least three out of six months, on the assumption that the subsidy would be passed to the worker; takeup was very low (OECD, 2013[20]). A series of projects have provided training to residents for employment in the construction sector, in some cases followed by job subsidies, bringing wages up to 50% above the minimum wage. While this did lead to some take-up, the main occupations relying on foreign workers, are so-called "wet-work", high paid but onerous jobs in plastering, tiling and sealing.

Attempts to train for these jobs have met more difficulty, especially when employers also have access to foreign workers. Stigmatisation is an obstacle (Economic Affairs Committee, 2011[21]). In the health sector, beneficiaries of long-term care subsidies were granted 20% more hours if they hired a resident worker, but take up was minimal, as beneficiaries preferred foreign workers to whom limits on working hours did not effectively apply (OECD, 2011[22]).

National skills funds based on fees imposed on employers of labour migrants may also be used to try to train resident workers to fill jobs. In the United States, the H-1B programme requires employers to contribute to a training fund. Grants from the fund provide training targeted to occupations in demand, to reduce American dependence on foreign labour, although grants bear no relation to the distribution of H-1B workers or their occupations (OECD, 2014[6]). Australia introduced a "Skilling Australian Fund" in 2018 to which employers of temporary foreign workers are required to contribute; there is no statutory link to temporary foreign worker occupations.

In other cases, requiring a one-for-one hiring of local workers and foreign workers may represent an indirect subsidy. In Ireland, for example, a sector-specific agreement between the Department of Jobs, Enterprise and Innovation and the meat deboners industry granted a quota of work permits on the condition that the sector recruit at least one resident worker from the unemployment rolls for each foreign worker admitted. This approach is possible in Ireland due to the small size of the economy, the concentration of employers and workplaces in the sectors where such agreements are made, and the close monitoring possible.

Does programme design protect the local labour market?

One of the key questions in any labour migration programme is how to ensure that foreign workers do not have a negative effect on local workers. There are a number of safeguards which can be put in place. Some are designed to provide local workers a fair chance to apply for vacancies; this is the logic behind mandatory advertising procedures and periods prior to authorisation. In Korea, the mandatory advertising period serves this function, as does the point system to reward firms which recruit local workers.

However, given the specific characteristics of the less-skilled Korean labour force, the workers who are most likely to be displaced are not younger workers or new labour market entries, but rather older workers – including those who have retired from another job and are in the labour market.

One paradox of the foreign worker programme in Korea is that EPS programme design requires workers to receive at least the minimum Korean wage, since the mandatory contribution framework represents a form of compliance oversight. The gross monthly income of EPS workers is at least the minimum wage (KRW 1.35 million in 2017). In 2017, 58.3% earned more than KRW 2 million while no E-9 workers earned less than KRW 1 million[9]. At present, participants in

EPS are almost universally initially hired at minimum wage; due to overtime their gross monthly wage is above the Korean minimum. The working hours of foreign workers exceed, on average, 260 hours per month, with more than 20 hours per week of overtime (Table 3.6). This is all the more remarkable as it is the average, as reported by employers in 2015. Hours are longer in smaller firms (SMEs with fewer than five employees are exempt from limits on overtime) and firms outside of the capital region. Gross wages of about USD 5.05 were reported, suggesting that E-9 workers employed 40 hours per week would earn about KRW 1 million, or USD 875.

Table 3.6. Extensive overtime raises monthly income of E-9 workers

Working hours and wages and employer cost (USD) for E-9 workers, by region and firm characteristics, July 2015.

	Firm characteristics	Overtime hours worked	Total hours worked	Hourly wage	Monthly Gross Wages	Additional employer costs	Employer contributions as a share of total labour costs
Area	Metro	81	254	5.06	1491	272	15.4%
	Non-Metro	96	270	5.04	1602	260	14.0%
Firm size (employees)	<10	79	253	5.11	1492	265	15.1%
	10-49	91	264	5.03	1558	276	15.0%
	50+	96	269	5.05	1603	231	12.6%
Total		89	262	5.05	1549	266	14.6%

Note: Overtime is calculated based on gross wage, assuming 40 hours weekly at hourly wage and overtime at 1.5 times hourly wage. Exchange rate is KRW/USD for July 2015, the survey period.
Source: Survey of 620 SMEs employing E-9 workers conducted by the Ministry of Public Administration and Home Affairs, Current Status and Improvement Plan of Foreign Workers, SME Researcher, 2015) cited in (KOSBI, 2016[15]).

The same cannot be said for Korean workers, many of whom earn less than the statutory wage. Raising the wages for foreign workers might make it more attractive to hire local workers, as long as the compliance framework remains in place. However, overtime among Korean workers is below the level of foreign workers.

As a result of extensive overtime, the estimated wage distribution of all foreigners in Korea shows a concentration around the minimum wage level and around the maximum monthly earnings for minimum-wage workers employed for the maximum time allowed (in 2015, 68 hours weekly) (Figure 3.16). This figure shows all foreigners, so includes those such as H-2 workers who may work fewer monthly hours, and higher-paid technicians. Some E-9 and H-2 workers however clearly earn above the minimum wage, even taking into account the overtime hours. The income distribution for Koreans is shifted significantly toward higher income.

Figure 3.16. Foreigner income is concentrated around minimum wage and minimum wage with maximum overtime

Estimated wage distribution of foreigners, 2015.

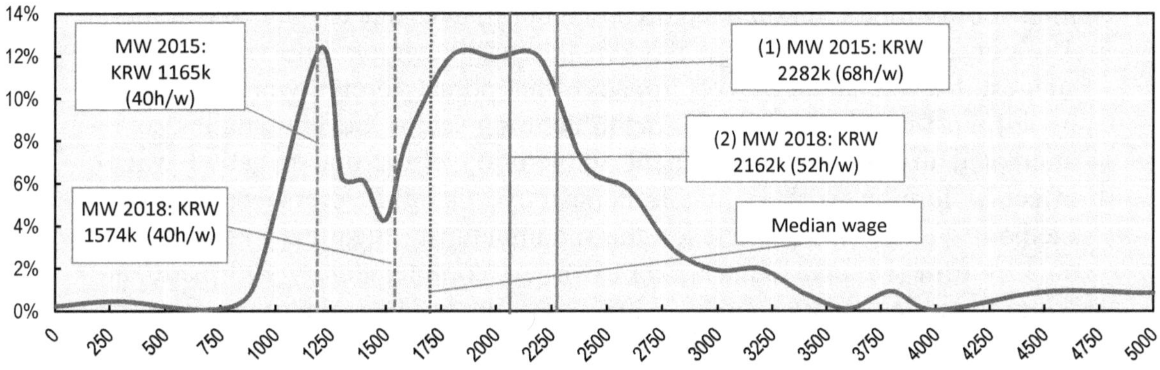

Note: MW = Minimum Wage. (1) MW 2015 for 68h/week is calculated based on 50% overtime bonus for 12 hours during weekdays and eight hours in weekend/holiday and 100% overtime bonus for more than eight hours in weekend. (2) MW 2018 calculation for 52h/week assumes 50% overtime bonus for 12 hours on condition of less than eight hours in weekend/holiday. Wage above KRW 5 000 is not shown. Based on a sample of all foreigners employed.
Source: Unofficial estimates by the Ministry of Justice (Ministry of Justice, 2018[23]).

This question will be put to the test in 2018, when the hourly minimum wage increased to KRW 7530, a 16% increase. This will have a disproportionate effect on categories of workers where most are paid minimum wage, as is the case for newly hired EPS workers.

The EPS programme is gradually upskilling, with the addition of the points-based selection mechanism. A rise in minimum wage will also lead firms to expect higher productivity from their foreign workers. In addition, current regulations foresee a decline in the maximum number of working hours, which will fall to 52 hours a week in 2020, in firms with five or more employees.

Box 3.9. Studies on the Labour Market Impact of Migration in Korea

Despite the large inflows, there has been relatively limited literature on the impact of immigration on the Korean labour market due to data constraints. The concentration of foreign workers in certain sectors and firms would suggest that the labour market impact of temporary foreign workers would be felt most in the SMEs in the manufacturing sector. Several studies have attempted to test the employment substitution effect and negative wage effect of foreign workers in this perspective using different econometric methods. A first study analysed the manufacturing business in the Seoul area by firm size and found foreign workers complementary with national workers in elementary labour in businesses under 100 employees (Kwon, Lee and Cho, 1995[24]). Another early study analysed the trend of relative employment rate by skill levels in manufacturing during the Industrial Trainee Program from 1997 to 2001 (Hahn and Choi, 2006[25]). Later results point to the possibility of national male semi-skilled workers, such as machine operators and assembly workers, being displaced by industrial trainees (Hahn and Choi, 2006[25]). However, these results in the early phase of temporary labour migration policy in Korea are difficult to generalise because of methodological issues - and weak evidence of impact on wage was found in both studies.

More recently, research has been conducted with the increased inflow of foreign workers and cumulated administrative data. One study using the employment insurance database investigated the impact of foreign worker inflow on national worker employment in August 2004 and December 2005, the period during which employment insurance was mandatory for EPS workers (Kim, 2009[26]). This analysis estimated that a 10% increase of foreign worker employment rate increased national worker unemployment risk by 0.12-0.24% in the same occupation, with a stronger effect on national workers with a middle school education or less. By industry, the substitution effect was not found in manufacturing, while it was in the service sector on business unit analysis. Looking at the period from 2004 to 2008, during which employment of Koreans in most sectors fell while employment of foreign workers increased, one analysis reported the same findings as the previous study; employment of foreign workers had a negative effect on Korean worker employment, mainly in construction and in the restaurant industry (Lee and Park, 2008[27]). A study applying the aggregate factor proportions approach to the labour force survey and population census tested foreign worker's impact on national male workers' wage, in which skill level is defined by educational attainment and work experience (Choi, 2013[28]). This study found that the inflow of foreign workers since the 2000s reduced wage increase of the low skilled youth (25-34) by 20%. Due to data constraints, none of the above studies examining EPS program effects look separately at the effect of E-9 and H-2 workers.

A recent study combining EPS and the employment insurance database is the most comprehensive analysis to date on the EPS program separating temporary foreign workers into E-9 and H-2 workers over the time period between 2004-13 (Lee et al., 2016[29]). The analysis found that by industry the complementary effect exists between national and foreign workers in manufacturing (not significant since 2012) and that the substitution effect in the service sector intensified since the 2009 global economic crisis. The results also found that women, more than men, and older male workers were more vulnerable in terms of job competition with foreign workers. When looking at wage, a 1% increase in the share of foreign workers decreases wages of Koreans by 0.2-1.1%. The wages of domestic female workers are more affected by the employment of foreign workers than the wages of male workers. Since the wages of older Korean workers are higher than those of other age groups, the impact was found to be more negative on older workers. The change in employment of E-9 and H-2 visa holders were not significant factors. Lastly, this study compared the turnover rate of national workers in business with and without foreign workers using propensity score matching. The results also demonstrated that businesses employing foreign workers had a higher turnover rate of national workers and shorter-term employees. The labour market exit rate of national workers was 2.7% higher in businesses with foreign workers than that of businesses without foreign workers. As implied in this report, the national worker's higher turnover rate needs to be interpreted with caution; whether job instability in businesses hiring foreign workers can be attributed to substitution effects induced by foreign workers, or to unfavourable working conditions of the business, or the interaction of the two factors needs to be further examined.

More recent studies have also examined the broader aspects of the introduction of foreign workers as well as the firm-level labour market impact. A study on the business panel analysis from 2007-11 on manufacturing in the Incheon area found that the employment of foreign workers substituted national workers in small firms with less than 50 employees while no significant effect was found in the larger firms. No wage effect was found regardless of firm size (Oh, 2017[30]). A study using the Korean Workplace Panel Data investigated firm performance impact of foreign workers in SMEs from 2009 to 2011 (Nho and Hur, 2017[31]). The workers were a mix of EPS and H-2 workers as well as other foreign workers. The study found that temporary immigration has a positive impact on firm profitability. Presence of foreign workers had a positive effect on labour productivity, and weak effects of lowering the wage of low-skilled native workers and of reducing labour shortage.

Most analyses above examined the total foreign population rather than the impact of specific programmes. For more viable policy implication of labour migration policy in Korea, the effects of other category of foreign workers should be taken into account considering that most F-4 and F-5 holders work in same sector as EPS workers. Future analyses should look at firm level effects of employment of different categories of foreign workers. Particularly useful would be studies comparing firms *eligible* for E-9 workers, but not assigned E-9 workers, with those which employ E-9 workers.

Balancing rights of workers with those of employers

Binding workers to employers, sectors and regions

Korea has, as noted, a mix of different labour migration channels. The extent to which foreign workers are bound to their employers or sectors varies, with the E-9 workers facing the most strict conditions, bound to employment in a specific sector and with their job changes conditional on employer approval, illegal employment practices by their employer, layoffs or firm closure. Most other work permits require an employer but allow changes to any other eligible employer as long as the conditions of the visa are respected. A number of permits, such as the F-2 or the F-5 and F-6 permits, do not impose any restrictions on the type of employment.

The E-9 programme, when first introduced, allowed four grounds for job change:

- The employment contract is annulled (e.g., the worker arrives but the firm no longer requires the worker) or ends (e.g., the contract was for one year)
- The business closes or shuts down temporarily
- The business loses its right to employ the foreign worker
- Workplace injury or disability

Workers were allowed three changes of employer over the course of their employment period, not counting those changes cited above where they were not at fault. Unemployed workers had two months to find a new employer, or their permit was withdrawn. During the economic downturn in 2008, the number of E-9 workers who were laid off and seeking employment reached 14 700 from 8 500 in 2007.

The constitutional court considered the question of job-change restrictions in 2010 and left the restrictions standing; if it had abolished them, the sector restrictions would also have been abolished, allowing full labour market access to E-9 workers and throwing into question the Employment Permit-based scheme. The court justified the restrictions by linking admission to the labour market test and the need to protect resident workers. This justification explains why foreign workers are only allowed to occupy jobs for which vacancies are demonstrated, but does not address the question of job mobility among firms which have demonstrated labour shortages which cannot be filled by locally available labour.

The system for matching dismissed E-9 workers to new employers was changed in 2012. Until then, workers could be sent to new employers, or given a list of ten potential employers, which workers could contact directly. If no match was found, a second list of ten could be requested, and so on. Since many workers did not have language skills or capacity to contact employers, unlicensed brokers stepped in and often mediated, taking rents and leading some workers to lose legal status. From 2012, the employment centre has taken on the role of placing unemployed E-9 workers, offering three months job-search support. Based on worker preference for the region, conditions and occupation, text messages with contact of employers are sent; the employment centre also hosts interviews and provides translation if necessary. If the job seeker fails to find a job after two months, the centre proposes at least five employers.

On the employee side, job mobility is of enormous interest; call-centres serving foreign workers in Korea report that job-mobility is the top question they receive from EPS workers. On the employer side, mobility is seen as one of the negative aspects of the programme. Employers are concerned that employers who fail to authorise mobility will see their foreign workers lose motivation and productivity until they are let go.

In practice, job changes are not infrequent. The number of E-9 changes has tripled over time, from 19 000 (12% of E-9 workers) in 2006 to 56 500 in 2015 (about one in five workers). During 2016, 25.4% of E-9 workers applied for workplace change; the MOEL approved 94.3% of them. Most of these are voluntary job changes; involuntary job changes represented just 16% (MOEL, 2017[32]). The rate of change reflects survey data on the intention of workers. According to the survey results of the 2017 Survey on Immigrant's Living Conditions and Labour Force, 24.4% of E-9 workers wanted to change their current job, of which 32.2% cited the low wage as a reason to change the job.

This rate of job change is also reflected in the employer survey. About 40% of employers of E-9 workers had management difficulty due to the job change of their workers. Among those who had difficulty, the main response measure to retain workers was to raise the wage (49%). Improvement of work environment and accommodation followed (Noh, 2015[16]). About one in four employers facing retention difficulty was unable to take any step to retain workers.

It is surprising that employers would raise wage and improve conditions for retention, since low wages and poor conditions were among the main reasons for which, in the same survey, it was difficult to recruit local manpower (Noh, 2015[16]). The voluntary turnover rate is surprising given the high value assigned to diligent worker status by E-9 workers. In the 2017 FLFS, 77% of E-9 workers intend to stay in Korea after visa expiration, of which 87% cited visa extension (i.e., the returning migrant status) as a way to stay in Korea. To be eligible to be a returning diligent migrant, there should be no voluntary job change during the entire four years and 10 months of stay, and this policy plays a considerable role to prevent E-9 workers from voluntary job change of the employer to which they are originally assigned.

The Employment Permit System makes efforts to find the equilibrium point between employers and foreign worker's sides by rewarding workers when they do not change job, while creating and improving the arbitration system in case where the job change is deemed to be necessary. The fact that neither worker nor employer are fully satisfied with current provisions suggests that the system is a successful compromise.

Temporary work programmes in OECD countries are always conditional on an initial job offer with a specific employer, but job mobility is generally granted. Few European OECD countries restrict workers to a sector or employer. In European countries, workers have labour market mobility among employers, as long as the new job offered meets the requirements of the work permit. In Spain, foreign workers must remain in the region and sector for which they were recruited for the first year, although they may change employers; after one year, they have full labour market access. In Italy, foreign workers have full access to the labour market immediately, and are not required to start employment with the employer who sponsored them. However, outside Europe a number of temporary work programmes do bind workers to sectors and employers. This is true in the H-2A and the H-2B programmes in the United States, and the temporary foreign worker programme for lower-skilled workers in Canada, where workers are bound to the employers who admitted them as long as their job continues and the employer respects the terms of the contract. Australia's temporary 457 programme bound workers to employers but allowed some occupational change within the workplace; its 2018 revision (into the 482 programme) further specifies that workers may only work in the nominated position. As neither Canada nor Australia impose numerical limits, job change is subject to the same requirements as initial admission. In Israel, workers must remain in the sector for which they were recruited, but may change among authorised employers or employment agencies. In numerically limited sectors – agriculture and construction – there are more authorised employers than workers, so there is some competition among employers. Ireland included numerical limits in a pilot for lower-wage employment introduced in 2018, targeted at horticulture, meat-packing and dairy. Workers are required to remain within the sector, but may change among employers and positions meeting the programme requirements.

The challenge in these programmes is to find a balance between the acute labour needs of the employer, which justify recruitment from abroad, and the ability of the worker to maintain bargaining power to reduce the chance for exploitation. Binding can be more attractive for employers: employers are less likely to participate in a labour migration scheme if they suspect they will lose their workers to competitors offering more favourable working conditions or higher salary. Further, when admission is meant to provide labour to a specific sector or region, allowing workers to leave for other sectors undermines the labour market test or shortage which justified their admission.

The awarding of employment permits to firms in Korea under the EPS is an example where the logic of the shortage decrees that workers only be able to change among employers holding employment permits. Indeed, authorisation is not for employment in a specific sector but for employment in specific authorised positions. Issuing a higher number of employment permits to firms than workers admitted would however lead to a degree of competition. Restrictions could be placed on sectors and regions of employment, as in other countries, without binding workers to a single firm. The "diligent worker" provisions are an alternative incentive for workers to stay with their employer, so as to return for a second five year spell of employment.

Strengthening the ability of workers to improve compliance

Under EPS, there are no requirements for employers or workers to report effective payment of salaries.

Korea has a high use of internet and high penetration and use of smartphones. The foreign worker programme is no exception and Korea is using new technology to allow foreign workers to monitor their employers' compliance with labour law and to track their own salary and contributions. Participants in EPS can use an app developed by HRD Korea to monitor their rights, including to calculate the accumulation of severance pay (Departure Guarantee Insurance). However, the weakness of this application is that it relies on the self-reported pay.

In the case of dispute between employers and workers on the amount of severance pay and DGI, the burden is on the employer to prove the actual amount paid.

The use of apps to increase compliance and oversight can be expanded. One example is the "Record my Hours" application developed by the Australian Fair Work Ombudsman, which records arrival and departure time from the workplace using geofencing technology. Manual recording is also possible when there is no connectivity. The multilingual app also assists recording shifts, photographing and saving pay slips, and cloud backup of work diaries. "Record My Hours" is not meant to substitute employer record-keeping, but to allow workers to track their hours and address discrepancies between employee claims and employer records.[10] However, geolocation is not as reliable a means for recording working hours when workers live on site, as is often the case with E-9 workers whose housing is provided by the employer.

Within the agricultural sector, compliance issues are more of a concern, due to relative isolation of workplaces, the on-site lodging in often low-quality barracks, and lack of coverage of the Labour Act's provisions on working hours, rest times and vacations[11]. In order to address this, a proposal is to grant agricultural workers the right to change employer if housing is considered substandard, or if room and board deductions are excessive or occur without a signed agreement. This provision, if adopted, would create competition among employers to respect minimum standards and improve housing quality, as well as lower housing deductions, as long as sufficient alternatives exist for E-9 workers in agriculture.

A further means for improving the position of workers is to offer training. HRD Korea has offered training to EPS workers during their stay in Korea. From 2010 to 2017, it offered 25 600 places to workers, for 48 hours training, held on

Saturdays through job training centres across the country. Training comprises basic and advanced vocational programs, based on the sector of employment. Advanced courses, for the manufacturing sector, focused on technical skills such as automotive repair and welding. The objective of the courses was to improve productivity; additional skills also allow workers a chance at higher-wage jobs within their firms and the transition to E-7 visas. Since 2014, the number of courses offered by HRD Korea and the number of participants fell. However, employers organise training through direct contracting with training institutes. Relative to the total number of EPS workers, take up of training opportunities is fairly limited (about 3% of EPS workers participate).

Box 3.10. The use of employer levies in managing labour migration

One mechanism used to increase the cost of use of foreign workers, to encourage employers to invest in capital or hire resident workers rather than recruit from abroad, is the employment levy. Employment levies are regular taxes imposed on employment of foreign workers throughout their period of employment. Levies can be a fixed monthly or annual fee, or a percentage of gross wages. While levies are used in many non-OECD Asian countries such as Singapore and Malaysia, they are not used in OECD countries with the exception of Israel.

In Israel, the use of levies and annual fees has varied over time. A payroll levy is imposed on workers in agriculture (10%, but suspended from 2016 to 2020), construction (15%) and other sectors (20%), with the sole exception of care, where no levy is imposed. This levy was introduced in 2003 and increased in later years, with the 20% levy extended to employment of asylum seekers. In addition to the levy, there is also an annual fee which varies among sectors (NIS 7 130, about USD 2 000, in construction, NIS 1 190 in agriculture and NIS 9 500, or USD 2 700, for experts). This fee is in addition to the initial hiring fee, which also varies. Due to lower wages and to fewer social contributions, the average total cost to employers of foreign workers remains below that of Israeli employees even with the levy.

Annual fees may be similar to levies. Australia's Temporary Skills Shortage (TSS) Visa, introduced in 2018, imposes an annual AUD 1 800 fee on employers. Similarly, while not a levy, Canada imposes a CAD 1 000 fee on employers of foreign workers subject to labour market test; since the labour market test must be renewed annually, the fee amounts to an annual tax on continued employment of the foreign worker.

Alternatives to levies include requiring employers to pay at or above the prevailing wage. In Estonia, for example, through 2017 foreign workers were authorised only if their salary was 1.24 times the national average; this was lowered to the average in 2018. In the United States, the H-1B and H-2B visas both impose the "prevailing wage rate for the occupational classification in the area of employment". A public benchmark is calculated, and employers can also ask to use a private wage survey.

The levy is meant to increase the cost of employment to the employer. However, a statutory wage increase can achieve the same effect, with the added benefit of increasing the perceived wage in the workplace by resident workers. The risk of government levies is that if compliance and enforcement are insufficient, employers will be able to extract the additional cost from foreign workers themselves through illegal employment practices such as unpaid overtime. Further, levies, once in place, can come to represent a revenue stream of such importance that policy makers are reluctant to reduce the size of the foreign worker programme.

When applied to non-labour migrants, levies raising the cost of employment may indeed discourage employment. Switzerland imposed a 10% tax on annual income of certain categories of refugees and asylum seekers during the first ten years of residence in Switzerland, as a means of reimbursing social costs related to their stay. This tax was eliminated in 2018 due to its negative effect on employment of people in this category.

If the objective of the levy is to protect national jobs, as is stated in the Third Basic Plan in Korea, raising the cost of employing foreign workers can be achieved through market mechanisms – with higher wages accruing to workers – rather than regulatory surcharges.

Reducing overstay

One of the main concerns in the programme is workers overstaying the end of their permit and becoming irregular. This is a frequent problem in temporary labour migration programmes for less-skilled workers in OECD countries. In 2002, the foreign workers were able to complete one year as a trainee and then remain two years of employment. That year, the government increased the number of industrial trainees by 20 000 to 145 000 (Park, 2004). Although this scheme guaranteed their labour rights for a longer period, it could not entirely overcome the limited scope of the original trainee programme. As the programme kept generating problems, it became a prominent social issue. It escalated the debates as the number of undocumented foreigners who were assumed to be working illegally continued to rise to 290 000 in 2002 (Park, 2013). At the end of 2008, foreigners living in Korea without authorisation amounted to 200 000, a 10% decrease from the previous year. In 2016, overstayers amounted to about 10% of the total foreign population, but most were overstaying short-term visiting and tourist visas, rather than work visas. The only longer-term visas with a large number of overstayers, and a high overstay rate relative to the number of visa-holders, were the E-9 visa and, to some extent, sailors (E-10 visa holders), and students who came to Korea to study in Korean language institutions and not in tertiary educational institutions (D-4).

Overstay within the EPS programme was initially very high, as the first group of regularised interns reached the end of their work extension, but fell until 2009 (Figure 3.17). When the first cohorts of EPS workers reached the end of their five-year work term in 2009, the overstay rate began to tick upwards. Recruitment halts and greater co-operation with countries of origin from 2012 led to a decline in the share of overstayers. Overstay – which includes workers abandoning their authorised employers – is higher in sectors where working conditions are relatively poor, such as fisheries (38%) and waste treatment services, but also construction. Overstay of workers admitted into the manufacturing sector was below 12% in 2017, substantially lower than in other sectors. The manufacturing sector also has far more employers than other sectors, giving workers who are unhappy with employment more opportunity to change jobs.[12]

Figure 3.17. The EPS programme has grown, while overstay rates have declined

Panel A. Stock and flow of E-9 workers, 2004-16, and overstay rate.
Panel B. Stock of E-9 workers and overstay rate by nationality, October 2017.

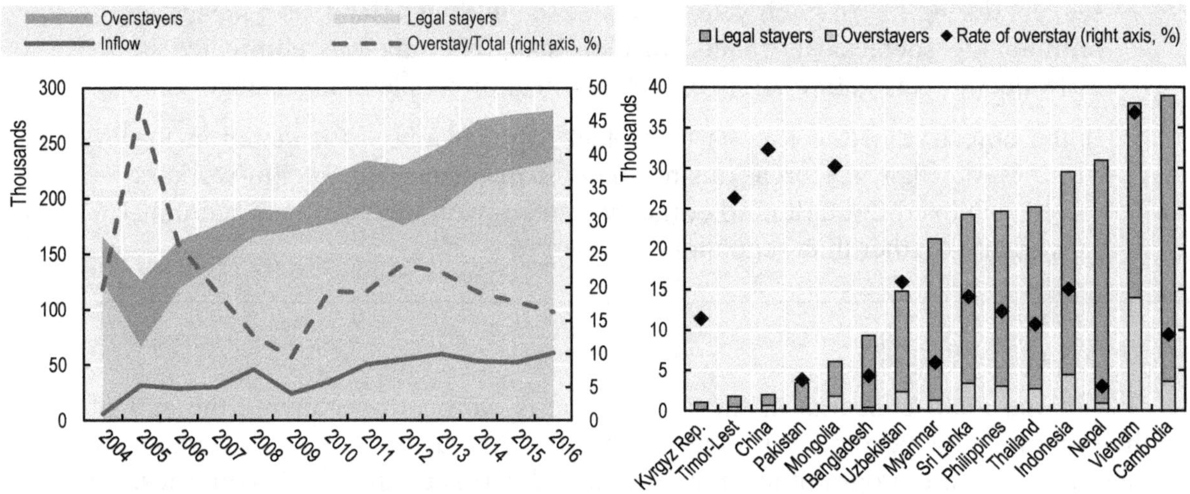

Source: Panel A: Korea Immigration Statistics. Panel B: HRD Korea (Woo, 2018[33]).

There is a strong desire among E-9 workers to extend their stay in Korea (Figure 3.18). In 2017, only 23.3% said they would prefer to return to their home countries after the end of their stay in Korea, while more than 67% said they would like to extend their stay under the same status. These shares have been constant since the question was first asked in 2012. For other categories of workers and residents, the intention to remain was high. The intention to extend stay or acquire nationality was high among ethnic Koreans (H-2 and F-4 permits). Intentions have been constant for most other groups in the past six years, although the share of working visit (H-2) permit holders hoping to naturalise or acquire permanent residence has declined, in part due to the fact that many of those eligible have changed status to F-4.

Figure 3.18. Most foreign workers would like to extend their stay

Desired outcome when permit expires, by permit type, 2017

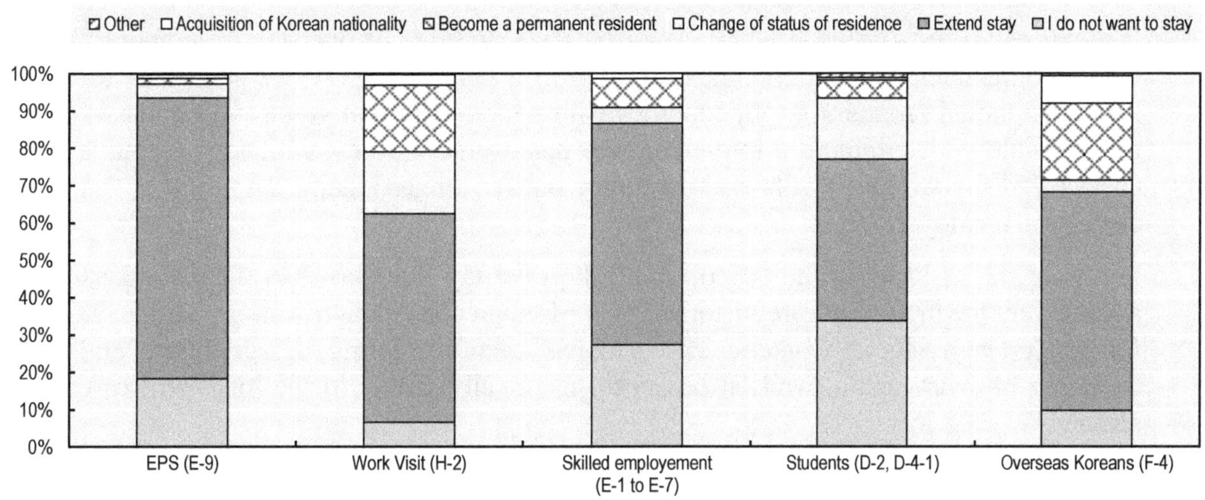

Source: Survey on Immigrant's Living Conditions and Labour Force, 2017.

The high level of intention to remain among E-9 workers (at least, those covered under the survey) suggests that they are not only satisfied with the programme and their job opportunities in Korea but that they are willing to remain under the same programme conditions during an extension.

Overstay is also an issue because of the large pool of employers willing to hire foreign workers without legal status. Many of the former EPS workers have acquired experience and language skills sought by employers; in addition, as overstayers, they do not require dormitories. Some firms have been excluded from EPS due to the PBS distribution, and can only hire foreign workers illegally. If a clear path back to access to EPS is provided, some of these employers may return to legal hiring.

The overstay rate in EPS has been declining, and represents a substantial improvement over the overstay rates of previous labour migration channels. The rate was 16.9% in 2014, 15% in 2015, and 14.1% in 2016, although it increased slightly in 2017 (14.5% in October 2017).

This can be compared with overstay rates in some other temporary labour migration programmes (Box 3.11).

Box 3.11. Overstay rates and contrasting measures in employment programmes in other OECD countries

It is difficult to establish a benchmark for the expected rate of overstay of temporary work programmes. Not all countries are able to accurately report overstay rates for labour migration programmes. In countries with double-card (entry-exit) visa controls, it is possible to determine if a foreign worker has overstayed or – with administrative checks – if the worker is still in the country but no longer legally employed by an authorised employer.

For example, in Israel at the end of 2017, the overstay rate was 20.9% for workers admitted for the long-term care sector, 6.9% for foreign construction workers, and 5.3% for foreign agricultural workers. The rate has been increasing in agriculture and declining in construction, while it has been historically steady in the long-term care sector.

In the United States, estimates for overstay were produced for Fiscal Year 2015 and 2016 (Department of Homeland Security, 2017[34]). While temporary workers (H visas) were only one of many categories included in the calculation of overstay rates (for "other in-scope nonimmigrant classes"), rates for the main nationalities of temporary workers were generally between 5% and 10%, although some approached 20%.

In Japan, the total rate of overstayers relative to legal residents was under 3% in 2017. Overstay rate by admission category is not available. However, in additional to illegal overstay, an emerging issue has been opportunistic asylum applications by workers whose trainee period of employment expired – such applicants do not appear as overstayers, as they are granted temporary leave to remain and, until early 2018, were also granted employment access while awaiting a decision on their application.

In seasonal programmes, ensuring that workers can return the following season is one measure used with success to reduce the risk of overstay (Merwood, 2012[35]). Indeed, overstay rates in New Zealand's seasonal programme are around 1% (Gibson and McKenzie, 2014[36]). New Zealand employers in the seasonal scheme pay the costs of removal (up to NZD 3 000) for each worker who overstays; this encourages employers to select workers likely to return. In Spain, employers with many overstayers lose their right to recruit in the future, providing an incentive to select workers likely to return and to make efforts such as provide transportation to the point of departure at the end of their stay (OECD, 2008[37]). In Italy, any employer sponsoring a work permit (seasonal or non; first, renewal or change of employer) must assume responsibility for the return costs of foreign workers. The interpretation of this 2002 requirement, however, is that it applies only to forced returns and in the event that the state requests reimbursement of related costs; no such requests have ever been made. Partner countries in bilateral agreements may also apply their own measures; Samoa, for example, excludes relatives of overstayers from participation in the bilateral seasonal work programme with New Zealand.

HRD offers training in the home country after return. In 2014, about 8.5% of all EPS workers who went home participated in training following their return to the home country. HRD also puts ex-EPS workers in contact with Korean companies in the origin country seeking foremen and local staff managers for their operations in the country. These opportunities are a powerful incentive to return, since a quality job where their new skills can be used is valuable for workers. The opportunities are primarily available where Korean companies have a strong presence, such as Viet Nam, Indonesia, Cambodia and Mongolia.

To ensure the quality of home-country post-migration training, providers are paid in full only if at least 45% of participants find employment; this encourages good co-operation between training institutes and Korean companies.

HRD also supports successful ex-EPS workers to serve as representatives in their home countries to speak with the local community, to encourage quality candidates and to provide evidence that return can be positive. For this purpose, HRD Korea maintains a database on returned workers. It also issues work experience certificates to departing workers.

How long is too long?

Two considerations underlie the restriction on stay in EPS. First, the indefinite need for the worker is not demonstrated in a context where the long-term need for non-professional labour is not known with certainty. The second is the restriction on family reunification, which makes an indefinite stay difficult to reconcile with family life. The restriction on family reunification is in turn justified by the low wages paid for the jobs filled by EPS workers, which are not enough to support a family without assistance from benefit programmes. Further, the gruelling working hours of E-9 workers – consistently averaging 20 hours weekly overtime (as seen in Table 3.6) – are incompatible with a sustained rhythm of employment.

The maximum stay under the EPS is 10 years (more precisely, nine years and eight months), a limit which was reached by the first cohort of workers in 2017, covering those who returned after five years. There are two separate grounds for returning workers after their first five year period: the diligent worker option and the language exam. Diligent workers are those who stay with their employer for the entire period in which they are in Korea; SMEs with fewer than 100 employees (50 employees prior to 2019) may request their return. The advanced language exam is administered in the country of origin and successful applicants may return to Korea for a second period of employment, with a new employer or with their old employer. It was decided in 2017 that these cannot be cumulative, capping stay at 10 years.

The number of workers allowed to return is set annually as part of the quota-setting exercise (Figure 3.2), and has been around 10 000 since 2011. Most go back into manufacturing sector jobs. About 6.2% of returning EPS workers are women.

This is the longest stay allowed in any temporary labour programme for low-skilled in OECD countries. In the United States, the maximum stay is three years, for example. Canada eliminated its four-year limit for temporary workers in 2016. In Israel, the maximum stay is five years (although care workers may extend their stay for the lifetime of their patient).

Box 3.12. Maximum duration in temporary work programmes

The maximum duration of stay in temporary work programmes may reflect different and competing policy objectives.

In the United States, the maximum stay is three years, for example, in the H-2B programme, although the permit must be renewed annually. After three years, there is a three-month required exit before applying for re-entry. Canada eliminated its four-year limit for temporary workers in 2016, at the same time as additional restrictions were imposed on recruitment for the programme. The elimination of the limit was related to the situation of specific industries with chronic difficulty in recruitment (especially seafood processors) in certain regions of the country. In Israel, the maximum stay is five years (although care workers may extend their stay for the lifetime of their patient). In Japan, the maximum stay period in the technical intern and industrial trainee programme was set at three years until 2017, when it was increased to five years.

In most European countries, two EU directives constrain the ability to limit stay: a right to family reunification and a right to permanent residence. First, the family reunification directive (2003/86/EC) grants a right of family reunification – subject to conditions - "where the sponsor is holding a residence permit issued by a Member State for a period of validity of one year or more who has reasonable prospects of obtaining the right of permanent residence". The directive allows countries to impose a maximum two year stay before eligibility. The second constraint is the long-term residents directive (2003/109/EC) which requires a possibility of permanent residence after five years legal stay. While conditions may be imposed on family reunification and qualification for permanent residence, in practice most EU countries cannot offer permits which, in the persistence of original grounds for admission, require departure after a stay of several years.

EU countries not covered by the directives have time-bound permits. The Tier 2 (General) skilled visa in the UK, for example, can be held for up to six years, although holders are potentially eligible for settlement after five years, subject to certain conditions.

Seasonal programmes may allow, and even encourage, repeat returns. Most seasonal programmes have high repeat rates, whether the H-2 programmes in the USA, the Canadian seasonal programme, or European programmes. In some cases, continued compliance with seasonal work allows transfer to regular residence (after as little as two seasons, in Italy). Until June 2002, Switzerland had a seasonal workers programme that allowed foreigners who were employed at least 36 months in four consecutive years under nine-month seasonal permits to "earn" an annual - and eventually a permanent – residence permit. This entitlement to status change was a particular feature of Swiss immigration policy, and meant that most labour migrants were low-skilled former seasonal workers (Martin, Abella and Kuptsch, 2006[38]).

Intra-company transfer permits may be subject to maximum duration of stay without extension in many countries. In the UK, maximum stay depends on the level of remuneration and role. Under the EU intra-corporate transfer directive (2014/66/EU), the maximum duration is one or three years, depending on the level, with a cool-down period (mandatory absence) of up to six months, but change of status is allowed. In the United States, the L-1 visa for intra-company transfers is valid for up to seven years, and requires a one-year period of employment outside the country before a new visa can be issued. It allows in-country status change, however.

In practice, there is some evidence that E-9 workers form families in Korea (although if they have children with other E-9 workers, the children do not have a right to a residence status), or bring their spouse from their home country through other means.

Can seasonal workers be a response?

The decline and aging of the rural workforce and the agricultural workforce have driven the increase in the use of foreign workers in the agriculture and livestock sector. Seasonal workers were not considered for many years. Seasonal work programmes are widely used in OECD countries to meet the needs of the agricultural and tourism sectors in particular, where labour demand is regular and seasonal and local labour in rural areas is not always readily available. In Korea, the national authorities were reluctant to create a seasonal agricultural programme out of fear of overstay due to the difficulty of seasonal workers to recoup their costs. EPS is not designed for seasonal stay. Nonetheless, local governments pushed for a pilot to test the programme, and in 2015, Korea introduced a pilot for seasonal workers. Unlike most countries, where selection occurs through agencies and is mediated or overseen by the regional government, Korea's pilot used two channels, in both cases through local municipalities, either through direct relations between rural municipalities in Korea and towns in the origin countries of workers; or through contact with workers through the "marriage migrants" who identify family members in their countries of origin and propose that the local authority sponsor them. Initial findings of the pilot with 150 workers have been favourable in terms of limited overstay, although the short-stay programme (less than three months) provides few guarantees to workers (Choi and Lee, 2016[39]).

Short-term seasonal work programmes do not give workers the opportunity to earn large amounts, so the use of channels such as family ties where the risk of rent-taking and abuse is reduced is a positive step. The Korean pilot applies to single employers, but it may be useful to consider allowing local agricultural consortia to employ seasonal workers more effectively during their stay. Similarly, allowing employers to rehire previous workers and allowing workers to return each season can be a means to ensure compliance with programme rules.

Options for permanent migration

The temporary labour migration programmes for non-professional workers introduced in the 2000s were meant to be temporary, with no explicit pathway to permanent residence. Employers, however, expressed interest in retaining the most talented and reliable foreign workers. Further, a solution had to be found for the ethnic Koreans who were nearing the expiration of their stay and were well settled, especially those who were working in regions or occupations in demand.

For the first group, a provision was put in place offering a small window for status change from E-9 to E-7. The increase in E-7 visas, however, cannot be attributed to this, since few E-9 holders met these strict conditions. The requirements were eased in 2015. There were 249 status changes from E-9 to E-7 in 2015, a small number compared with the number of expiring E-9 visas. The vast majority of E-9 visa holders do not qualify for the bridge to E-7. They are more likely to qualify for an F visa due to marriage with a Korean national; indeed, in 2015, 428 E-9 workers acquired permanent residence through this channel.

In mid-2017, a second provision for bridging from E-9, E-10 and H-2 visas to the E-7 visa was created, using a points-based system. This visa, the E-7-4, allows candidates to qualify by scoring points on different criteria (work experience, income, age, Korean language proficiency and level of education, as well as considerations such as employment in "root" industries). The E-7-4 was introduced as a pilot scheme and capped at 300 visas, which were immediately taken up; a further 300 were made available for 2017. Only SMEs with fewer than 150 employees may sponsor a change, unless they are in root industries. A firm-level limit on status change is imposed, with firms only allowed one or two changes to E-7-4 per round, depending on the firm size and sector: root industry firms with five employees or more are allowed to sponsor a status change for one employee; other firms must have at least 10 employees. Firms with 50 to 149 employees may sponsor two employees. Root industry firms may sponsor additional E-7-4 applications, up to five according to firm size.

In light of the complexity of the PBS used for E-7-4 (Annex Table 3.A.4), and the requirement to remain in the same employment, careful monitoring of beneficiaries will be necessary in the first years of the pilot to ensure that income levels remain at the level initially considered in the PBS. Evaluation of the outcomes of these visa-holders, in terms of their later status change behaviour, their family reunification patterns and the outcomes of their family members, will be important to adjust the PBS and decide whether to lift caps. This is particularly relevant if the E-7-4 PBS replaces the previous E-7-1 bridge.

A further provision is available for E-9 workers, the F-2-6 visa. This visa, also open to E-10 and H-2 visa holders, is available for workers who have worked for at least three years in the manufacturing, construction, agriculture and fishery sector. It requires a salary above the national average for the previous two years; about USD 18 000 in liquid assets, and a medium level of Korean language ability (TOPIK 3). A language exemption is available for those who have a skill certificate.

What prospects do low-wage foreign workers have for settlement?

Most but not all OECD countries offer much more generous possibilities for temporary labour migrants to acquire permanent residence status. This is also true for low-skilled temporary labour migrants in those EU countries where such migrants are admitted from outside the EU. In addition, most OECD countries allow temporary workers to bring family members, especially if their stay is over a year and they meet income and housing requirements. Korea thus stands out in its policy setting; only Israel imposes a similarly rigid temporary labour migration system for long-staying labour migrants.[13]

A strong argument against allowing E-9 workers to bring their families – even temporarily – is that the family would be in a situation of likely social exclusion and extreme vulnerability. Unlike Korean families, foreign workers do not benefit from existing capital in the country (neither social, in terms of networks, nor financial, in terms of household wealth) nor are they eligible for the social transfers which represent an important share of the income for low-wage Korean families. Further, for workers with children, it could be difficult to bear the additional expenses most Korean families invest in supplementary private education services for their children, putting their children at a disadvantage. According to the Private Education Expenditure Survey, in 2017, on average, 70.5% of all students pay for supplementary education service in privation institutions in Korea, of which their family spend KRW 384 000 per month and per child. This amount is equivalent to 21% of the average monthly gross wage level of E-9 workers – KRW 1.8 million (Noh, 2016[40]). Assuming one breadwinner in four-person household, a household with KRW 1.8 million would be eligible for the housing and education benefit under Basic Livelihood scheme, which is not the case for a household composed of only foreigners.

In practice, the prospect of permanent residence already granted by the chance of status change is a powerful incentive to achieve certain goals and to encourage workers to make an investment in their own human capital. It is not clear whether E-9 workers who aim to qualify for this status change are motivated by a desire to stay longer in Korea, remitting to their families at home, or to bring their families and settle. In the latter case, prospects appear poor without access to integration support.

Working Holiday Makers

Korea has signed Working Holiday Agreements with 20 countries, although outflows from Korea are much higher than inflows. Korea had about 4 500 WHMs incoming in 2015, a decline from the peak year of 2014, when inflows stood at 6 400 (Kang, 2016[41]). Most are Japanese, followed by Chinese Taipei and Hong Kong. Most came to learn Korean, rather than to earn money. Due to their generally low level of Korean language skills, the job opportunities of WHMs in Korea are more constrained than in the English-language destination countries of WHMs. While WHMs might be able to play a minor role in certain jobs – and changes of status towards for example language teaching or students should be examined more closely – this channel is not intended to - and not likely to - address labour shortages.

Conclusions

The EPS is working very efficiently to meet its objectives, but a number of questions remain.

The success of a low-skill and low-wage temporary foreign worker programme lies in ensuring that there is equal pay for equal work with resident workers. In turn, this requires means to enforce respect of wages and working hours, including contract conditions. Most low-wage temporary work programmes are considered high-risk for abuse by unscrupulous employers, due to the vulnerability of the worker. EPS, by providing a framework for training and support has put in place a number of safeguards. However, the sector of employment is one where Koreans face poor working conditions.

In the selection process for foreign workers, there remains some margin for discriminatory behaviour by employers, especially as regards age, gender and nationality. It is important that the candidates proposed by the Job Centres include profiles which reflect the characteristics of the roster, in terms of gender, age and nationality.

Korea's EPS is designed to provide workers at the lowest possible wage level to specific types of firms in certain sectors of the economy which suffer from low productivity and low quality jobs. The demand for this labour is driven by persistent demand in these firms – which are characterized by a high mortality rate – due to the collapse in the low-educated cohorts entering the labour market and the declining productivity and rapid turnover among the available workers. EPS – and more specifically, the E-9 visa – is a form of support to firms which would otherwise be forced to invest in physical or human capital, raising wages and productivity, or move production to lower-cost foreign locations.

Consequently, the objective to maintain low labour costs within the foreign worker programme constrains its ability to give workers more bargaining power – e.g., by allowing them more mobility among authorized employers – since the scope of the programme is to provide low-cost labour. Imminent increases in the minimum wage may put to the test the demand for foreign workers as the impact will be strongly felt in firms hiring EPS workers. Introducing employer levies would also undermine the objective of providing low-cost labour; in any case, favouring mechanisms such as mobility or assigning workers to higher-paying firms would be more effective than levies in increasing employer costs.

The programme has been successful in achieving its objective of temporary stay. Although the programme is expected to remain in place, due to a presumed structural need for labour in these sectors and firms, Korea does not allow workers to stay in the country indefinitely. There is an implicit element of EPS that if demand should dry up for low wage non-professional workers, the programme could be quickly curtailed or even expire. Meanwhile, restricting family reunification also ensures that workers do not face the need to support their families in Korea on minimum wage income, without income support.

The question of the impact on resident workers has not been resolved. One issue in the EPS is that it is a large programme targeted at a very small sector of the labour market, so that the positive and negative effects are concentrated on a relatively limited area. The absence of job mobility may be thought to limit spillover effects in non-authorised employment sectors, but what may be occurring is rather a spill-over effect on lower wage workers as they are forced out of these jobs. More analysis at firm level would be necessary to understand the impact of the programme in firms dependent on EPS workers.

Indeed, the mandatory advertising period – which functions in other countries as an additional safeguard against adverse impact on resident workers – is of little relevance when wages are below the local reservation wage.

Since programme design limits the possibility for E-9 workers to use high demand to bargain for higher wages, the principal safeguard against a negative impact of the programme on resident workers is the quota system. The quota applies to the industry as a whole, rather than individual firms. EPS allows firms, in principle, to be entirely dependent on E-9 workers for their non-professional labour needs. This is in contrast to the firm-level ceiling which applies to skilled workers holding E-7 permits (see Box 4.2 in the next section). A firm-level ceiling could be established to ensure that firms which survive only due to temporary foreign workers are pressured to reorganise.

Notes

[1] EPS workers remit, on average, 63.5% of their earnings in 2010 and 69.1% in 2013 (Kang, 2014[74]). More than 90% of E-9 workers remit. The figure was lower for H-2 workers, about 56% in 2013.

[2] The FWPC is chaired by the Minister of the Prime Minister's Office and consists of the Vice Minister of the Ministry of Strategy and Finance, the Ministry of Foreign Affairs and Trade, the Ministry of Justice, the Ministry of Knowledge Economy, the Ministry of Employment and Labour (MoEL), Administrator of the Small and Medium Business Administration, Vice Ministers of other related central government administrative agencies (the Ministry of Culture, Sports and Tourism, the Ministry for Food, Agriculture, Forestry and Fisheries, the Ministry of Health and Welfare and the Ministry of Land, Transport and Maritime Affairs) and other related experts.

[3] "Root industries" are SMEs in basic manufacturing industries, defined as using one of six process technologies (casting, die, welding, surface treatment, plastic processing, and heat treatment), under the Root Industry Law of 2012. Until 2014, the firm size was determinant of root industry firms. From 2015, annual sales volume is the criteria; firms with less than 150bn KRW (about USD 135m) in sales qualify.

[4] Individuals convicted for sexual violence may not sponsor visas for five years following completion or suspension of the sentence.

[5] From February 2017, employers can choose whether they will charge the costs of food and lodging to E-9 workers. Utilities costs may not be charged to workers, but may be included as gross labour cost by employers.

[6] In contrast to practices in many OECD countries, contracts for the centres are not awarded through tenders but through direct award (Surak, 2017[73])

[7] One-time training costs borne by employers are below USD 150 per worker. Amounts vary by industry: employers pay KRW 195 000 in manufacturing, KRW 210 000 in agriculture and fisheries, and KRW 224 000 in construction.

[8] Construction sector employers of H-2 visa holders are exempt.

[9] These figures are taken from the public data on 2017 Survey on Immigrant's Living Conditions and Labour Force which report income in increments of 1 million RW.

[10] https://www.fairwork.gov.au/how-we-will-help/how-we-help-you/record-my-hours-app

[11] Article 63 of the Korean Labour Standards Act stipulates that workers in agriculture, livestock and fishery are not subject to the regulations on rest time and vacations. This applies to foreign and Korean workers alike.

[12] Workers may shift from manufacturing into agriculture, but not vice versa.

[13] Some OECD countries may restrict labour market access for family members of temporary labour migrants, as in the United States for the H-4 Family Members of temporary workers. In EU countries covered by the EU framework on legal migration, eligibility for family reunification is granted – subject to conditions – and family members are given labour market access (OECD/EU, 2016[29]).

References

Abella, M. and P. Martin (2014), *Migration Costs of Low-skilled labor migrants: Key Findings from Pilot Surveys in Korea, Kuwait and Spain*, KNOMAD, https://www.knomad.org/publication/migration-costs-low-skilled-labor-migrants-key-findings-pilot-surveys-korea-kuwait-and (accessed on 23 November 2017). [8]

Chaloff, J. (2014), "Evidence-based regulation of labour migration in OECD countries: setting quotas, selection criteria, and shortage lists", *Migration Letters*. [4]

Choi, K. (2013), "The Impact of Foreign Worker Inflow on the Natives in Korea (외국인력 유입의 내국인에 대한 영향)", *Economics Research*, Vol. 61/3, pp. 153-194. [28]

Choi, S. and C. Lee (2016), "A Policy Review of Korea's Seasonal Worker Pilot Scheme", *IOM MRTC Policy Report Series*, No. 2016-02, IOM MRTC, Seoul, http://iom-mrtc.org/eng/business/business02_3.php?admin_mode=read&no=360&make=&search=&s_url= (accessed on 24 October 2017). [39]

Department of Homeland Security (2017), *Fiscal Year 2016 Entry/Exit Overstay Report*, https://www.dhs.gov/sites/default/files/publications/Entry%20and%20Exit%20Overstay%20Report%2C%20Fiscal%20Year%202016.pdf (accessed on 04 April 2018). [34]

Economic Affairs Committee (2011), *Meeting on 2/2/2011: The shortage of manpower in the construction industry*, Israeli Knesset, Jerusalem, http://www.knesset.gov.il/protocols/data/rtf/kalkala/2011-02-02-01.rtf. [21]

Gibson, J. and D. McKenzie (2014), "Development through seasonal worker programs: the case of New Zealand's RSE program", in Lucas, R. (ed.), *International Handbook on Migration and Economic Development*, Edward Elgar Publishing, https://doi.org/10.4337/9781782548072.00011. [36]

Hahn, C. and Y. Choi (2006), "On the Economic Impact of Foreign Labor Inflows in Korea", *Journal of Economic Policy*, Vol. 28/1, pp. 1-28, http://journal.kdi.re.kr/eng/info/paper_view.jsp?art_no=1211&pub_no=9695 (accessed on 29 October 2017). [25]

Kang, D. (2016), "Case Study of Working Holiday Programs in Overseas Countries and Its Implications for Korea", *IOM MRTC Policy Report Series*, No. 2016-03, IOM Migration Research and Training Centre, Seoul, http://iom-mrtc.org/eng/business/business02_3.php?admin_mode=read&no=361&make=&search=&s_url= (accessed on 24 October 2017). [41]

Kim, J. (2009), *Analysis of the economic impact of low skilled foreigners (저숙련 외국인 유입의 경제적 영향 분석)*, Korea Development Institute, http://www.kdi.re.kr/report/report_download.jsp?list_no=11412&member_pub=2&type=pub. [26]

KOSBI (2016), *Are Employer Levies Necessary?*, Korean Small Business Institute, Seoul, http://www.kfca.or.kr/boardview.php?table=100245&num=55 (accessed on 24 May 2018). [15]

Kwon, J., B. Lee and J. Cho (1995), "A Study on the Substitutability of Foreign Labour: Focused on Seoul Area (외국인 노동의 대체성 분석: 서울 지역을 중심으로)", *Economics Research*, Vol. 44/2, pp. 135-158. [24]

Kyung, K. (2013), *Update on the Employment Permit System*. [7]

Lee, G. et al. (2016), *Changes in Labor Market Environment: Issues in Foreign Workforce Policy (노동시장 환경변화에 따른 외국인력 정책 쟁점과 과제)*, Koreal Labour Institute, Seoul, http://www.prism.go.kr/homepage/theme/retrieveThemeDetail.do;jsessionid=CF3A28E4C08BA8588157FBD55F944A21.node02?cond_research_name=&cond_organ_id=&cond_research_year_start=&cond_research_year_end=&cond_brm_super_id=NB000120061201100031424&research_id=1490 (accessed on 17 November 2017). [18]

Lee, H. (2008), "International marriage and the state in South Korea: focusing on governmental policy", *Citizenship Studies*, Vol. 12/1, pp. 107-123, http://dx.doi.org/10.1080/13621020701794240. [46]

Lee, K. et al. (2016), *Policy for utilization of foreign labor force: policy direction of foreign manpower in the age of low birthrate and aging society*, Ministry of Employment and Labor. [29]

Lee, K. and S. Park (2008), "Employment Structure and Effects of the Foreign Workforce", *KLI Monthly Labor Review*, Vol. September, https://www.kli.re.kr/kli_eng/selectBbsNttView.do?key=220&bbsNo=31&nttNo=100745&searchY=&searchCtgry=&searchCnd=all&searchKrwd=&pageIndex=7&integrDeptCode= (accessed on 13 November 2017). [27]

Martin, P., M. Abella and C. Kuptsch (2006), *Managing labor migration in the twenty-first century*, Yale University Press, https://books.google.fr/books/about/Managing_Labor_Migration_in_the_Twenty_f.html?id=gnkFAQAAIAAJ&redir_esc=y (accessed on 19 April 2018). [38]

Merwood, P. (2012), *Return Migration and Earnings of Workers in New Zealand's Recognised Seasonal Employer Scheme*, Labour and Immigration Research Centre, Department of Labour, http://www.mbie.govt.nz/publications-research/research/migration/return-migration-and-earnings-of-workers-in-nz-rse.pdf (accessed on 04 April 2018). [35]

Ministry of Justice (2018), *Labour Migration to R. O. Korea: Policy Perspectives*, https://www.adb.org/news/events/8th-adbi-oecd-ilo-roundtable-labor-migration-asia. [23]

MOEL (2017), *Elucidation on the article Newsis 「Urgent revision of Employment Permit System that violates human rights of migrant workers」 : 「이주노동자 인권 침해하는 고용허가제 개정 시급」 기사 관련 해명.* [32]

Nho, Y. and J. Hur (2017), *The Impact of Temporary Low-skilled Immigrants on Firm Performances: Evidences from the Korean Small-Medium Business Sector.* [31]

Noh, M. (2016), *Is the levy for employment of foreigners really needed? (외국인 고용부담금제 과연 필요한 것인가)*, Korea Small Business Institute(KOSBI) 중소기업연구원, http://www.kfca.or.kr/getFile.php?fName=16-8.pdf. [40]

Noh, M. (2015), "A Study on Improving Work Permit System (외국인 근로자 활용현황 및 개선방안 연구)", *Basic Studies (기본연구)*, No. 15-08, KOSBI, Seoul. [16]

OECD (2017), "A portrait of family migration in OECD countries", in *International Migration Outlook 2017*, OECD Publishing, Paris, http://dx.doi.org/10.1787/migr_outlook-2017-6-en. [47]

OECD (2017), "A portrait of family migration in OECD countries", in *International Migration Outlook 2017*, OECD Publishing, Paris, http://dx.doi.org/10.1787/migr_outlook-2017-6-en. [49]

OECD (2016), *OECD Economic Surveys: Korea 2016*, OECD Publishing, Paris, http://dx.doi.org/10.1787/eco_surveys-kor-2016-en. [11]

OECD (2014), "Managing labour migration: Smart policies to support economic growth", in *International Migration Outlook 2014*, OECD Publishing, Paris, http://dx.doi.org/10.1787/migr_outlook-2014-6-en. [48]

OECD (2014), "Managing labour migration: Smart policies to support economic growth", in *International Migration Outlook 2014*, OECD Publishing, Paris, http://dx.doi.org/10.1787/migr_outlook-2014-6-en. [6]

OECD (2014), *Recruiting Immigrant Workers: Austria 2014*, OECD Publishing, Paris, http://dx.doi.org/10.1787/9789264226050-en. [3]

OECD (2013), *Review of Recent Developments and Progress in Labour Market and Social Policy in Israel: Slow Progress Towards a More Inclusive Society*, OECD Publishing, Paris, http://dx.doi.org/10.1787/9789264200401-en. [20]

OECD (2011), "International Migration to Israel and its Impact", in *International Migration Outlook 2011*, OECD Publishing, Paris, http://dx.doi.org/10.1787/migr_outlook-2011-9-en. [22]

OECD (2011), *Recruiting Immigrant Workers: Sweden 2011*, Recruiting Immigrant Workers, OECD Publishing, Paris, http://dx.doi.org/10.1787/9789264167216-en. [12]

OECD (2010), "Better Managing Labour Migration", in *OECD Reviews of Labour Market and Social Policies: Israel*, OECD Publishing, Paris, http://dx.doi.org/10.1787/9789264079267-8-en. [45]

OECD (2009), "International Migration and the Economic Crisis: Understanding the Links and Shaping Policy Responses", in *International Migration Outlook 2009*, OECD Publishing, Paris, http://dx.doi.org/10.1787/migr_outlook-2009-3-en. [50]

OECD (2009), "Workers Crossing Borders: A Road-map for Managing Labour Migration", in *International Migration Outlook 2009*, OECD Publishing, Paris, http://dx.doi.org/10.1787/migr_outlook-2009-4-en. [13]

OECD (2008), "Management of Low-Skilled Labour Migration", in *International Migration Outlook 2008*, OECD Publishing, Paris, http://dx.doi.org/10.1787/migr_outlook-2008-6-en. [37]

OECD (2001), *Trends in International Migration 2001: Continuous Reporting System on Migration*, OECD Publishing, Paris, http://dx.doi.org/10.1787/migr_outlook-2001-en. [1]

OECD/ADBI/ILO (2018), *Labor Migration in Asia: Increasing the Development Impact of Migration through Finance and Technology*, ADBI, Tokyo, https://dx.doi.org/10.1787/9789264289642-en. [2]

OECD/EU (2016), *Recruiting Immigrant Workers: Europe 2016*, Recruiting Immigrant Workers, OECD Publishing, Paris, http://dx.doi.org/10.1787/9789264257290-en. [14]

Oh, J. (2017), "The Labor Market Effect of Foreign Workers : An Empirical Study on the Incheon Metropolitan Area (외국인근로자의 고용이 노동시장에 미치는 영향 분석 : 인천지역을 중심으로)", *Journal of the Korean Regional Economics*, Vol. 36, pp. 22-51. [30]

Oh, J. et al. (2012), "Migration Profile of the Republic of Korea", *Research Report Series*, No. 2011-01, IOM Migration Research and Training Centre, Seoul, http://iom-mrtc.org/eng/business/business02.php?admin_mode=read&no=119&make=&search=&s_url= (accessed on 18 October 2017). [44]

Park, Y. (1991), *Foreign Labor in Korea: Issues and Policy Options*. [42]

Park, Y. and M. Kim (2016), *Employment Permit System: Korea's Temporary Low-skilled Foreign Worker Program*, Human Resources Development Service of Korea, Ulsan, Korea. [5]

Seol, D. and G. Han (2004), "Foreign Migrant Workers and Social Discrimination in Korea", *Harvard Asia Quarterly*, Vol. 8/1, pp. 45-50. [43]

Seol, D. and J. Ko (2015), *Foreign Migrant Workers Survey in Korea 2015 (외국인근로자 고용허가제 만족도 조사 연구)*, HRD Korea (Human Resources Development Korea), Ulsan, http://www.hrdkorea.or.kr/4/2/2?k=46890&pageNo=&searchType=&searchText= (accessed on 24 May 2018). [9]

Seol, D. et al. (2015), *Designing foreign worker levy prgram for Korea (고용부담금제 도입 및 운영방안 연구)*, http://www.prism.go.kr/homepage/researchCommon/downloadResearchAttachFile.do;jsessionid=C3F67425543EFB019C8A176143C55F60.node02?work_key=001&file_type=CPR&seq_no=001&pdf_conv_yn=N&research_id=1490000-201600009. [17]

Skrentny, J. et al. (2007), "Defining Nations in Asia and Europe: A Comparative Analysis of Ethnic Return Migration Policy", *International Migration Review*, Vol. 41/4, pp. 793-825, http://dx.doi.org/10.1111/j.1747-7379.2007.00100.x. [10]

Woo, B. (2018), *Employment Permit System*, ADBI, Incheon, https://www.adb.org/news/events/8th-adbi-oecd-ilo-roundtable-labor-migration-asia. [33]

Zimring, C. (2004), "Dirty Work: How Hygiene and Xenophobia Marginalized the American Waste Trades, 1870-1930", *Environmental History*, Vol. 9/1, p. 80, http://dx.doi.org/10.2307/3985946. [19]

Annex 3.A. Supplementary tables

Annex Table 3.A.1. Occupations open to participants in the H-2 Visa, 2018

Occupation	Code
Growing of crops	11
Farming of animals	12
Inshore and coastal fishing	3112
Aquaculture	321
Manufacturing	10~33
Sewage, waste water, and human waste treatment services	37
Waste collection, disposal and materials recovery	38
Construction	41~42
Wholesale of live animals	46205
Wholesale of other agricultural raw materials and live animals	46209
Wholesale of household goods	464
Wholesale of machinery equipment and supplies	465
Collection and wholesale of recycling materials	46791
Retail sale of other household equipment	475
Retail sale in other specialized stores	478
Retail sale not in stores	479
Transit and ground passenger transportation	492
Refrigerated warehousing	52102
Hotels (limited to grade 1, 2, and 3 tourist hotels pursuant to the Tourism Promotion Act)	55111
Inns (applicable only to ethnic Koreans holding foreign citizenship at the age of 45 or older.)	55112
Restaurants	5611
Lunch counters	5619
Publishing of books, magazines and other publications	581
Publishing of music and other audio	59201
Business facilities support management services	741
Building general cleaning services	74211
Cleaning of business facilities and industrial supplies	74212
Activities of travel agencies & tour operators and tourist assistance activities	752
Social work activities	87
General repair services of motor vehicles	95211
Repair services of motor vehicles specializing in parts	95212
Maintenance and repair services of motorcycles	9522
Saunas	96121
Industrial laundry services	96911
Private nursing and similar services	96993
Activities of households as employers and undifferentiated goods (and services) producing activities for own use	97~ 98

Source: Ministry of Justice.

Annex Table 3.A.2. Sector limits imposed on ethnic Koreans only in the late 2000s have expired

Sectors of employment – ceilings on H-2 Work Visit employment.

Year	Agro-livestock	Construction	Fishery	Manufacturing	Services
2007	1700	10500	200	27200	20400
2008	1000	12000	400	16000	30600
2009	1000	0	100	10000	5900

Source: Ministry of Employment and Labour.

Annex Table 3.A.3. Occupations not allowed under the F-4 visa, 2018

Occupations which are ineligible for holders of the F-4 permits

Non-professional Occupations	9. Elementary Workers	Elementary Workers in Construction	91001
		Elementary Workers in Mining	91002
		Loading and Lifting Elementary Workers	92101
		Moving Helpers	92102
		Other Loading and Lifting Elementary Workers	92109
		Postmen	92210
		Door to Door Deliverers	92221
		Other Door to Door Deliverers	92229
		Food Deliverers	92230
		Beverage Deliverers	92291
		Newspaper Deliverers	92292
		Other Deliverers	92299
		Hand Packers	93001
		Hand Trademark Attaching Labourers	93002
		Building Cleaners	94111
		Transport Vehicle Cleaners	94112
		Other Cleaner	94119
		Garbage Collectors	94121
		Sweepers	94122
		Recycling Products Collectors	94123
		Other Sweepers and Recyclables Collectors	94129
		Apartment Guards	94211
		Building Guards	94212
		Other Guards	94219
		Ticket Examiners	94220
		Fastfood Restaurant Workers	95210
		Kitchen Helpers	95220
		Petrol Pump Attendants	95310
		Store Arranging Elementary Workers	95391
		Bill Distributing and Posting Workers	95392
		Other Sales Related Elementary Workers	95399
		Forest Fire Watchman	99104
		Meter Readers, Gas Readers	99211
		Gas Readers	99212
		Money Collectors	99220
		Parking Manager	99231
		Parking Service Workers	99232

		Shoe Cleaners	99910
		Laundry and Ironing Workers	99920
		Environmental Pollution Watchman	99991
		Other Service Related Elementary Workers	99999
Occupations Against Public Interest and Employment Order	4. Service Workers	Foot Care Specialists	42233
		Bath Attendants	42235
		Wedding Ceremony Workers	42320
		Hotel Service Workers	43221
		Other Lodging Facilities Service Workers	43229
		Karaoke Workers	43232
		Other Entertainment Facilities Workers	43239
		Caddies	43292
		Catering Service Workers	44221
		Beverage Service Workers	44222
		Alcohol Service Workers	44223
	5. Sales Workers	Street Stall Salespersons and Vendors	53050

Source: Ministry of Justice.

Annex Table 3.A.4. Points Grid for Status Change to E-7-4, 2018

Category	Max Points	Characteristic			Points
Must score points in each category (max 80)	20	Income or Skills	Annual Income	Certified Skill	
			33m+ KRW	Engineer	20
			30-33m KRW	Industrial Engineer	15
			26-30m KRW	Certified craftsman or Skill equivalency verification	10
	20	Education	Bachelor or more		20
			Associate degree		10
			High school graduate		5
	20	Age	<24		20
			24-26		15
			27-28		10
			29-31		7
			32-33		5
			34-38		2
	20	Language	Level 5+		20
			Level 4		15
			Level 3		10
			Level 2		5
Additional points (up to 100)	35	Liquid Assets	Two-year deposits	100M KRW	15
				60M KRW	10
				30M KRW	5
			Household Assets (excluding deposits	100M KRW	20
				80M KRW	15

Category	Max Points	Characteristic			Points
			counted above)	50M KRW	10
	15	Korean work experience	Root Industry	At least 6 years	15
				At least 4 years	10
			General manufacturing, construction industry etc.	At least 6 years	10
				At least 4 years	5
	10	Education in Korea in relevant fields	More than Bachelor level		10
			Associate degree		8
		Training in Korea (in recognised inst.)	More than 1 year		5
			6 months to 1 year		3
	40	Experience in domestic study	More than MA		10
			Bachelor or less		5
			Associate degree		3
		Ministerial recommendation by ministry responsible for field of employment			10
		Work experience in Eup, Myeon (rural) area	At least 4 years		10
			At least 3 years		7
			At least 2 years		5
		Social Contribution (not cumulable)	Recognition		5
			Community Service		3
		Income tax paid in previous year	3M KRW+		5
Deductions: Up to -50 points	-50	Immigration Control Act violation		Once	-5
				Twice	-10
				3+ times	-50
	-50	Other violations of domestic laws		Once	-5
				Twice	-10
				3+ times	-50

Note: Community Service is more than one year with at least 200 hours of volunteer. Recognition is from the local authority.
Source: Ministry of Justice.

Chapter 4. Talent, innovation and investment through migration

This chapter examines the framework for skilled migrants in Korea, including students, investors and intra-corporate transferees. Korea offers highly qualified foreigners a variety of permit categories with relatively generous conditions for initial residence and rapid access to permanent status. Yet there are few high-skilled foreign workers. The chapter explores the obstacles beyond labour migration policy itself for highly-skilled workers to arrive and remain in Korea. Highly-skilled labour migration policy is analysed in light of the saturated labour market for tertiary-educated residents. It examines the articulation of visa categories for professional foreigners and whether these are suited to the policy objectives. The chapter discusses how these could be adjusted. Finally, the chapter considers the possible relevance of a Secretariat for analysis on the impact and direction of labour migration policy going forward.

The statistical data for Israel are supplied by and under the responsibility of the relevant Israeli authorities. The use of such data by the OECD is without prejudice to the status of the Golan Heights, East Jerusalem and Israeli settlements in the West Bank under the terms of international law.

High-skilled workers, international experts and talent

Is Korea attractive?

Despite the large increase in migration to Korea in the past decade, the share of highly qualified workers in Korea relative to both the total migrant population and the highly qualified Korean population remains very low. The total number of foreign workers on permits for highly qualified was about 60 000 in 2016, including more than 15 000 language teachers and about 2 500 tertiary-level professors. The largest group, more than 21 000 specialised workers (E-7), does not necessary have tertiary qualifications. Inflows are very limited. From 2004 to 2015, average annual inflows of E-1 (professors) was under 500; that of researchers (E-3), about 730 annually; and that of professionals (E-5) about 110. Intra-company transfers and temporary employees of Korean firms are counted separately, but amount to fewer than 2 000 annually, with most staying only the time their firm posts them to Korea. In addition to these temporary permits, some skilled foreigners have obtained permanent residence (F-2 and F-5, primarily), but in very small numbers.

The first factor business environment in Korea is not considered, in international comparison, among the attractive destinations for foreign talent in OECD countries (Figure 4.1).

Figure 4.1. Korea is not one of the most attractive destinations for talent in the OECD

"Foreign high-skilled people are attracted to your country's business environment" (index from 0 to 10)

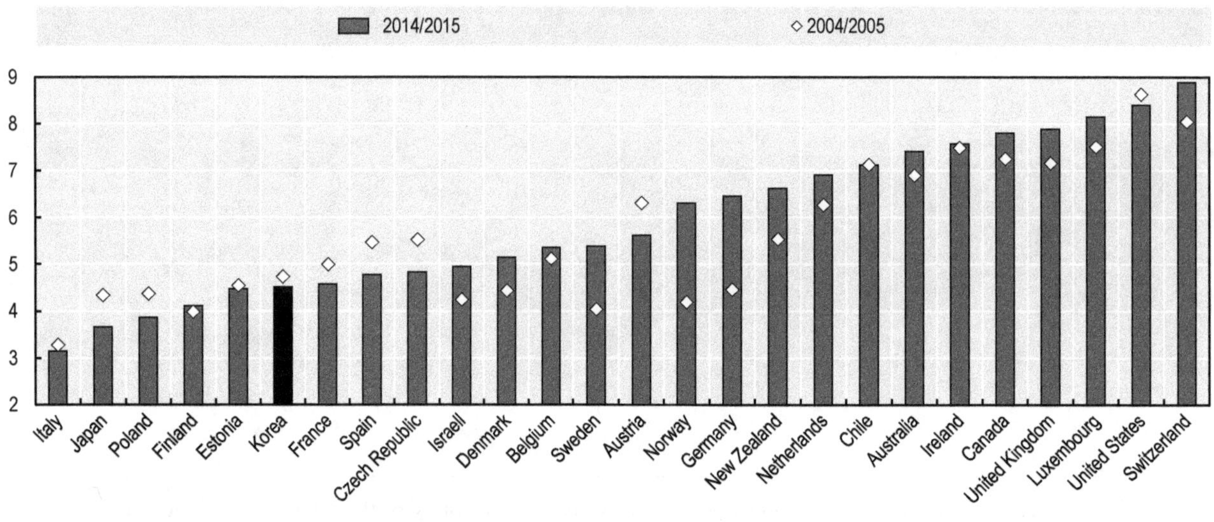

Source: World Competitiveness Yearbook, 2004-2015.

Skilled migration inflows in Korea are limited, and much lower than in other OECD destinations in both absolute terms and relative to population (Figure 4.2). Inflows are about 5 400 in the main skilled worker categories annually, or about 0.1 per thousand inhabitants, lower than in other major destinations.

Figure 4.2. Korea has very low levels of skilled migration

Skilled labour migration permit flows, 2015 or most recent year, selected OECD countries, absolute value and as a share of population.

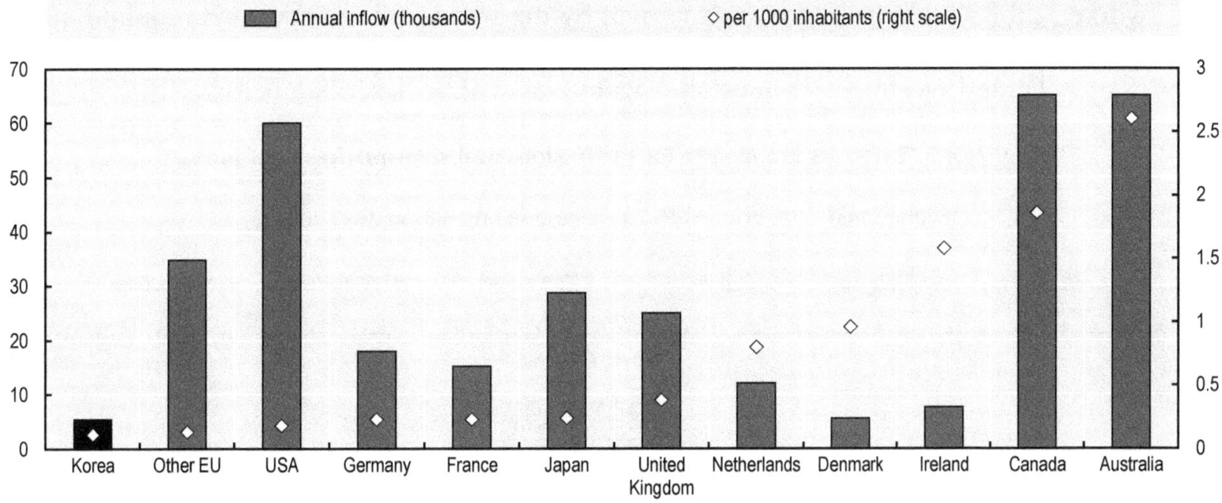

Note: For USA, Canada and Australia, primary applicants approved under permanent economic migration channels. For other countries, qualified migrants with temporary permits allowing indefinite renewal and change to permanent status. For Korea, E-1, E-3-5 and E-7 visas.
Source: National immigration authorities.

The permit framework for skilled labour migration

Migration policy for the highly qualified has historically been open in Korea, with few limits placed on migration for employment for researchers, executives and managers, and highly-qualified foreign professionals. Specific visa categories have been in place since the late 1980s for teachers and international personnel.

The framework for skilled migrants comprises a number of different visa categories, primarily E-1 through E-7, but also including several D visas, especially D-7 through D-9.

There is no labour market test for any of the visas, in the traditional sense of a mandatory job advertisement period or a requirement that employers seek resident workers prior to recruitment from abroad. However, a number of visas in the E category, notably the E-5 and the E-7 visa, require a letter of recommendation of employment from the head of state administration or a document which can prove the necessity of employment. Without these documents, the Korean Immigration Service will not approve the visa application.

The main category is the E-7 visa for Specially Designated Activities, for skilled work in a number of authorised occupations. The E-7 permit is divided into a number of separate grounds for admission. First, applicants must work in one of the eligible occupations (see Annex Table 4.A.1). The list of eligible occupations is determined by and announced by the Minister of Justice. The number of occupations on this list vary; in 2014 there were 78 jobs eligible for the E-7, rising to 85 in 2015, cut back to 82 in 2017 and back to 85 in 2018. Not all of these jobs required a tertiary degree or advanced skills; the list includes cooks, as well as tourism-related jobs where foreigners might be employed, such as hotel receptionists and event planners. It also includes a generic category "skilled worker", for which discretionary approval by the Immigration Service is required based on supporting documents such as an official recommendation by KOTRA (Korea Trade-Investment Promotion Agency), as will be described below.

Figure 4.3. E-7 visas are mostly for professions and semi-professional jobs

Occupational categories of E-7 visa holders, by nationality, 2014.

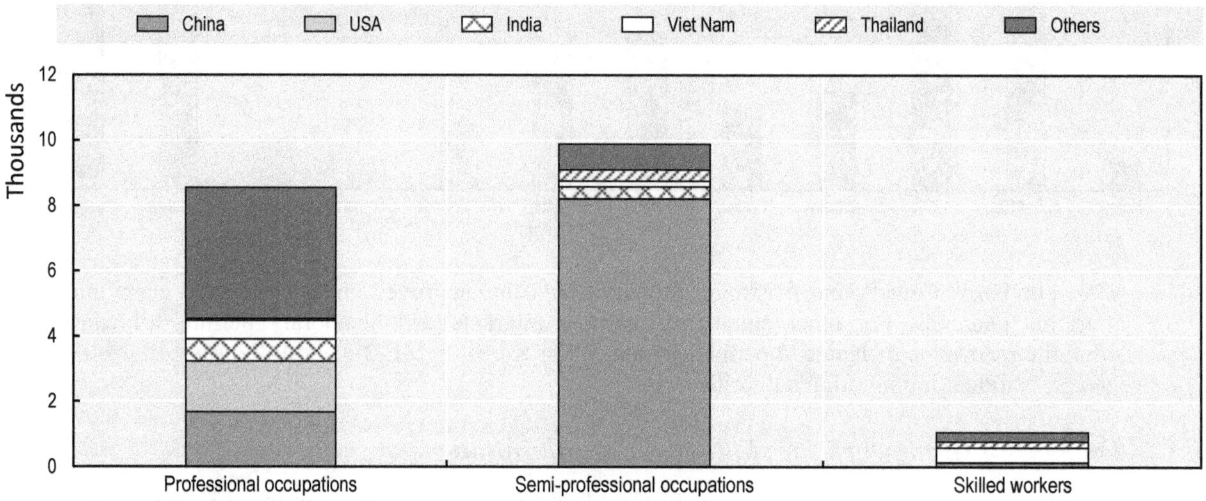

Source: KLI (Lee et al., 2016[1]).

The eligible occupation list is not, strictly speaking, an occupational shortage list. Most of the occupations on the list are specialised occupations requiring specific professional, linguistic and cultural competencies which, while not in shortage in Korea, may justify recurrence to a global talent pool. The less qualified jobs on the list, on the other hand, reflect occupational priority rather than a verified shortage. Occupations classified into group three are eligible only if the employer has a workforce with less than 20% E-7 workers. An employer could have 20% E-7 workers, but also a large number of foreign workers on other permit grounds employed in the same firm.

The E-7 occupation list is different from shortage occupation lists used in most migration schemes in OECD countries (Box 4.1), which are based on vacancies or priority occupations and which often exempt from a labour market test.

Box 4.1. Occupation lists for migration in OECD countries

Korea does not use a shortage occupation list (SOL) in its labour migration management system. SOLs may be used for two purposes: to identify which occupations are eligible for recruitment of foreign workers, or to exempt recruitment from requirements such as salary thresholds or labour market tests which apply to recruitment of foreign workers.

Most often, SOLs are used to exempt from the labour market test, on the basis that there is little point in advertising vacancies when the shortage of labour has already been demonstrated. This accelerates recruitment.

In other cases, the SOL is used to justify a lower salary threshold (e.g., the EU Blue Card) or eliminates it altogether (as in Austria's Red-White-Red card).

In several countries, the SOL determines which occupations are open to recruitment, as in Greece or under several admission programmes in Australia and New Zealand.

Finally, the SOL can be used to prioritise applications in a PBS (used in New Zealand and Canada).

Developing a SOL is often a complex procedure in the hands of an expert body (Chaloff, 2014[2]), requiring regular update to remain relevant (some countries update the list every six months, although the United States has not revised its list in decades). Some SOLs are based on short-term labour market indicators such as vacancy rates (e.g., in Spain), while in other countries they are meant to take into account structural or long-term needs (the Australian Skilled Occupation List or New Zealand Long-Term Skill Shortage List). The effort to develop a SOL needs to be weighed against its effective use in the migration system; in the United Kingdom, the SOL involves regular and onerous consultation and study, even as it only covers a fraction of labour migration flows, most of which are labour-market tested. Nonetheless, the Migration Advisory Committee in the United Kingdom, originally established to determine the SOL, gradually received a broader mandate to conduct analysis and propose policy solutions in response to government queries.

The E-7 visa requires proof of qualifications, either through a masters-level degree, a bachelor-level degree with one year experience, or five years' experience in the relevant field for those with no tertiary degree.

There were more than 20 000 foreign residents holding E-7 visas in 2017, indicating a sharp increase since 2010 (Figure 4.4). While inflows of E-7 visa holders from abroad have also increased over the period, the annual inflow is below 5 000.

Figure 4.4. The number of E-7 visa holders has risen sharply in recent years

Panel A. E-7 visa holders, stock and inflow, 1998-2017.
Panel B. Nationality of E-7 visa holders, 2017.

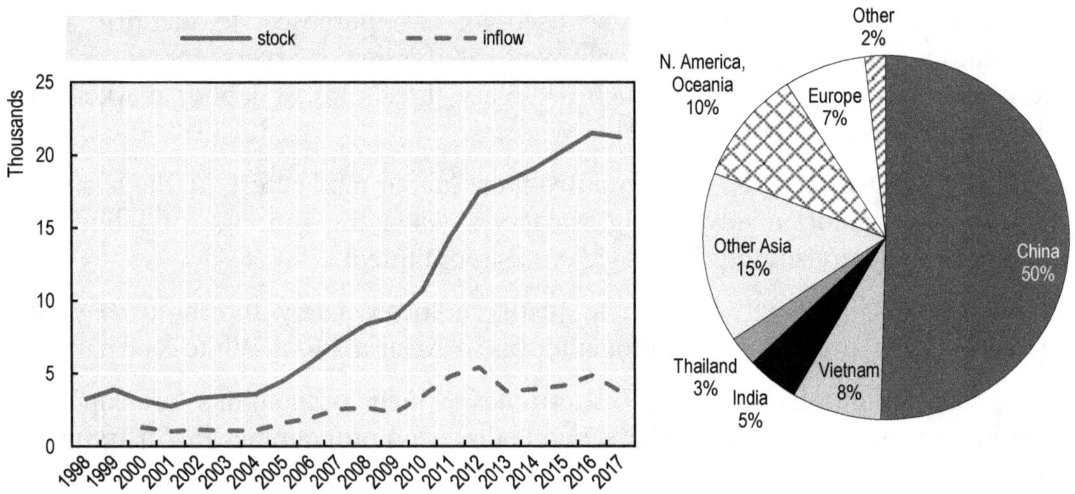

Source: International Migration Statistics of Statistics Korea for inflow, Korean Immigration Service fo stock.

Graduates of universities in Korea who find employment are also eligible for an E-7 visa regardless of the job, as long as it is requires tertiary-level education.

The E-7 visa is subject to a firm-level restriction, as a safeguard, that no more than 20% of all employees of the firm are foreign nationals, and firms with fewer than five employees (registered with the National Insurance Scheme) may not request an E-7 visa.

Box 4.2. Firm-level ceilings as a migration management tool

Korea imposes a variable firm-level limit on employment of E-9 workers (Table 3.3) and a 20% limit on employment of E-7 workers. This is meant to prevent firms from becoming overly reliant on foreign workers. Several other OECD countries use this firm-level cap within their skilled migration programmes.

In Canada, since 2014, there has been a cap on the number of low-wage positions in a firm – specific work location – which can be filled by temporary foreign workers. The cap applies wherever the wage is below the provincial or territorial median hourly wage. The cap was set at 20% for firms with low-wage TFWs hired prior to the introduction of the cap, and 10% for firms hiring low-wage TFWs following the introduction of the cap. Exemptions to the 10% cap are in place for some categories of firms and some occupations.

Turkey imposes a firm-level limit on employment. In general, there is a five-to-one ratio required, with at least five Turkish workers employed full-time for each new foreign worker hired at a firm. Some exemptions are in principle allowed, but in practice have not been implemented. Work-permit-exempt employment may also be subject to a ratio; for example, public-benefit associations may employ up to one-third of their staff permit-exempt. Employment of Syrians under temporary protection is ratio-exempt in agriculture.

Chile has a largely open work permit regime for foreigners in the country legally, but the Labour Code imposes restrictions on larger firms. Employers with more than 25 employees must certify that at least 85% of their total employees working in Chile are Chilean nationals. Some foreign nationals are however included as citizens in the calculation: foreign spouses and surviving spouses; parents of Chilean nationals; and foreigners resident in Chile for more than five years. Other exemptions apply to certain expert technical staff. Foreign investment firms can also apply for an exemption by providing detailed justification.

Ireland has a "50:50 rule", under which an employment permit will not be issued unless half of the employees in a firm are EEA nationals. Exceptions apply for certain start-up firms and for one-person firms.

Employment ratios may also be taken into account in fee structure and compliance mechanisms. The United States, for example, considers "H-1B dependent employers" those which have above certain share of their workforce employed under H-1B visas. The threshold is 15% for firms with more than 50 employees, but higher for smaller firms. Firms classified as "dependent" are subject to a more rigorous labour market test. Higher-salary and higher-education workers are exempt from this more rigorous labour market test. Australia introduced a "non-discriminatory workforce test" in 2018 to its Temporary Skills Shortage visa. The discretionary test adds review to requests for workers from firms with a high (or above-the-norm) share of foreign workers in their workplaces.

Within the E-7, there are a number of channels meant to favour migration by individuals with specific skills, through "recommendation" by a trusted body which attests that the individual has the specific skills on the occupation list.

The so-called "Gold Card System" for technology talents was introduced in November 2000 for one occupation (e-commerce). The E-7 visa issued as a Gold Card offers a longer duration (three years instead of two maximum, raised to five years in 2007). In 2003, the number of eligible occupations for the Gold Card was expanded to include seven additional fields (nano-, bio-, transport, material, environment and energy technology), and in 2006 technology management was added. Initially, the Ministry of Industry, Commerce and Energy provided a recommendation; since 2011, the government body providing the recommendation is KOTRA. The service is provided for the IT field, for anyone with a master's degree; for applicants with a bachelor degree in the field of expertise; for those with a bachelor's degree in a related field and one year experience; or for those with five years of experience. KOTRA evaluates the degrees and certification of experience and provides a recommendation letter for the E-7 visa.

Also in 2000, two other special cards were offered, for information technology (the "IT Card") and for scientists and engineers (the "Science Card"). The IT card was issued following recommendation from the Ministry of Information and Communication; in 2009 it was merged with the Gold Card under KOTRA. The Science Card requires support of the Ministry of Science and Technology. Like the Gold Card, they offer three-year duration. The Gold and Science cards allow cardholders to employ foreign domestic workers (under the F-1-24 visa sub-category), who would otherwise not be admitted for employment in Korea.

KOTRA also offers a recommendation service for skilled workers hired by export-oriented Korean firms through its ContactKorea service. ContactKorea was created in 2008 by KOTRA to target global professionals for work either in Korean companies, to increase their capacity for global markets, or for Korean companies in Korea for employment in export-oriented positions. ContactKorea is meant to bring talent to Korea. While ContactKorea focuses on professional employment, ContactKorea can also support applications by foreigners for E-7 visas, which require demonstration of a "special ability". ContactKorea can attest to the special ability justifying the issuance of this visa.

Visa procedures for a number of skilled worker categories was introduced in 2010 as "HuNet Korea", an on-line application to join pool for foreign skilled workers interested in working in Korea. Recommendation was limited to a subset of occupations eligible for E-1 to E-5 permits and the higher-skilled professions under the E-7 permit. HuNet Korea relied on "visa nominators", unpaid third parties approved by designated attachés within Korean embassies and by the Korea Business Centres (under KOTRA). The role of the designated visa nominators was to review applications by individuals and recommend they be included in a database (pool) of human resources. Korean companies were allowed to search this pool, while individuals in the pool could consult job vacancies.

The use of a designated third-party nominator to validate candidate qualifications represented a novelty in the international migration system, in terms of certification of the legitimacy of applications. While corporate third parties such as professional bodies, universities or arts boards are used to validate the competences of individual applicants (as under the United Kingdom's nomination system for its Tier 1 exceptional talent visa), no country uses trusted individuals. HuNet relied on the assumption that neutral and disinterested experts could be found, providing review of candidates in return solely for recognition of their own expertise and motivated by a desire to strengthen ties between their country of residence and Korea. This assumption proved difficult to realise, and the HuNet nomination system ended in 2011. KOTRA continues to nominate candidates under the ContactKorea scheme, and is the only body which can verify the academic and professional qualifications of candidates in the job pool; it does so only after a job offer has been found.

HuNet introduced on-line visa application for the first time. Approved profiles in the HuNet database were granted access to on-line visa application, eliminating the need to go to a Korean consular representative in person. This facilitation is maintained for skilled workers and investors.

The E-7 visa requires that the holders remain in the occupation for which they were recruited and with the employer for whom their permit was authorised. They are allowed to seek employment with other employers who meet the same conditions. However, there is no job search period in case of unemployment. It is noteworthy that about 8% of E-7 permit holders switched into the D-10 job-search permit in 2015; this was more common than acquisition of permanent residence (Figure 4.5). The job-search permit is the only grounds on which an unemployed E-7 permit holder can switch employment.

E-7 holders may bring family members, but their family members may not take up employment without changing their visa.

Figure 4.5. Many Specialty Workers use the D-10 bridging visa

Status change from E-7 visas to other visas, 2015, by destination visa

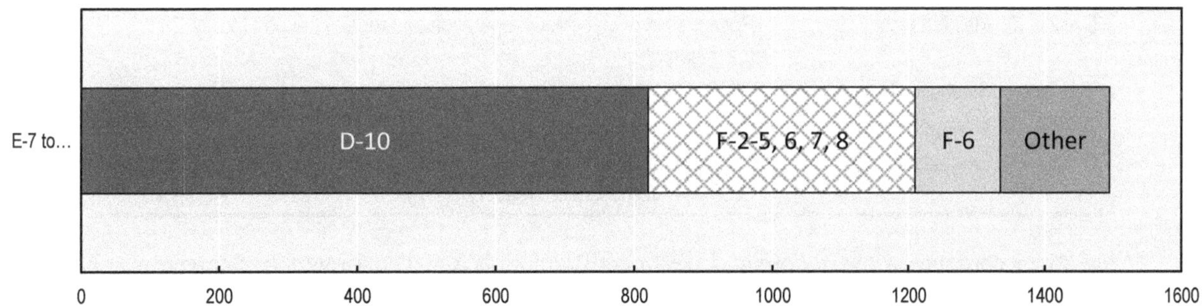

Source: Korea Immigration Service, 2016.

Intracorporate transfers and employees of multinational firms

One of the main channels for skilled migration into Korea has not been local hiring of foreigners by Korean enterprises, but different forms of mobility within multinational firms operating in Korea or Korean forms bringing employees from abroad for training and knowledge transfer. Intra-company transfers and related detached workers in Korea, holding D-7 to D-9 visas, amounted to more than 10 000 workers in 2017; until 2011, workers holding these visas outnumbered locally hired E-7 visa holders.

Table 4.1. D-7 through D-9 visas

Sub-categories of detached workers and intracorporate transfers.

Visa code	Subject	Type of beneficiary
D-7-1	Intra-Company Transferee (Foreign Company)	Employee of a least 1 year at a foreign public institution or of a foreign company, dispatched to affiliates, subsidiary, or branch Korea in a field requiring expertise
D-7-2	Intra-Company Transferee (Domestic company)	Employee of a least 1 year at an overseas corporation, branch of a public organization or listed company, dispatched to head office in Korea for training or teaching professional knowledge / technology
D-7-91	Intra-Company Transferee (by FTA)	Intracorporate transfer under an FTA
D-7-92	Contractual Service Supplier (by FTA)	An employee affiliated with a company of in an FTA contract dispatched to Korea for providing or supporting contract services
D-8-1	Incorporated Enterprise	A required professional to work in manufacturing·technical or management·administration at a foreign-invested Korean corporation*
D-8-2	Business Venture	A person who has established a venture business pursuant to the Act on Special Measures for the Promotion of Venture Business or who has been confirmed as a preliminary venture business
D-8-91	FTA transferee	Intra-company transferee according to FTA
D-8-3	Unincorporated Enterprise	Required professional to engage in the management of foreign-invested enterprises or in the fields of production and technology*
D-9-1	International Trade Visa	Traders with granted trader identification number, ex-foreign students with retail experience, trained traders
D-9-2	Maintenance	Responsible of installation, operation and repair of export facility machinery
D-9-3	Shipbuilding supervisor	Shipbuilding supervisor sent by client of shipyard
D-9-4	Manager	Company management and commercial operators
D-9-5	Ex-student	Trade management who was student. Individual firm. Korean degree and >300M KRW investment required

Note: *in accordance with the Foreign Investment Promotion Act. The foreign investment must be more than KRW 100m.
Source: OECD Secretariat analysis of Korean legislation.

There are a little over 1 300 people with a D-7 visa in Korea, a figure which has been steady for more than a decade (Figure 4.6). About one in three ICTs with a D-7 is from China, and 22% and 23% each from India and Japan. Other OECD countries besides Japan comprise most of the remainder.

D-8 visas, with about 6 000 foreign residents, are notable for the predominance of Japanese (47%), followed by Chinese (22%) and nationals of other OECD countries outside Asia (20%), but also Pakistan (6%) and India (4%).

D-9 visas are mostly granted to foreign nationals representing clients of Korean shipyards (in 2017, the D-9-3 visa comprised about 82% of all D-9 visas), so that the number varies according to the contracts underway in Korean shipyards. The number sharply fell from its peak in 2014 to below 3 000 in 2017. Top countries in 2017 were Norway, Great Britain and France. Overall, OECD countries comprised 49% of the foreigners holding D-9 visas in 2017.

One notable aspect of D visa holders in Korea is that they are overwhelmingly men: more than 85% of the visa-holders in each of the D-7, D-8 and D-9 categories are men.

Figure 4.6. Intracorporate transfers are more numerous than skilled workers

D-7, D-8 and D-9 visa holders in Korea, by year (Panel A) and by nationality in 2017 (Panel B).

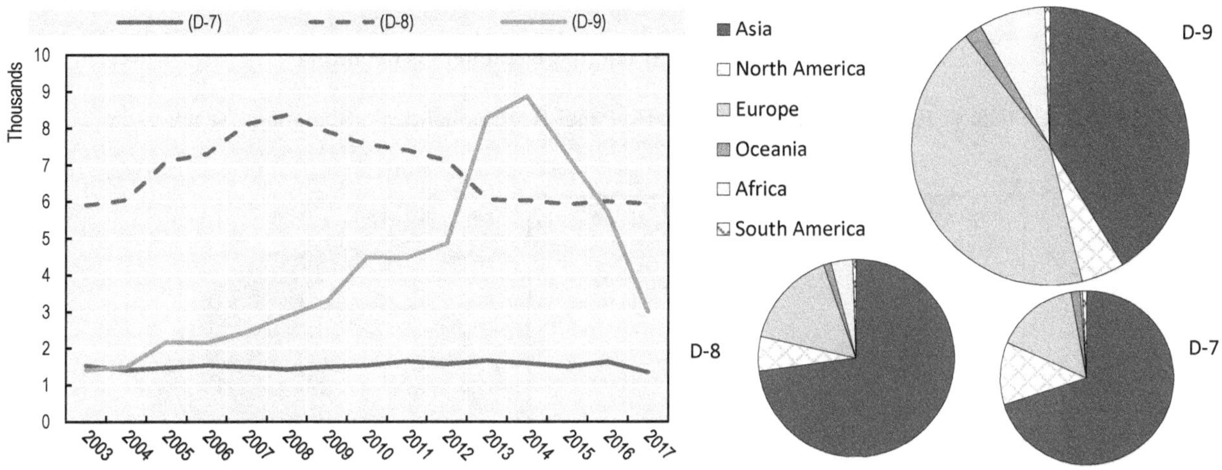

Source: Korea Immigration Statistics.

The D-7 through D-9 visas can be renewed indefinitely. This makes the D-7 visa, in particular, unusual in international comparison, as most intra-corporate transfers are subject to a maximum stay followed by a cool-down period or mandatory absence from the country (see Box 3.12). At the same time, it opens opportunities for intra-corporate transfers to become familiar with the country and potentially shift to local hire with a view to remain.

Foreign Language Teachers

The educational system in Korea has a particular interest in English language education. As English proficiency is one of the main criteria for assessing the ability of students to enter top universities or hiring after graduation, a large number of Korean parents pay to offer private English language lessons to their children. In 2017, half of middle school students and 30% of high school students were taking private English language lessons[1]. Korea has the highest expenditures on supplementary private education among the OECD countries. This specific demand led to a creation of E-2 visa for Foreign Language Instructor in 1993. Issued to native English speakers who wants to teach English in Korea and meet the following requirements: a 4-year-university degree from English-speaking countries (the US, the UK, Canada, South Africa, New Zealand, Australia and Ireland) and holding the nationality of one of these countries. The number of E-2 visa holders peaked in 2011 and has been falling since then (Figure 4.7). The

E-2 visa is the only visa among skilled work visas where more than half of recipients (55.2% in 2017) are women. For other skilled E visas (excluding E-6), only 38.4% were women in 2017.[2]

Exceptions have begun to be made for nationals of other countries. Indian nationals who are qualified as teachers benefit under the India-Korea Comprehensive Economic Partnership Agreement (CEPA) which came into effect in 2010. University graduates from India who majored in English and acquired a teaching certificate can apply for the E-2 permit to teach English in Korea for a year. The number using this visa, however, has been very limited.

Figure 4.7. The number of language teachers is declining

Panel A. Stock of E-2 visa holders, 1993-2016. Panel B. Nationalities of Language Teachers in 2017

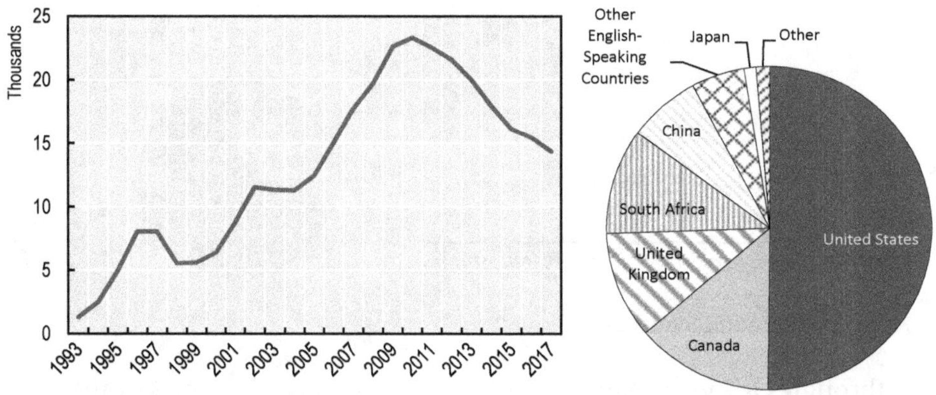

Source: Korea Immigration Service, 2017.

Since native speakers are a top selling point for private language institutes, they compete to hire native speaking teachers. Public schools also compete by offering English classes taught by a native speaker. About one-fourth of language teachers in Korea are employed by public schools. Salaries are not particularly elevated relative to other qualified employment in Korea: the wage level of the language teachers varies between KRW 1.5 million and KRW 3 million (about USD 1 500 to 3 000) depending on their experience and the type of workplace. Low-wage and underpaid English language teachers have been a problem in the unregulated sector of language schools; in 2013, the Ministry of Justice set a minimum wage for acquiring the E-2 visa at KRW 1.5 million to prevent underpaid foreign language teachers and reduce the number of undeclared language teachers. This salary requirement, along with the declining demand for English-language instruction as there are fewer young people in the school-age cohort, has led to a decline since 2012.

Japan is the only other OECD country with a similar work visa, and has a smaller number of English teachers from abroad at around 7 000 permit holders, including language teachers at public schools with Instructor visa and teachers at private institute with Specialist in Humanities / International Services visa.

There are several programmes under the E-2 scheme. The English Program in Korea (EPIK) helps improve English proficiency of both students and teachers in Korean schools by recruiting native speakers. The NIIED's Teach and Learn in Korea (TaLK) scholarship programme launched in 2008 is designed for university graduates to participate in six months to one year of working partnerships with the Korean university to prepare and engage in the after-school English programmes at the elementary schools.

The only other language allowed under the visa is Chinese; there were more than 1 000 Chinese teachers in Korea in 2017. The Chinese Program in Korea (CPIK) invites Chinese teachers with a university degree and a teaching certificate. CPIK teachers can stay up to two years to give Chinese lessons.

Most E-2 teachers do not settle in Korea. In-country status changes are allowed, although rare. The permit is not designed to bring in talent; E-2 permit holders are granted a stay a month longer than the length of contract. Those who require additional time to change jobs or sectors and stay in Korea can also apply for a job search visa (D-10-1).

Global talent attraction initiatives

Among the policy priorities in the migration area is attraction of global talent, particularly in research and innovation. This is a response to the fact that, while Korea invests heavily in R&D, its integration into global innovation networks – as measured by levels of international co-authorship and co-patenting – are among the lowest in the OECD (Figure 4.8). To address this, Korea has launched a wide range of different programmes to attract international talent.

Figure 4.8. Korea lags behind in international collaboration in science and innovation

Co-authorship and co-invention as a percentage of scientific publications and IP5 patent families, 2003-12.

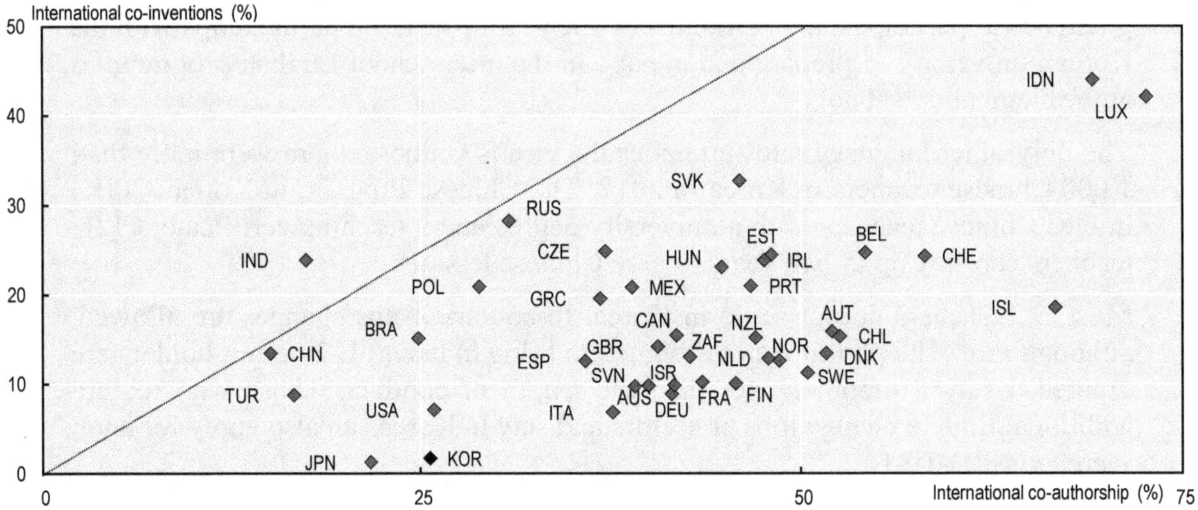

Note: International co-authorship of scientific publications is measured in terms of the share of articles featuring authors affiliated with foreign institutions (from a different country or economy) in total articles produced by domestic institutions. A scientific document is deemed to involve an international collaboration if institutions from different countries or economies are present in the list of affiliations reported by single or multiple authors. Estimates are based on whole counts from information contained in the Scopus database. International co-inventions are measured as the share of patents with at least one co-inventor located abroad in total patents invented domestically. Data refer to IP5 patent families with members filed at the EPO or the USPTO, by first filing date and according to the inventor's residence using whole counts.

Source: OECD, STI Micro-data Lab: Intellectual Property Database, http://oe.cd/ipstats, June 2015; and OECD and SCImago Research Group (CSIC), Compendium of Bibliometric Science Indicators 2014, http://oe.cd/scientometrics.

The points-based system for skilled foreigners

Korea offers fast-track permanent residence for qualifying high skilled foreigners. Under a points-based system (PBS) it evaluates professionals who have been living in Korea for at least a year under a different permit. Points are given by checking academic qualifications, Korean language proficiency, income and age. If eligible, they are entitled to residence status (F-2). Obtaining F-2 status allows full labour market access as well as permits for family members. Permanent residence status is allowed after three years of having F-2 status, rather than five years as would normally be required. About 800 people received this status in the first 18 months of application.

Table 4.2 Age and education count for status change to permanent resident

Points grid for status change to F-2-7 Permanent Residence Permit.

Category	Criteria	Points Available	Description
Standardized criteria	Age	15-25	Increasing from 20 for age 18-24 to 25 for age 30-34, decreasing to 15 points for more than 51 years old
	Education	15-35	PhD level: 33 Masters: 30 Bachelors: 26 Associate: 23 Extra 2 for multiple degrees or degree in science or engineering.15 for high school.
	Korean language ability	10-20	10 for the lowest level, 2 points for each additional level up to 20 points for level 6
	Current income	1-10	1 point for less than 20m KRW annual income. 1 point for each 10m KRW up to 100m (10 points)
Extra points	Million KRW of income tax payments	1-5	1 point for 1-2m KRW in tax payments, one additional point for each million up to 5.
	Korean study	1-5	1 point for language study, 2-5 points for degree from associate to PhD
	Volunteer activity in Korea	1-5	1 point for 1-2 year, 3 points for 2-3 years, 5 points for 3+ years.
	Overseas professional work experience	1-5	1 point for 1-2 year, 3 points for 2-3 years, 5 points for 3+ years.
Penalties for violation of Korean laws	By the applicant	-1 to -3	depending on number of offences (1-2 or more) and total amount of fines imposed
	By a family member or (sponsored) invitee	-1	for multiple offences or fines over 1m KRW
	Sponsored family member overstay by >3 months	-1	
Total		Must score 80 out of possible 120	

Source: Ministry of Justice.

The PBS in Korea privileges education more than other criteria, offering up to 35 points, or 40 points for study in Korea; this is half the points necessary to qualify for the threshold. Language and age appear to be the criteria with the most weight following education. However, the ranking also provides a minimum score for a number of variables, the real weight of age, for example, is reduced, since all applicants score at least 15 points, converting the real minimum score to 65 instead of 80 for calculating the share contributed by each factor. While the grid requires some top-scoring in basic categories, a 30-year old graduate, with a bachelor degree from a Korean institute, a medium level of Korean knowledge and a job paying the median salary would not qualify for the F-2 permit.

Korea joins a number of other OECD countries in using a PBS for high skilled migrants. Since introduction in Canada in 1967, PBSs have been used as an instrument to manage selective migration policy. All PBS assigns points per migrant characteristics (e.g. Master's degree, three years of professional experience) grouped in factors (e.g. education, professional experience). PBS are either pass/fail or ranked: in the first, a pass score determines eligibility, while in the second total points are used to prioritise admission.

PBSs are meant to be flexible, as the point allocation can be easily changed, and transparent, as applicant score and admission chances are easy to calculate. They also signal that authorities have control over migration inflows and that only migrants with certain skills are admitted to the country.

Table 4.3. Points-based selection systems tend to focus on highly-skilled workers

PBS in different OECD countries, by year of introduction and target group.

Country (year of introduction of PBS)	Scheme	Target group
Canada (1967)	Federal Skilled Worker Program; Canadian Experience Class; Federal Skilled Trade; Provincial Nominee Programme (optional)	Skilled migrants
Australia (1979)	Skilled Independent visa (subclass 189); Skilled Nominated visa (subclass 190); Skilled regional visa (subclass 489)	Skilled migrants
	Business Innovation and Investment Visa (subclass 188) T	Investors and entrepreneurs
New Zealand (1991)	Skilled Migrant Category	Skilled migrants
	Investor 2	Investors
Czech Republic (2003-2009)	Selection of Qualified Foreign Workers	Highly skilled workers
Denmark (2007-2016)	Green Card	Highly skilled workers
United Kingdom (2008)	Tier 2 - general	Skilled workers
Netherlands (2008)	Self-employed person	Entrepreneurs
Korea (2010, 2011, 2015)	Long-term residence (F-2 visa)	Migrants who have resided in Korea for one year and want to apply to the long-term residence
	Employment Permit System (E-9 visa)	Low skilled workers
	Start-Up visa (D-8-4)	Start-up entrepreneurs
Austria (2011)	Red-and-White Card	Highly skilled migrants
Japan (2012)	Preferential treatment for highly skilled foreign professionals	Highly skilled workers
Germany (2016)	PuMa (pilot project) only in the Land of Baden-Württemberg	Medium skilled workers with a profession which is not in the shortage list
Turkey (2017)	Turquoise Card	Highly skilled workers and investors

Source: OECD Secretariat.

PBSs have a twofold objective: to improve selection and to improve case management. PBSs improve selection by weighting factors differently, by equally considering different profiles, and by introducing factors with multiple dimensions. Case management is an issue when the number of applications exceeds the number of available places or the administrate capacity. In either case, authorities may want to prioritise some applications over others. A PBS, thanks to its ranking feature, can be used to this end if applications scoring more points are processed earlier.

Korea uses the PBS exclusively for selection, rather than case management; indeed, there is no backlog of high-skilled workers to prioritise. In this, its system is similar to that of European countries and Japan.

Compared with points-based systems used to select permanent economic migrants in other OECD countries, Korea's F-2 PBS relies more heavily on education, and much less on the characteristics of the occupation (Figure 4.9). The occupation of the applicant does not affect points ranking.

Figure 4.9. The F-2 Points-Based System relies more on education and less on occupation

Value of different factors in points systems for skilled migrants in selected OECD countries, 2018.

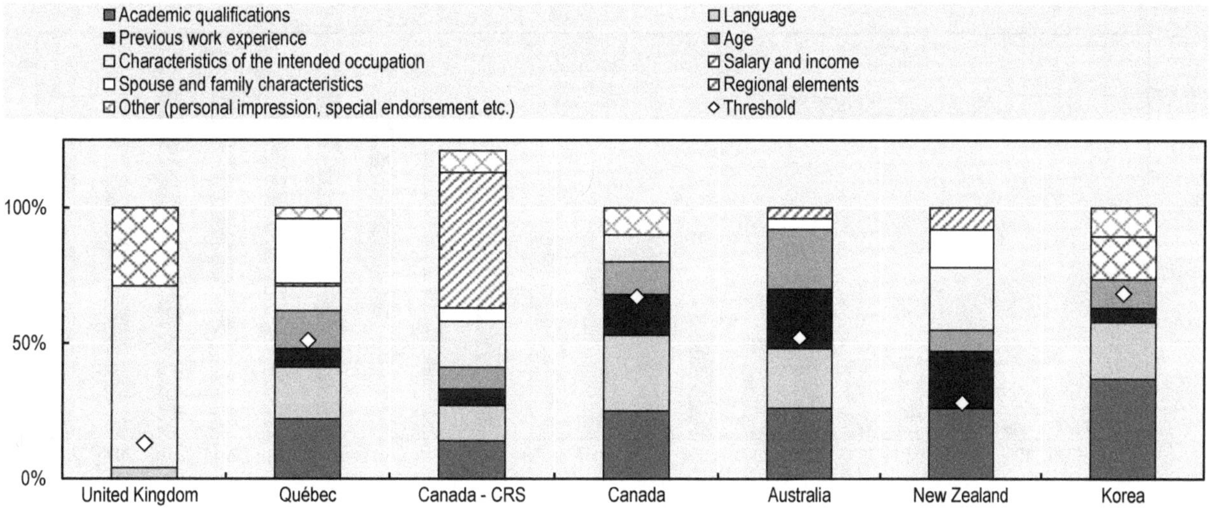

Source: OECD Secretariat.

The F-2 under the PBS is not available to applicants who are not already resident in Korea. Family members of F-2 PBS visa holders are allowed to come to Korea (as F-1 visa holders), but their employment is restricted, and they must apply for separate work authorisation.

In OECD countries using PBS in selection, PBS criteria and weights are regularly reviewed and reweighted in light of evaluation of the outcomes of recipients, in order to improve the ability of the system to select candidates who are able to maintain their employment over the long term. An adequate evaluation framework needs to be in place to adjust and refine the PBS. This appears especially important for Korea, which weights academic qualifications very highly. Other OECD countries have noted that academic qualifications, in the absence of a high degree of language skills, have not assured long-term employability.

Researchers and R&D programmes

Most of the effort in the field of research has focused on researchers and academics for university and research centre staff. The objective of internationalisation of the higher education sector is a long-standing one; in 2002, the objective was set to increase the share of foreign academic staff in higher education to 30% (Kim, 2005[3]). The number of foreign professors increased along with the expansion of the higher education sector but has been in decline since 2012 (Figure 4.10). The number of foreign faculty has also been declining as a share of total faculty (now about 6.3%). Institutional barriers to inclusion remain strong (Kim, 2016[4]).

Figure 4.10. The number of foreign professors has started to decline

Foreign teaching staff, Korean higher education institutions, 1970-2017.

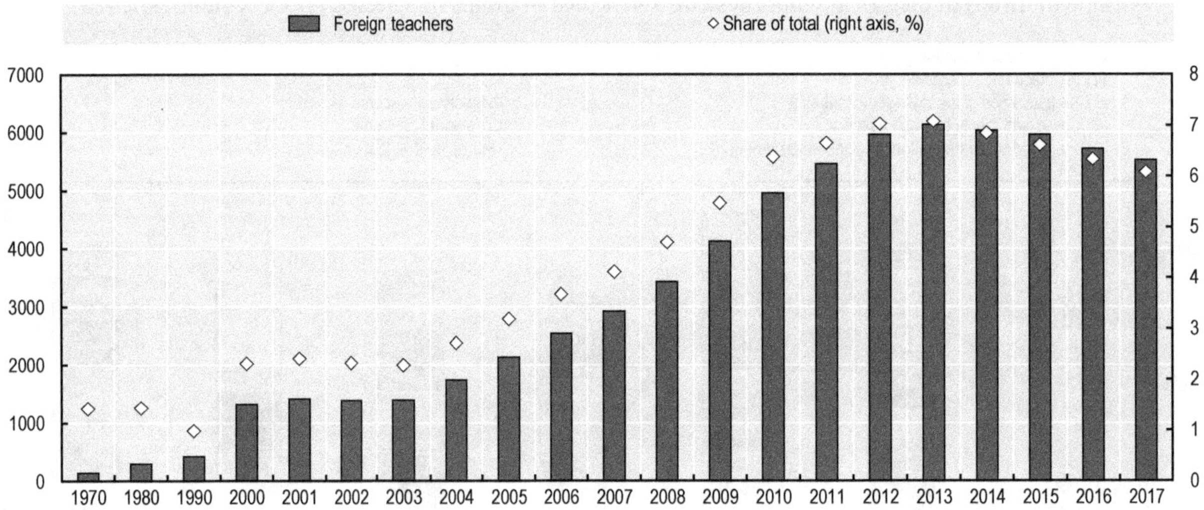

Source: Ministry of Education.

To attract highly skilled, one such programme was the World Class University (WCU) program, which ran from 2008 to 2012, with the objective of attracting outstanding foreign talent. The programme was funded (KRW 825 bn, or about USD 620M) by the Ministry of Education, Science, and Technology (MEST), and run by the National Research Foundation. The project was divided into three types: establishing departments with hired foreign scholars; hiring individual foreign scholars to existing departments; and attracting world renowned scholars (Um, 2012[5]). The programme attracted more than 1 000 academic applicants (Noh, 2014[6]). By early 2011, more than 340 recruits had begun. The costly programme can be evaluated positively in terms of its impact on the participating universities. However, after the World Class University Programme expired, only 14% of foreign participants remained in Korea.

In January 2014, the Korean government introduced a new plan to attract more global talents, with the aim of increasing the number of the high-skilled foreigners by nearly 50% by 2020. This initiative was launched to strengthen the global competitiveness and the R&D capabilities. The plan aimed to increase the number from 25 000 in 2012 to 36 650 by 2017, reaching 7 500 E-1 and E-3 visas. The increase over the period was only half what was necessary, and the target is unmet.

As Korea has endeavoured to develop itself into a knowledge-based economy, several programmes to bring more foreign experts already existed, such as Brain Korea, which dates back to 1999, when the first initiative included a component of international mobility to bring more than 400 scholars in the first five years. Although the number of foreign experts has grown since 2007, most of those visiting experts and students have left the country soon after the programme or scholarship ended.

Responding to these outcomes, the government decided to involve and allocate specific tasks to each Ministry in order to attract more foreign labour primarily for long-term. The plan distinguishes foreign workers into three different categories: researchers (scholars); workers in SMEs including start-ups; and students.

To attract researchers and scholars, the Ministry of Education and Ministry of Science, ICT and Future Planning collaborate to reinforce the infrastructure for research. The Ministry of Science programme, Korea Research Fellowship, offers scholarships and additional supports for maximum five years for scholars who wish to stay to work in companies or institutions. The BK21 Plus programme will be used to approach the top scholars in the world. Research collaboration with the EU began in 2014 exchanging 40 researchers per year.

Another project to absorb more intellectuals to Korea is Brain Return 500 Project, which began in 2012, promoted by the Ministry of Education, Science and Technology (MEST). It aimed to attract 500 top scientists and young researchers in the coming years. Funding for research is provided; up to USD 500 000 annually for two years, for senior scientists, and up to USD 300 000 annually for three years. Extensions of funding can be provided – one year for the first group, and two years for the second. By March 2014, it had attracted almost 100 scientists, of which 1/3 were Korean nationals and the remainder foreigners.

To import more high-skilled workers in SMEs, the Ministry of Science and Ministry of Trade, Industry and Energy focused on recruiting and a better environment for start-ups. Contact Korea supports active recruitment in SMEs; job fairs have been held in Korea and abroad. Ministries also run numerous contests to give opportunities and support the start-ups.

Lastly, the Ministry of Education and Ministry of Science offers various programmes and scholarships to bring outstanding students around the world. The Ministry of Education introduced "Study Korea 2020", to invite outstanding students in the national strategy. The Korea Research Fellowship programme targets only researchers and talented students. Increasing exchanges between local universities and foreign universities will be encouraged. The Ministry will offer counselling services for the foreign students in Korea to support their stay.

For researchers and high-skilled foreigners to make long-term commitments in Korea, however, their engagement in Korean society would have to increase. On the side of foreign researchers, voluntary classes and counselling services to support their journey to adapt and engage more in the community could help. Only 13% of the foreign researchers in Korea in 2016 were women, suggesting that there are also gender issues to address in this channel. A further obstacle is the difficulty of acceptance in Korean university culture, and changes here can only occur on the Korean side (Kim, 2005[3]).

Non-tertiary technical personnel

In Korea, attempts are being made to encourage students in tertiary education to leave university and enrol in university-offered non-tertiary technical vocational certification programmes, in order to work in skilled jobs in "root industries" (SMEs in basic manufacturing). These firms require technical skills but face labour shortages, as Korean students have been reluctant to take the technical training and to work in these SMEs. In 2015, the Ministry of Trade, Industry and Energy (in collaboration with the Ministry of Justice) launched a pilot project to bring foreign students into these jobs. Three participating universities have created non-tertiary technical skills institutes, "Training Institutes for Foreign Engineers in Human Resources of the Root Industry". The pilot recruited students from university programmes into short-term training courses (less than two years) for professional certification, e.g., as industrial welding engineers. Courses were organised with a simplified Korean, for easier understanding, and offered only to these foreign students. In addition, the pilot provided subsidised workplace-specific Korean language instruction and progressive subsidies for studying for the TOPIK exam. Companies were identified who were ready to hire students upon programme completion. The pilot was designed for up to 100 students; 23 were admitted in the first group; by 2017, eight universities were running vocational certification programmes under this pilot with 123 students.

The pilot is based on the existing E-7 visa, for which skilled manufacturing workers are already allowed, and provisions to transfer from the student visa to the E-7 visa at graduation from the programme. However, the E-7 visa requires, for skilled industrial workers without higher-education qualifications, five years of experience. In 2017, this requirement was exempted for graduates of the Training Institutes, allowing them to change status. Similar measures were applied in 2016 to E-9 workers offered technical jobs in "root industry" SMEs, who are now allowed to change status.

Non-migration policy challenges to international recruitment and responses

Despite the introduction of a number of programmes to attract talent from abroad, it is difficult to expect large inflows or their long-term stay. They are likely to confront cultural barriers, language problems and higher costs of private education for children. A 2014 survey by the Hyundai Research Institute – albeit small-scale, with about 115 interviewees – found that work-life balance was the main complaint (Jeon, 2014[7]). Half were certain they wished to leave Korea at the end of their contract, with the main reason cited "corporate culture and values". The sample was mostly male (68%), single (50%) or married without children (20%) and young (36% under age 30, 46% between 30 and 39). All those with children cited their children's education as a difficulty in settling.

The challenges faced by international scientists and engineers to migrate to, or remain in, Korea are similar to those facing Korean expatriate scientists and engineers. These include important differences in wages and working conditions, gender disparity in education and employment, and a highly competitive job market (Song and Song, 2015[8]). Song and Song further point to the issue of children's education: many educated Koreans prefer to enrol their children in education abroad rather than the Korean system, with foreigners even more hesitant to put their children in Korean schools, despite their outstanding record.

Kraeh et al. (2015[9]) identify a number of factors which affect retention of foreign professionals in Korean firms, indicating the long working hours, communication culture, strict hierarchies, and difficulties in integrating. These factors cannot be addressed by migration policy but require a cultural change (Herting, 2016[10]). Similarly, Shin and Choi (2015[11]) point to a number of factors which hinder skilled migration, including a hierarchical and gendered work culture, concerns about the perception and treatment of foreigners in Korea, and closed social networks.

Some local governments have taken steps to support the foreign resident population. Two noteworthy approaches are in Ansan, a city with a relatively large and long-standing foreign population, and the Seoul Global Center.[3] Both centres are run by the municipality, and provide support for foreign residents of all kinds. The Seoul Global Centre, on the other hand, was launched by the municipality of Seoul in 2008 as a multi-lingual, comprehensive support centre. It provides free counseling (in almost a dozen languages) on daily life, with a number of services related to employment (job fair, dispute resolution). The centre also provides language training. Experts provide counselling on issues faced by foreigners living in Seoul in ten different languages on subjects such as starting a business, legal disputes, labour disputes and real estate transactions among others. The Seoul Centre offers support for entrepreneurship (starting a business) and even a business incubator for start-ups, offering office space and mentoring for the first year. The centre is funded by the municipality, but also makes use of volunteers.

Highly qualified talent is also brought to Korea by large Korean companies with global presence or commercial relations, such as the large technology and shipbuilding firms. However, large firms in Korea make sparing use of foreign workers. According to the 2016 Foreigners Labour Force Survey, large firms (more than 300 employees) accounted for just 3% of employment of foreigners in Korea, compared with 13.6% of Korean workers.

A number of factors need to be in place beyond a favourable permit regime to attract foreign talent: career opportunities for the skilled worker and any accompanying spouse, education for any children of the migrant, and the possibility of a community. In the capital region, a sufficient network of support has developed so that large firms can rely on the labour market and existing international schools. In other parts of Korea, large firms employing large numbers of foreign skilled workers have had to support the creation of expatriate compounds, social centres, international schools, newsletters and other elements to ensure that foreign talent is willing to accept employment; this is the case in the shipbuilding centre of Ulsan, for example. This model of expatriate compounds, where international skilled workers are segregated in housing, education and civic life, hinders long-term retention.

Regarding opportunities for spouses, according to the 2016 Foreigners Labour Force Survey, 83% of the foreign employees of large firms were men, a wide gender gap suggesting that there are many spouses of qualified workers. Without job opportunities for spouses, it is unlikely that married couples will wish to settle in Korea; indeed, employed spouses increase the retention rate for skilled immigrants (OECD, 2014[12]).

Korea has also offered foreign high-skilled employees significant tax breaks, although these are gradually being withdrawn (Box 4.3).

Box 4.3. Favourable tax treatment

Starting in January 2003, fiscal incentives for highly skilled immigrants included tax-free allowances of up 40% of salary to cover cost of living, housing, home leave and education. For certain foreigners - employed under a tax-exempt technology inducement contract, or a foreign technician with experience in certain industries – the salary was made tax-exempt for up to five years (OECD, 2005[13]). The general exemption was later reduced to 30% and eliminated in 2010. For technicians and engineers providing services to a Korean company, there is a 50% income tax exemption on salary for the first two years of employment (this exemption will be withdrawn in 2019).

Foreign employees working in Korea have been eligible to elect to pay a flat income tax rate on earned income in Korea, rather than the progressive rate to which Koreans are subject (which goes up to 40%). This flat rate on earned income in Korea has varied in recent years, rising from 15.5% prior to 2013, to 17.5% in 2013, 18.7% in 2015 and 20.9% in 2017. At these levels, the flat income tax becomes attractive for high-income foreigners, currently those earning more than USD 100 000 annually. The flat rate can be applied for up to five years from arrival. The government has announced that it will withdraw this favourable treatment for foreigners arriving from 2019, except for those in certain firms.

Such tax incentives are unusual to offer to immigrants, except in very high tax countries to eliminate strong disincentives for talents to migrate (OECD, 2011[14]). It is not clear whether these personal tax incentives have influenced the attractiveness of

Korea for highly-compensated foreign professionals, since the numbers remain relatively low. More direct policy tools such as supporting educational opportunities for children and ensuring equal access to housing may be more effective. Furthermore, tax concessions create equity concerns by treating differently high-skilled and less-skilled workers, and often foreign and domestic workers.

International students

International study is one of the main drivers of migration movements, the globalisation of higher education, and circulation of higher educated. In many OECD countries, a large share of higher skill migrants are former international students. The number of international students studying in OECD countries increased by more than one third between 2004 and 2015 (Figure 4.11). Korea's share of this growing international market rose from 0.5% to 1.7% over the same decade.

Figure 4.11. Korea has a small but growing share of global international student flows

International students enrolled in OECD countries, 2004-15, by destination (thousands), and share of Korea of total.

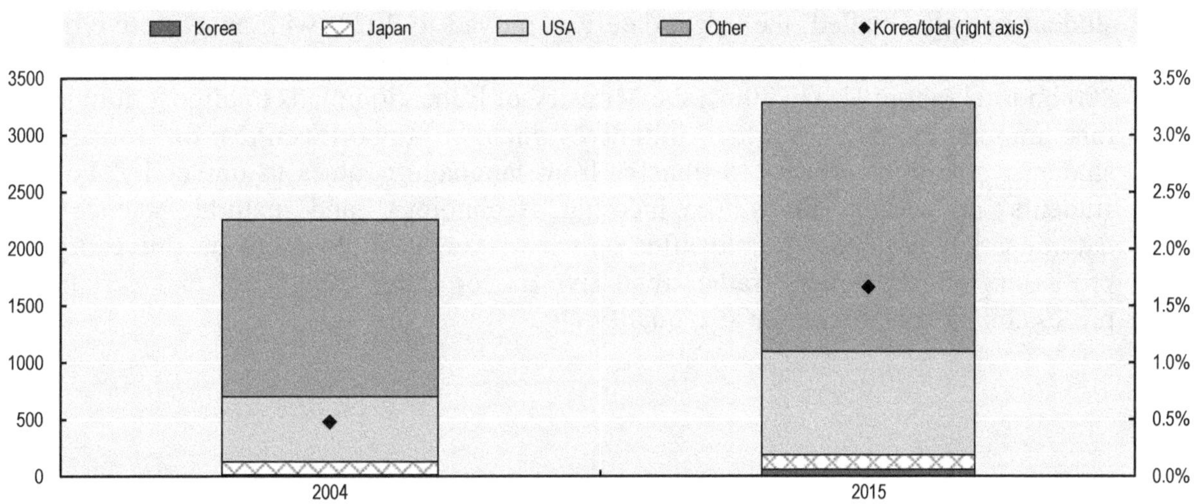

Note: Dates refer to the academic years 2003/04 and 2014/15. For notes see http://dx.doi.org/10.1787/migr_outlook-2017-table16-en.
Source: OECD, *Education at a glance* database.

Korea has seen a rapid expansion of its international student population in the past decade, although this fell from 2010 to 2014, and has been increasing since (Figure 4.12). The number stood at 123 900 in 2017, of which 72 000 were in degree programmes, and 35 700 in language programmes. Foreign students comprised almost 2% of total enrolment in universities, and almost 8% of total enrolment in Master's level and PhD programmes.

Increasing the number of foreign students has been a major policy goal for some time. "Study Korea", a policy programme for 2005-12 launched in 2004, set an objective of bringing foreign student enrolment to 50 000 by 2010. One of the main outputs during the programme was the creation of a multilingual website studyinkorea.go.kr centralising information on admissions, scholarships and regulations. The objective of the first "Study Korea" was exceeded, and the next phase, "Study Korea 2020" was launched in 2011 to further increase the number of international students to 200 000 in 2020 (from 90 000 in 2011). This objective was set in order to internationalise its higher education sector, but also to support universities in the face of falling enrolment. High enrolment levels and shrinking youth cohorts mean that Korea is expected to have more university capacity than demand starting in 2018, making foreign enrolment an attractive means to compensate for fewer national students, and a means for universities to maintain their student body. Foreign student enrolment is not a component of the quality index used by the Ministry of Education to rate universities. However, international rankings such as the THE and the QS rankings incorporate foreign student enrolment, giving universities an incentive to increase enrolment.[4]

The 2012 programme included extra support for international students during their studies and their transition to employment, improving international recruitment into universities, and expanding scholarships. In addition, the government announced facilitated pathways to stay on in Korea. In 2015, with international student numbers stalled, the target date was moved to 2023, with an objective of 5% of total enrolment. In 2015, subsidies for foreign students amounted to KRW 800 bn total (about USD 730m); the Ministry of Education plans to almost double this amount by 2020. Further initiatives include support centres for foreign students, a simpler process to transfer from language courses to university. For students in certain fields (engineering, technology and natural science), naturalisation will be possible after only two years employment as university professors or researchers, rather than five as for other categories, and certain professional experience may also qualify.

Figure 4.12. International enrolment has varied

International students, 2000-17, by type of study and share of total enrolment.

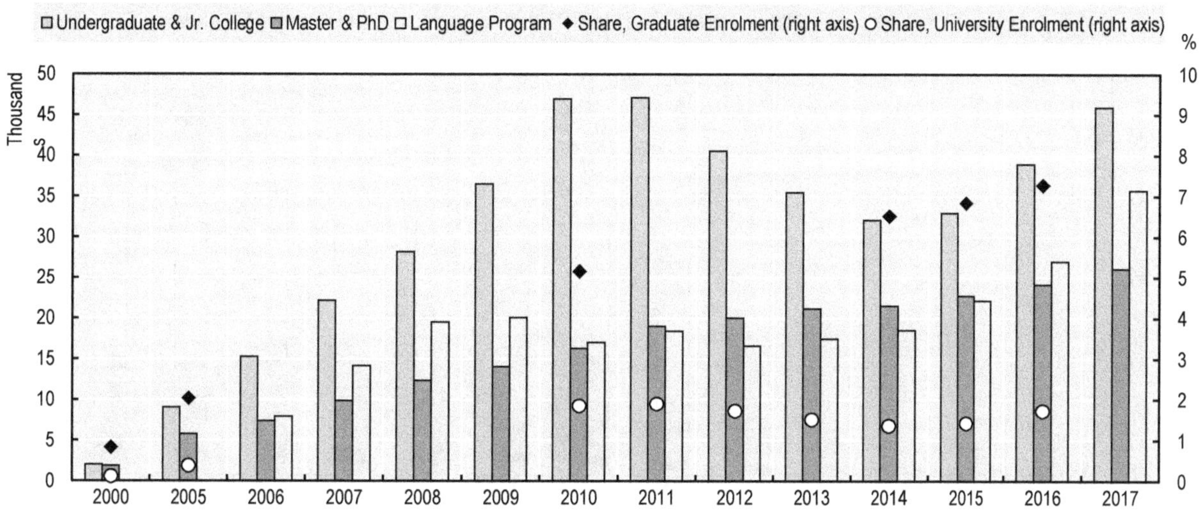

Source: Ministry of Education.

In terms of national origin, most international students are from China (Figure 4.13). The decline in the number of Chinese students from 2011 to 2014, related to stricter review of admission criteria and of actual participation, explains the fall in overall student numbers. As Chinese enrolment picked up again in 2015, total students numbers increased. Most of the remaining international students are from other Asian countries, led by Viet Nam (7.2% of the total in 2016). Historically, most Asian students came from Japan and Taipei,China. Those from other Asian countries have increased more sharply; notably, Mongolia accounted for 4.3% of total enrolment in 2016. Half of Vietnamese and Mongolian foreign students were enrolled in non-degree language courses in 2016, compared with 33% of Japanese students, 25% of Chinese students and 18% for those from all other countries.

Figure 4.13. More than half of foreign students come from China

Nationality of foreign students, all study programmes, 2003-16.

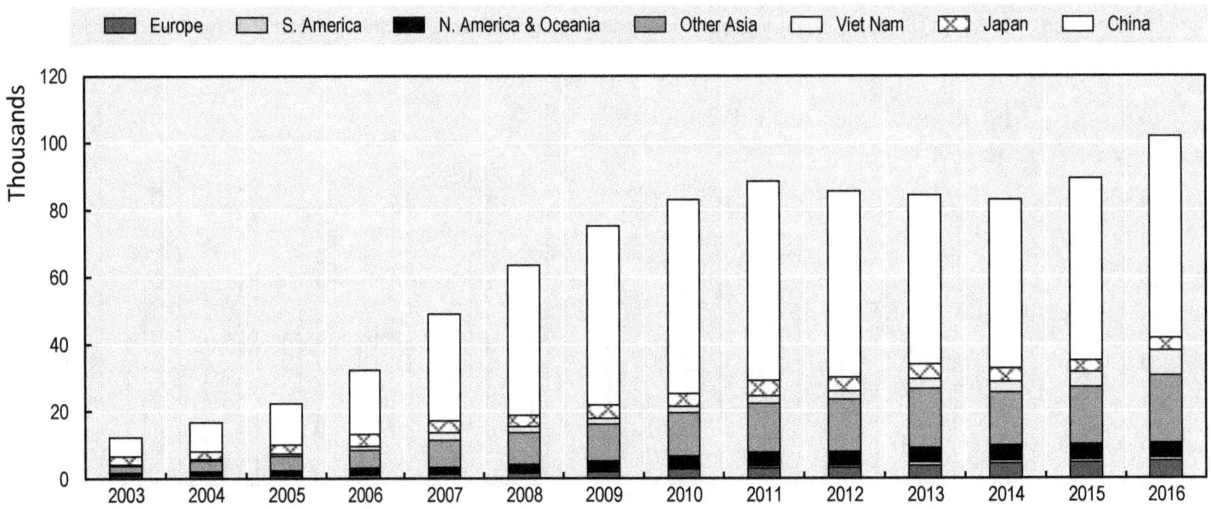

Note: Korean-Chinese students are not included.
Source: Ministry of Education.

Korea is a relatively competitive destination for international students in terms of cost (Figure 4.14), although international students in Korean-language courses will have to achieve a minimum level of Korean to study (TOPIK level 3) prior to study. Scholarships are available: the Global Korea Scholarship now funds almost 900 new students annually, primarily graduate students. Universities fund about three times as many scholarships. About 85% of students pay their own fees, so cost is an important consideration in promoting Korea as a destination. The share and the absolute number of foreign students with a scholarship has fallen from 2011 to 2016, despite government efforts to increase the scholarships offered to international students.

Figure 4.14. Korea is a relatively inexpensive destination for international students

Living costs and educational costs for international students in selected OECD countries, 2015, in euros

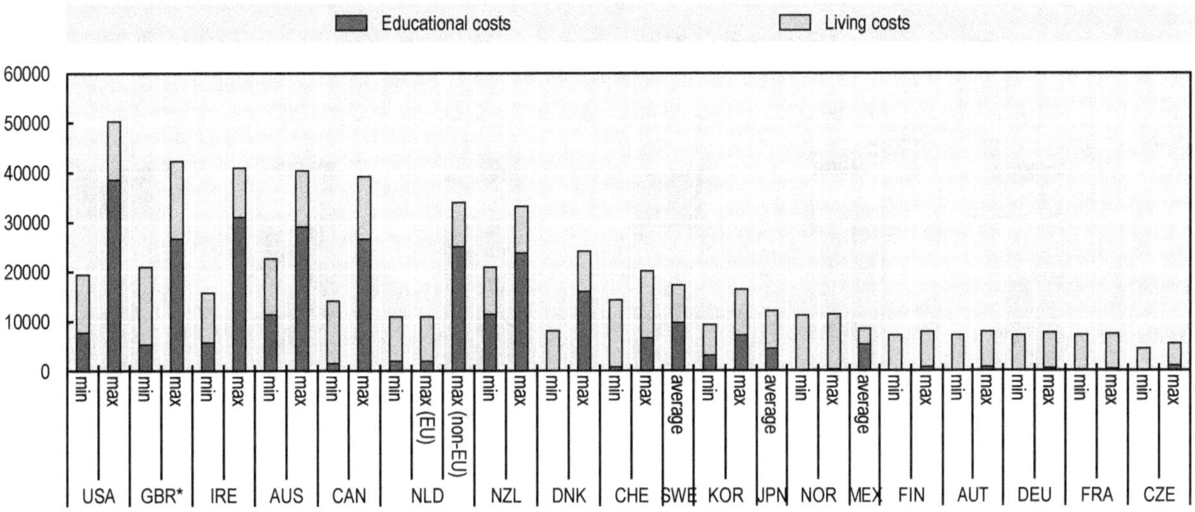

Note: * Excludes Scotland, min refers to lower bound of educational costs, max refers to an upper bound of educational costs. For the Netherlands the maximum possible fee refers to international students from non-EU countries.

Source: OECD (2013), *Education at a Glance 2013: OECD Indicators,* OECD Publishing, Paris, http://dx.doi.org/10.1787/eag-2013-en; Usher, A. and J. Medow (2010), "Global Higher Education Rankings 2010. Affordability and Accessibility in Comparative Perspective, Higher Education Strategy Associates", Toronto; and national governmental and university websites. For the Netherlands the source is Nuffic. For Korea, the source is Study in Korea.

Field of study of foreign students varies according to the level of study (Figure 4.15). Undergraduates are mostly enrolled in social sciences and humanities (two-thirds of these in social sciences). While there are fewer graduate students, a much larger share of them are in engineering (38%) and natural sciences (19%). About half of international students are in Seoul or other major metropolitan areas, while 47% are in provincial areas. There are few differences in field of study between those in major metropolitan universities and provincial universities.

Figure 4.15. Most undergraduates study liberal arts, most graduates engineering and natural sciences

Field of study of international students, share by level of study and total, 2013 and 2016.

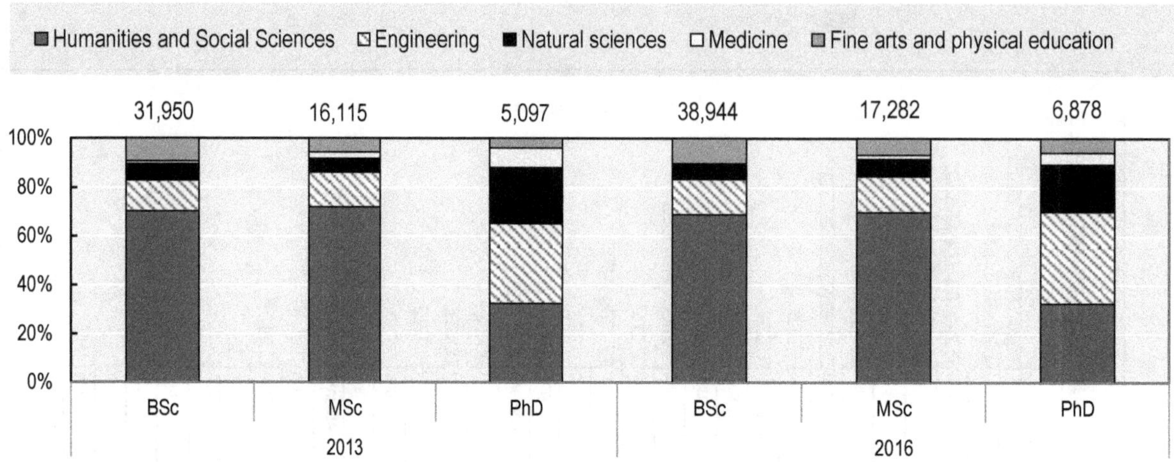

Note: Students in the joint MSc-PhD programs were aggregated into PhD category. Education is included in the "Humanities and Social Sciences" programme.
Source: KEDI international students annual statistics.

With the pressure to maintain international enrolment, there has been the risk that standards were relaxed for admission and international students accepted even if they did not meet requirements. The general language standard for international students was lowered from TOPIK 3 to TOPIK 2 in 2018. While scholarship students are subject to a high Korean-language requirement (TOPIK 5 for admission, or TOPIK 3 after one year of language education).[5] To deal with this, the government decided in 2011 to recognise certain higher education institutions for excellent selection and management of foreign students, easing the document requirements for foreign students enrolling in these universities, the International Education Quality Assurance System (IQEAS) (Table 4.4). IQEAS takes into account the share of international students who overstay or otherwise fail to comply with permit conditions, or who abandon the programme. In addition, institutions are expected to meet basic requirements.

In addition to the factors shown in Table 4.4, IQEAS is also based on a subjective evaluation of the capacity of the institution to support international students. This is based on a number of factors, reviewing: international vision and characterization; support for international students' adaptation and study; and the actual academic achievement of international students.

For institutions with IQEAS, more proof of actual competence, language skills and prior education is required before a student visa will be issued. The introduction of IQEAS is associated with the decline in student enrolment, before numbers resumed their upward trend.

Table 4.4. Korea ranks trustworthy universities

International Education Quality Assurance System (IQEAS) components.

Classification	Criteria	Standard	University	Community College	Graduate College
Compulsory criteria	Rate of undocumented foreign students	< 2 to 4%		at least 1 criterion	
	Foreign student dropout rate	< 6%			
Conditional criteria	International student tuition burden ratio	80%+	at least 3 of 4 criteria	at least 3 of 4 criteria	at least 2 of 3 criteria
	Health insurance purchase rate	85%+			
	Linguistic ability (Kor. /Eng.)	30%+			
	Rate of dormitories provided to freshmen	25%+			

Note: Undocumented foreign student rate is calculated based on total foreign enrolment; 4% is the threshold for smaller enrolments (<100) and 2% for larger (>500).
Source: NIIED.

This means of ensuring compliance is similar to that used in several other OECD countries, such as the United Kingdom, where "trusted sponsors" are able to admit students, while other institutions are granted sponsorship rights on a probationary basis. An alternative method is to develop an electronic monitoring and compliance platform, such as SEVIS in the United States, requiring universities to verify enrolment and performance of international students. Korea has a Foreign Student Information Management System (FIMS), which contains information on the identity of foreign students, whether they have a state scholarship, and their current enrolment status. FIMS is managed by NIIED, but is accessible by other public bodies.

Employment during studies

About one in eight international students is employed. This is a relatively low share compared with Australia and New Zealand, for example, where about one-third of international students are employed, and may reflect the difficulty foreign students have finding a job, especially compared with higher employment levels among Korean university students. In 2017, 76% of international students responded that they had not worked in the past year. Of those that held jobs, 10.9% worked for less than three months. Among those who are employed, most work in education (37%), most often as assistants, in restaurants (24%) and in trade (17%).

Most OECD countries do grant some employment rights to international students, although unrestricted access to employment carries the risk that the student visa becomes a channel for spurious students whose only scope is employment. In this light, the low employment rate of international students in Korea suggests that the student channel is likely used by legitimate students. There is a much higher share of students employed in Japan; in October 2017, there were about 260 000 employers reporting foreign students employed, compared with about 280 000 students total in Japan. Although one student may have multiple jobs with different employers, this still suggests that students in Japan have a much higher rate of employment than those in Korea.

Foreign students in undergraduate or language courses have the right to work up to 20 hours a week; those in graduate courses may work up to 30 hours a week. Work on weekends and holidays is not subject to this limit, so in practice foreign students may work much longer hours during their study. Work rights are not automatic; students must apply to the Immigration Service for a part-time work permit for each job. Authorisation requires a letter of recommendation from the educational institution for part-time work, or a transcript or certificate of attendance demonstrating that the student is in good standing. There are some restrictions on the type of work which can be accepted; any work allowed for Korean students is also allowed for foreign students. Work within the university is generally exempt from the work permit requirement. The work permit can be withdrawn, or extensions denied, if work appears to be having a deleterious effect on study (either through an attendance rate below 70%, or a GPA of 2 or lower).

Retention of international student graduates

According to the 2017 Survey on Immigrant's Living Conditions and Labour Force, 48.1% of international students declared their intention to return home after graduation. 41.2% of foreign students wanted to stay in Korea after graduation. 16.8% wanted to continue their studies in Korea and 24% to find employment in Korea. KEDI conducts and annual survey of all university graduates, including international students, which allows a comparison with actual post-graduation behaviour. In contrast to intentions, only about 17.5% actually end up staying, and less than 5.8% of students that receive their bachelor's degree in Korea found full time employment after graduation. The success rate was slightly higher at (7-15%, taking low and high ranges from 2007-17) for students who received a post-graduate degree (Figure 4.16).

Figure 4.16. A small share of international students ends up staying to work in Korea

Post-graduation status of foreign students, 2007-17 (thousands).

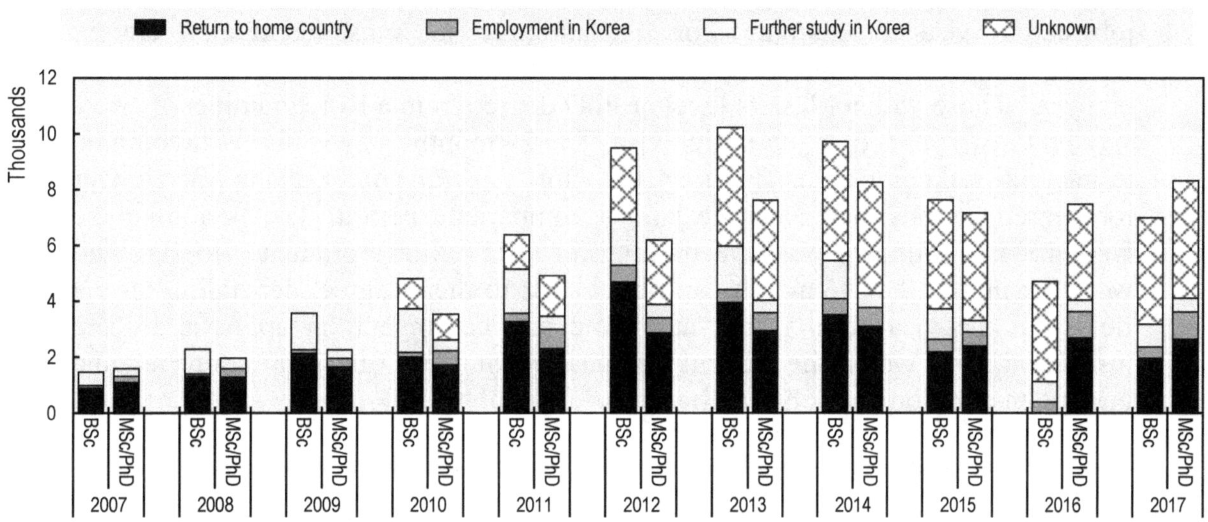

Note: "Unknown" category added after 2009.
Source: KEDI international students annual statistics.

The low employment rate during studies may partly explain the low retention rate, since employment during studies is positively associated with post-graduation retention (OECD, 2014[15]). Most students who stay in Korea transition to a job search permit, rather than directly to employment. In 2015, more than 4 200 graduates took the D-10 job-search permit (Figure 4.17). Only 430 transitioned directly to the main skilled employment visa, the E-7 visa.

Figure 4.17. Relatively few international graduates stay in Korea

Panel A. International student stay rates, selected OECD countries.
Panel B. Status changes from student permits, 2015.

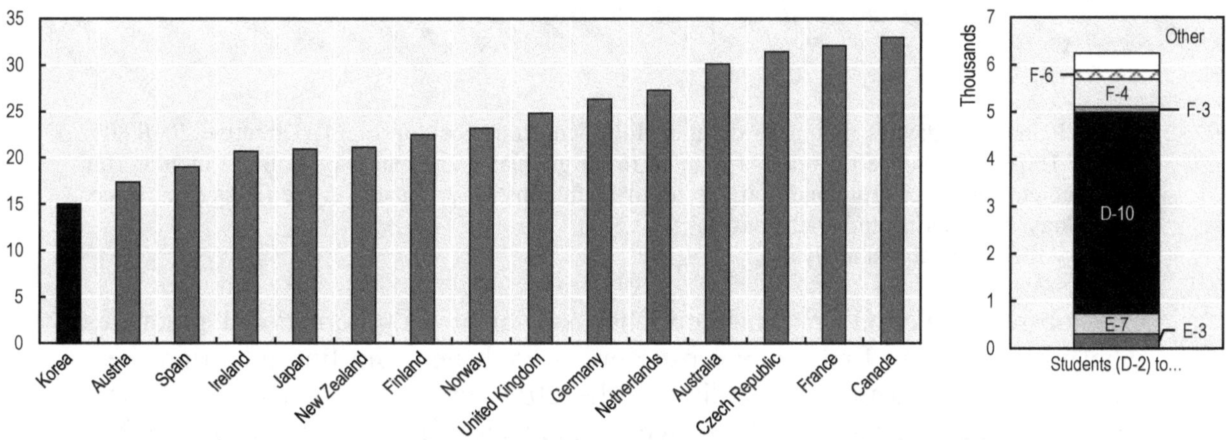

Note: Data for European countries cover only students from outside the European Economic Area. Data for Canada include changes from student to both permanent status and other temporary statuses.
Source: Panel A. Analysis by the OECD Secretariat. Panel B. Korea Immigration Service.

As in many OECD countries, foreign graduates of Korean universities have the right to stay in the country following their studies for a certain period, work and look for a job which will give them access to a work-related permit. Korea's job-search visa programme for is among the most generous among OECD countries. Graduates may stay for six months, renewable once for a total of one year. Those with a Masters level or PhD degree from a Korean university may stay up to two years on a job-search visa. The 24 months stay is highly favourable in international comparison (Figure 4.18). Only Australia and Canada offer longer job search periods, and New Zealand a comparable period. The period in the United States (optional practical training, or OPT) allows graduates to stay and work for up to 12 or 36 months in jobs related to their degree, depending on the field, but the visa grant is not automatic and contingent on approval by the institution from which the student graduated. For most European countries, the maximum duration of a job-search visa is 12 months.

Figure 4.18. Korea has a long job-search period for international graduates

Duration of job-search periods for post-graduate schemes in different OECD countries, 2018. In months.

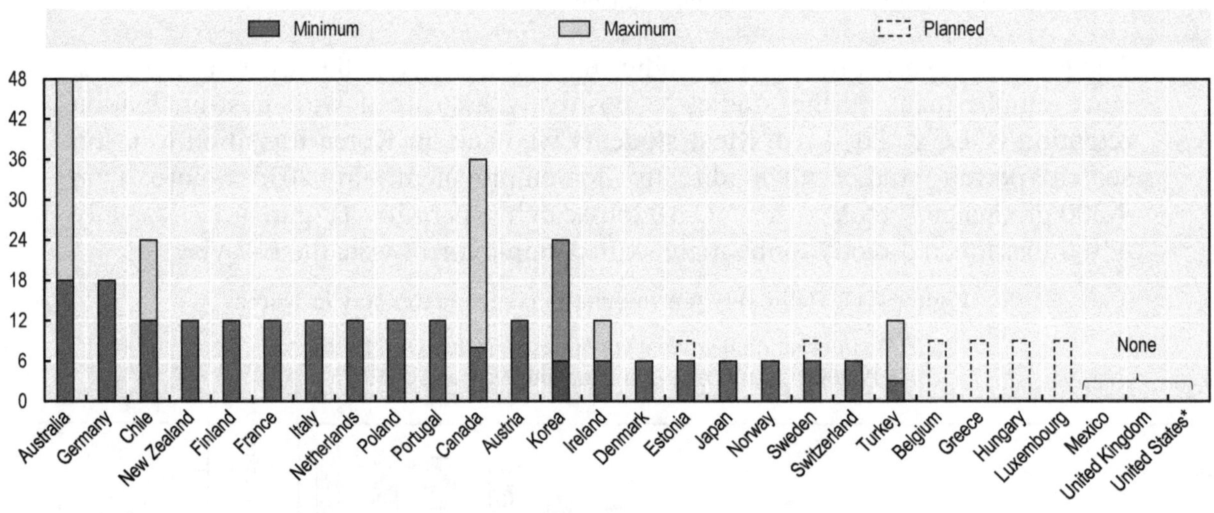

Note: "Planned" indicates minimum duration following transposition of EU Directive 2016/801. *In the United States, the OPT is not granted to all graduates and can vary from 12 months (for most subjects under certain conditions) to up to 36 months for graduates in the fields of Science, technology, engineering and mathematics.

Source: OECD Secretariat analysis.

The job-search period appears more than sufficient for international graduates who wish to stay to find a job; most Korean graduates who find jobs find them either before graduation. According to the 2013 survey of graduates in Korea, 48% of male graduates and 40% of female graduates found their jobs before they graduated. Almost 90% found their first job within a year of graduation. It is reasonable to expect that foreign students should also be able to find a job within a year of graduation.

International graduates must find qualifying tertiary-level employment to stay after the job search period ends. This is comparable to the conditions in most other OECD countries, although a few, such as Italy, allow students to take up employment of any kind. The definition of "tertiary-level" employment varies from country to country, however. In Germany and France, the correspondence between the field of study and the field of employment is considered important, and insufficient match a grounds for refusal of a work permit. International students cite many of the same obstacles to retention as other highly-qualified foreigners, related to exclusion from networks (Shin and Choi, 2015[11]).

The D-10 visa for job-search was introduced in 2009 to allow skilled workers an opportunity to seek work. Almost all of these visas are issued within Korea, as a bridge permit for students following graduation and for other professional employment categories to bridge periods of unemployment. The job search permit is often used as a bridge to language teaching; it is the only permit which allows extension of job search for language teachers who are between employers for more than a month. The main category of destination however is the standard specialty occupation permit, E-7 (Figure 4.19). According to a NIIED survey, only 6% of graduates in 2013 found employment during their job search period, primarily through vocational fairs.

Figure 4.19. The job search visa generally leads to language teaching or to skilled employment

Permit issued following the D-10 job search permit, 2015.

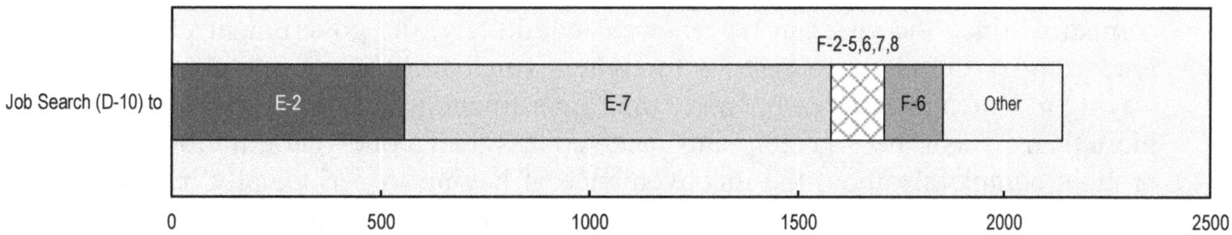

Source: Korea Immigration Service.

Investors and entrepreneurs

Korea has a framework for attracting investors, comprising a number of different visas. The business (corporate) investment visa (D-8) is issued to foreign entrepreneurs, investors, and essential-skilled professionals. There are a number of subcategories under the business investment visa, including essential skilled personnel of a company that meets Foreign Direct Investment (FDI) conditions, owners of venture business, investors of private business operated by Korean citizen, and founders of technology-based start-ups. The majority of the recipients are high skilled employees (executives, senior managers, and specialists) dispatched by foreign invested companies to work at local offices in Korea, under the D visas discussed above, but others are investors.

As one of the measures to attract foreign investment in Korea, individuals who qualify for the business investment visa are given favourable treatment during the application process. Foreigners can apply for the business investment visa at a Korean embassy of their native country or enter Korea on visitor status and change their status of sojourn at an immigration office in Korea. The most utilized method by investors is to apply for the visa change at the immigration office inside Invest KOREA, a national investment promotion agency that provides services related to pre-investment consultation, administrative support, and post-investment processes. At Invest KOREA, the visa processing time takes an average 30 minutes and all handling fees are waived. There is a high approval rate because applying for the visa is the last step of the investment process and the pool of applicants are highly qualified. For many foreign companies, communication has already occurred with Invest KOREA for their services during the foreign direct investment process. Project managers at Invest KOREA can arrange for the arrival of foreign investors and the company transferees. Foreigners also visit Invest KOREA for the issuance of visas for dependant family members and housekeepers, re-entry permits, visa extensions, and immigration priority cards (Financial Investor Card).

The maximum period of stay for the business investment visa varies by subcategory. Previously when there were no subcategories under the visa, the maximum period of stay per visa issuance was three years. However, the actual duration of stay has always been generally much shorter. The duration of stay is subject to the discretion of the immigration officer and depends on the size of business, investment amount, and performance records of the foreign invested company. Since the visa can be renewed indefinitely, the government prefers to issue shorter durations to restrict foreigners (including family members) from staying in Korea after an early end to their investment or dispatch period. In 2003, more than 50% of the visa recipients received less than a one-year duration, which brought complaints about the inconvenience of having to periodically renew the visa. In 2005, the government decided to separate investors into subcategories and lengthen the maximum sojourn period for dispatched employees and investors of private Korean businesses to five years. Venture business investors and technology start-up investors became limited to two years. Since then, the government also assented on issuing longer durations - on average at least oen year for first issuances and at least two years for renewals.

Since 2013, an “'Immigrant Investor Scheme for Public Business” has been in place to obtain an F-2 permanent residence visa immediately based on investment in either a public fund or a community development project designated by the Ministry of Justice. The thresholds are KRW 500 million (about 450 000 USD) in designated investment products; the threshold is reduced to KRW 300 million for investors over age 55 who also have KRW 300 million in demonstrable personal liquid assets. The F-2 visa for these investors can be converted to an F-5 visa after five years. The criteria to acquire permanent residence in fact been reduced over time. Prior to 2005, the threshold was at least USD 5m, lowered in 2005 to 2m as well as five jobs created, and in 2008 for investing USD 500m, create three jobs and stay for three years prior to applying for permanent residence.

The scheme for real estate investment allows investment in housing or recreational real estate – not for personal residence. Investment is only allowed in certain regions; the programme began as a special regional investor programme for Jeju Island (see Box 4.4) and has since been extended to other zones.[6] The two schemes – public investment and real estate – can be combined to qualify for the latter scheme. Investments which are made in either scheme with a locked duration of at least five years allow the investor to qualify immediately for the F-5 visa.

Foreigners who invest a minimum KRW 500 000 (about USD 450 000) and hire at least five Korean employees are offered permanent residence status. Foreigners with D-8 status that attract a minimum KRW 300 million and hire at least two Korean employees can apply for permanent residency after meeting additional requirements (i.e. passing Level 3 of the TOPIK). Foreign professionals of a foreign-invested company can obtain permanent residency by first living in Korea for three years on the business investment visa and five years on the long-term residency F-2 visa. According to Invest KOREA's studies, 90% of foreigners on the business investment visa are not interested in receiving permanent residency due to the difficult residence requirements or because they do not desire to live in Korea for a long time.

Box 4.4. The Jeju Island Investor Programme

Jeju province, an island located southwest of Korean peninsula with about 600 000 inhabitants, has a high level of autonomy in governing. In 2001, it was designated as a Free International City with tax exemption and foreigner friendly environment to boost its tourism industry and foreign investment. To attract foreign investors, its self-governing body introduced a special treatment since 2002. The advantages include governmental support for employment, housing supply and long-term stay in case foreigners meet certain requirements. In practice, the local government provides permanent residency, the F-5 permit, when the person invests over KRW 500 million (about USD 450 000) in local industries and employs more than five workers.

A further programme to foster foreign investment in real-estate business came into effect in February 2010. This policy applies to investors who purchase a recreational property designated by the local government such as condominiums, resorts and guesthouses worth more than KRW 500 million. After investment, they can apply for an F-2 residency permit. The first F-2 permit is valid for two years, renewable for additional three years. If they live over five years in Jeju or in elsewhere in Korea they may obtain an F-5 permit. The screening process occurs at the end of five years of residency under the supervision of Ministry of Justice. Once they receive the F-5, foreign investors and their families are entitled to benefit from social systems such as medical care, education and employment with the same rights as Koreans. As of 2017, 1499 investors have received the F-2 visa for Jeju (308 in 2013, 556 in 2014, 323 in 2015, 136 in 2016, and 33 in 2017). Among them, Chinese investors made up the largest proportion.

The visa drove Foreign Direct Investment (FDI) in Jeju. FDI was only USD 115 million from 1962 to 2010, but jumped to USD 126 million in 2011 alone. In 2015, it amounted to 708 million and 900 million in 2016. The total amount of foreign investment under "Permanent Residence Policy for Investors in Real Estate" policy was about USD 1.2 billion between 2010 and 2017.

The influx has not been universally welcomed. As the overall number of incoming foreigners for both tourism and investments grew rapidly in the past few years, concerns rose among residents and the local press. In response, the local government suggested an amendment to the Ministry of Justice to limit the number of investment immigrants at 6 000, equal to 1% of the total local population. It also proposed to raise the minimum investment amount to USD 1 million. Some experts criticised the proposal since it might deteriorate the foreign investment in Jeju as a whole. Thus the authorities try to encourage the locals to embrace incoming foreigners recognising the importance of foreign investment as a vital resource for the local economy.

Minimum investment criteria

Until 2010, the minimum investment requirement for the business investment visa had been as low as USD 10 000-50 000. The sum was small enough to provide a loophole for foreigners who wanted to live in Korea under the guise of an investor. In 2010, the government increased the minimum investment amount to KRW 100 million. In addition, owners of sole-proprietorships no longer qualified for the business investment visa as it became required that all businesses are of the corporate form. In 2013, the Ministry of Trade, Industry and Energy announced plans to increase the minimal capital requirements to KRW 300 million. There was strong opposition from both overseas foreigners who were planning on doing business in Korea and existing small and medium business owners who would need to meet the KRW 300 million requirement for their next visa renewal. Consequently, the government decided to retain the minimal capital requirement of KRW 100 million and make greater efforts to provide a business-friendly environment for foreigners.

There are a number of different investor visas in Korea now, offering thresholds ranging from about USD 100 000 to 500 000 (Figure 4.20).

There is a new D-10 "entrepreneurship" visa category that allows those that are interested in starting a start-up to stay in Korea and work towards the requirements for the D-8-4 Start-up visa. The basic qualifications for the D-10 entrepreneurship are a bachelor's degree and an intellectual patent. During the stay on the D-10 visa, the entrepreneur participates in a training programme, Overall Assistance for Startup Immigration System (Oasis). Oasis is run by the Small and Medium Business Administration (SMBA, now part of the Ministry of SMEs and Startups). SMBA's Points are given by the completing courses and sessions, and once the foreigner accumulates 80 out of 368 possible, he or she can apply for the D-8 visa.

While the migration policy framework for foreign investors has evolved, obstacles to investment often lie outside the permit status of the primary investor. With a few exceptions, foreign invested enterprises have a limitation on the employment of foreign workers up to 20% of the total number of contracted employees.

Figure 4.20. Korea has many competitively priced investor visas

Minimum investment thresholds in selected OECD and EU countries, 2017 (thousands of dollars)

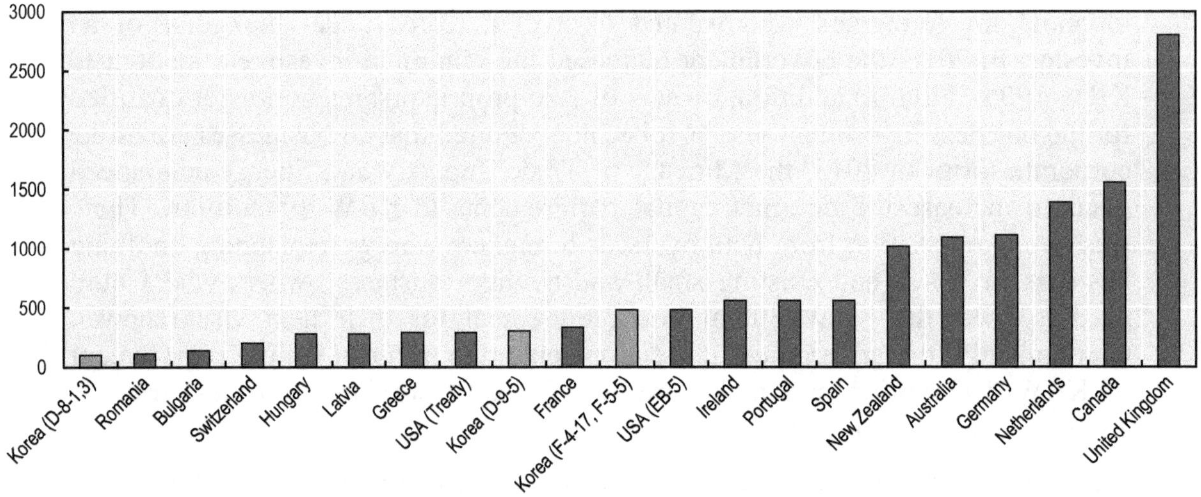

Source: OECD secretariat calculations.

The Start-Up visa

Following a common trend in OECD countries, in recent years Korea has introduced measures to attract foreign start-up entrepreneurs. In general, start-up visa programmes have both a migration and a business component, and aim at making it easier for foreign entrepreneurs to enter the country and to start up a new business. On the migration side, start-up entrepreneurs often fail to meet the requirements for existing entrepreneur or investor programmes, for instance the minimum investment requirement (in Korea, it is USD 93 000/KRW 100 million). To overcome this difficulty, start-up visa programmes introduce a brand new start-up visa or permit, or open up a specific track with different conditions to be granted an existing visa or permit. On the business side, start-ups face particular challenges compared to other types of businesses, due to their high-risk, technology and human capital-intensive, low initial financial investment business model. This is why start-up visa programmes tend to provide support, spanning from easing the procedures to set up a business, providing business counselling, facilitating access to capital and to the ecosystem.

Korea introduced its start-up visa (D-8-4) in 2013, on a joint initiative by the Ministry of Justice and SMBA. Candidates are assessed through a point-based system (PBS), and are considered eligible if they accrue 22% of available points (80/360).

While most start-up visa programmes do not impose human capital requirements on applicants, Korea requires them to have a Bachelor's degree and provides points for a PhD and Korean language skills. On business requirements, many countries demand an external validation of the business idea or project, often provided by start-up community members, investors and government agencies.

These are better placed than civil servants to assess the validity and innovation potential of a business idea. Similarly, Korea requires candidates to have an innovative externally validated project, such as patent ownership (or a patent application), winning a start-up competition, or being selected for a Korean start-up programme (Table 4.5).

Table 4.5. The points system for the startup visa favours patent holders

Requirements for D-8-4 Start up visa.

	Bachelor's degree	Compulsory
At least 80 points scored on:	At least one of the following:	Points:
	Intellectual property rights of a utility patent	80
	Ownership of a design patent	50
	Application for a utility/design patent	20/10
	Achievement of at least the third prize at invention, start-up exhibition?	25
	Selection by a central or local government-supported project?	25
	Additional elements:	
	OASIS courses: Advanced Intellectual Property Course	25
	OASIS courses: Start-up Class	25
	OASIS courses: Basic Intellectual Property Course	15
	OASIS courses: Start-up Coaching and Mentoring Service,	15
	Completion of Start-up incubator (Seoul Global Center)	15
	Capital of 100 million KRW	15
	PhD degree	10
	Korean language	10

The Korean government has set up a start-up visa acquisition programme, called OASIS (Overall Assistance for Startup Immigration System),[7] aimed at interested candidates who do not accrue 80 points in the PBS. It consists in start-up oriented courses, whose participation can give up to 80 points, that, if combined with at least one requirement in the compulsory list, give access to the start-up visa. The OASIS programme is delivered by the Ministry of Justice, in partnership with the Korea Invention Promotion Association (KIPA), Korea Productivity Centre (KPC), and Seoul Business Agency (SBA). Courses are short and intensive, approximately 20 hours long, and run throughout the year. Access to such courses is not selective and candidates can take part entering the country on a short-term visa (up to 90 days) or on a job-seeker visa (up to six months).

The Korean start-up visa programme has two unique design characteristics that distinguish it from other OECD countries' programmes: a points-based system (PBS) as selection method and a visa acquisition programme. In general, PBS makes the selection more flexible, as different point combinations can be made towards the threshold. In the start-up visa case, however, selection criteria in OECD countries tend already to be flexible, as often there are no rigid criteria ruling the assessment of the business project. It is therefore not clear whether the Korean PBS provides more flexibility or rather adds an element of rigidity in the selection. On the OASIS visa acquisition programme, little evidence is available to assess its effectiveness. These courses should prepare participants to be able to meet the remaining visa requirements. In 2014, however, only five out of the

126 foreigners participating in the programme obtained a start-up visa. In 2015, the number of participants was 132 but data on the transition to a start-up visa are not available.

Other initiatives to attract foreigner start-ups complement the D-8-4 visa. One of these is the K-StartUp Grand Challenge (KSGC)[8]. KSGC was introduced in 2016 and promoted by the Ministry of Science, ICT and Future Planning. There is no sector limitation, but ICT start-ups are favoured. KSGC comprises two contests. In the first, 50 start-up teams (40 in 2016) participate in a four-month acceleration programme, which includes free office space, 1-to-1 mentorship, information sessions and coaching, USD 12 000 (KRW 14m) to cover living expenses, support for visa application (using OASIS), and KRW 1m (USD 830) as a prize for participation. In the second contest (called 'demo day'), 25 of the 50 teams (20 in 2016) are selected and receive USD 27 000 (KRW 32m) on the condition that they set up a legal entity in Korea. In addition to that, the top four ranked start-up teams receive cash grants ranging from USD 100 000 for the top team to USD 6 000 for the fourth-ranked (KRW 120mand KRW 7.2m).

The first edition of KSGC drew much attention (2 440 applications) and led to the establishment of 14 start-ups in Korea. Other OECD countries have similar competitive capped start-up programmes offering attractive business packages, e.g. the French Tech Ticket, open to 70 start-ups; the New Zealand Edmund Hillary fellowship, capped at 100; and the British SIRIUS programme, open to 100 foreign graduates. The Korean programme is the only one that makes the competition a real contest, where participants get richer start-up packages depending on their ranking position. These programmes are important as they mobilise resources from other-than-migration departments and make the start-up scene more dynamic. However, it is important to co-ordinate them with visa programmes and make sure that selected applicants also qualify for a visa.

Conclusions

The framework for skilled migration in Korea is complex, comprising a wide range of overlapping permit categories. Initiatives targeting skilled migrants, such as researchers and global talent, as well as start-up visas, also overlap.

If Korea wishes to attract more international talent, the migration framework in place is largely sufficient; further multiplication of visa categories and points-based selection would only complicate unnecessarily. Rights for family members are in most cases less generous than in comparable skill streams in other OECD countries, particularly as regards unrestricted labour market access. The D-10 job search permit appears to be used by language teachers and specialty workers to bridge periods between jobs due to the short expiration date of these permits for workers whose contract ends. Permit duration could be extended from 30 days to three or six months beyond the end of the contract, as in many other OECD countries, to allow sufficient time to seek new work without requiring a bridge visa.

The main obstacle to attracting talent to Korea is not the migration framework but the highly competitive labour market for tertiary-educated workers, and the structural rigidities in the professional environment. These obstacles are not easily overcome by initiatives that focus purely on providing favourable visa categories and even subsidies.

Since there is no clear answer to the right role which foreign labour should play in the future, policy could be directed through a clearer process integrating information on the impact of the programme of firm productivity and survival, resident workers of different characteristics. This Review has identified some of the tradeoffs to be addressed in the design of the temporary low-skilled programme, and pointed to some of the processes used in other OECD countries to resolve these tradeoffs. One means to achieve this would be to grant the Foreign Workforce Policy Committee (FWPC) with a Secretariat and a mandate to co-ordinate analysis on the impact and direction of the policy. The Committee would have to be given a mandate to propose policy strategies to the government to achieve the objectives formulated by the government. Two examples cited here are the Migration Advisory Committee, in the United Kingdom, and the defunct process used in Italy for a triennial planning document for entry quotas. A Korean Secretariat would have to build on the strong empirical work done by public research agencies such as KLI and KDI, which obviate the need for in-house research, adding policy proposal for consideration by the government. Such a Secretariat could also address the overlapping and sometimes conflicting policy measures identified in this review.

Notes

[1] Source: the Private Education Expenditures Survey. Private English lessons cost an average KRW 210 000 and KRW 256 000 per month and per student in middle school and high school respectively.

[2] This calculation is based on the E-3, E-4, E-5 and E-7-1, E-7-3, and E-7-4

[3] Ansan, historically a city of settlement for foreign workers and other foreigners, started its centre in the mid-2000s, but serves primarily non-professional foreign workers.

[4] Foreign student enrolment counts for 2.5% of the THE and 5% of the QS ranking. Foreign faculty also counts separately.

[5] TOPIK 4 was requested in 2013, but the high fail rate of scholarship students led to maintain TOPIK 3.

[6] The other zones allowed are Gangwon-do Pyeongchang, Jeollanam-do Yeosu, and the East Busan Tourism Complex. For two additional zones, the Incheon Free Economic zone and the Busan Haeundae area, the investment threshold is higher, 700 million KRW.

[7] OASIS website, https://www.ipcampus.kr/oasis-visa/eng/about/info.jsp.

[8] K-Startup Grand Challenge 2017, http://www.k-startupgc.org/upfilePath/K-Startup%20Grand%20Challenge%202017.pdf

References

Chaloff, J. (2014), "Evidence-based regulation of labour migration in OECD countries: setting quotas, selection criteria, and shortage lists", *Migration Letters*. [2]

Herting, H. (2016), "A Closer Look at the Ranked: 10 Case Studies in Asia, Europe and North America", in *Universities, Rankings and the Dynamics of Global Higher Education*, Palgrave Macmillan UK, London, http://dx.doi.org/10.1057/978-1-137-46999-1_5. [10]

Jeon, H. (2014), "Foreign Professionals in Korea: Survey on their Life and Work", *Issues and Tasks*, Vol. 14/25. [7]

Kim, S. (2016), "Western faculty 'flight risk' at a Korean university and the complexities of internationalisation in Asian higher education", *Comparative Education*, Vol. 52/1, pp. 78-90, http://dx.doi.org/10.1080/03050068.2015.1125620. [4]

Kim, T. (2005), "Internationalisation of higher education in South Korea: Reality, rhetoric, and disparity in academic culture and identities", *Australian Journal of Education*, Vol. 49/1, pp. 89-103, http://journals.sagepub.com/doi/pdf/10.1177/000494410504900105 (accessed on 29 November 2017). [3]

Kraeh, A., F. Froese and H. Park (2015), "Foreign professionals in South Korea", in *After-Development Dynamics*, Oxford University Press, http://dx.doi.org/10.1093/acprof:oso/9780198729433.003.0010. [9]

Lee, G. et al. (2016), *Changes in Labor Market Environment: Issues in Foreign Workforce Policy (노동시장 환경변화에 따른 외국인력 정책 쟁점과 과제)*, Koreal Labour Institute, Seoul, http://www.prism.go.kr/homepage/theme/retrieveThemeDetail.do;jsessionid=CF3A28E4C08BA8588157FBD55F944A21.node02?cond_research_name=&cond_organ_id=&cond_research_year_start=&cond_research_year_end=&cond_brm_super_id=NB000120061201100031424&research_id=1490 (accessed on 17 November 2017). [1]

Noh, J. (2014), "Integrating and Retaining World-Class Scholars: The Key to Innovation in Korea", *U.S.-Korea Institute at SAIS Young Professionals Paper Series (YPPS)*, Vol. 1, pp. 6-25, https://www.uskoreainstitute.org/wp-content/uploads/pdf/YPPS_2014-Noh.pdf (accessed on 10 September 2017). [6]

OECD (2014), "Improving attraction and retention of labour migrants in Norway", in *Recruiting Immigrant Workers: Norway 2014*, OECD Publishing, Paris, http://dx.doi.org/10.1787/9789264226135-9-en. [12]

OECD (2014), "International graduates: An underutilised labour source in Norway", in *Recruiting Immigrant Workers: Norway 2014*, OECD Publishing, Paris, http://dx.doi.org/10.1787/9789264226135-10-en. [15]

OECD (2011), "The Taxation of Mobile High-Skilled Workers", in *Taxation and Employment*, OECD Publishing, Paris, http://dx.doi.org/10.1787/9789264120808-6-en. [14]

OECD (2005), "Counting Immigrants and Expatriates in OECD Countries: A New Perspective", in *Trends in International Migration 2004*, OECD Publishing, Paris, http://dx.doi.org/10.1787/migr_outlook-2004-3-en. [13]

Shin, G. and J. Choi (2015), *Global Talent : Skilled Labor as Social Capital in Korea*. [11]

Song, H. and E. Song (2015), "Why Do South Korea's Scientists and Engineers Delay Returning Home? Renewed Brain Drain in the New Millennium", *Science, Technology and Society*, Vol. 20/3, pp. 349-368, http://dx.doi.org/10.1177/0971721815597140. [8]

Um, M. (2012), *Centre of Excellence as a tool for capacity-building. Case Study: Korea*, IHERD, OECD, http://www.oecd.org/sti/Korea_case_study.pdf (accessed on 10 September 2017). [5]

Annex 4.A. Supplementary table

Annex Table 4.A.1. Occupations allowed under the E-7 visa, 2017

Skill level	Category	Occupation	
Professional Occupations	Manager Level	Executives of economic profit making organization	S110
		Executives of corporation	1120
		Business Management	1202
		Education Administrator	1312
		Insurance and Financial Manager	1320
		Culture, Arts, Design and Image Related Manager	1340
		Manager for Information and Communication	1350
		Professionals in Service Industries	1390
		Manager in Construction or Mining	1411
		Manager in Manufacturing Products	1413
		Manager in Agriculture or Fisheries	14901
		Sales Manager	1511
		Shipping Manager	1512
		Manager in Accommodation, Travel, or Sports	1521
		Manager in Food Service	1522
	Specialists	Specialist in Life Science	2111
		Specialist in Natural Science	2112
		Physicist or Physics Expert	21121
		Chemistry Expert	21122
		Astronomy or Meteorology Expert	21123
		Researcher in Social Science	2122
		Computer Hardware Engineer	2211
		Telecommunication Engineer	2212
		Computer System Designer and Analyst	2221
		System Software Developer	2222
		Application Software Developer	2223
		Database Developer	2224
		Network System Developer	2225
		Computer Security Specialist	2226
		Web and Multimedia Planner	2227
		Web Developer	2228
		Architect or Architectural Engineer	2311
		Civil Engineer	2312
		Landscape Architect	2313
		City of Traffic Planning Specialist	2314
		Chemical Engineer	2321
		Metal or Material Engineer	2331
		Environmental Engineer	2341
		Electrical Engineer	2351
		Electronic Engineer	2352
		Mechanical Engineer	2353
		Plant Engineer	23532
		Engineer for Automobile, Marine, Aircraft, and Railroad Car	S2353
		Textile Engineer	2392

Skill level	Category	Occupation	
		Gas and Energy Engineer	2393
		Computer-Aided Design, CAD	2396
		Nurse	2430
		Instructor at Global Technical Institution	2543
		University Lecturer	2512
		Other Education-Related Expert	25919
		Foreigner's School – Foreign Education Institution – International School – School for Gifted Children's Teachers	2599
		Legal Expert	261
		Government Administration Expert	2620
		Special Institution Administrative Officers	S2620
		Management and Diagnosis Experts	2715
		Finance and Insurance Expert	272
		Merchandiser	2731
		Travel Package Developer	2732
		Advertisement and Promotion Expert	2733
		Research Expert	2734
		Event Planner	2735
		International Sales Clerks	2742
		Technology Sales Representative	2743
		Technology Management Expert	S2743
		Translator / Interpreter	2812
		Announcer	28331
		Designer	285
		Image Related Designer	S2855
Semi-professional	Office worker	Sales Staff in duty-free shop or Jeju English City	31215
		Air Transport	31264
		Hotel Receptionist	3922
		Medical Coordinator	S3922
	Service Worker	Shipping Service Worker	431
		Tourism Interpretation Guide	43213
		Casino Dealer	43291
		Chef or Cook	441
Skilled Labour	Agriculture, Livestock, Fishery	Skilled Technician in Agriculture, Animal Husbandry, and Fishery	610
		Zookeeper	61395
		Sea Cucumber Farming Specialist	63019
	Functional Worker and Skilled Practitioner	Instrument Maker or Tuner	7303
		Skilled Worker in Specific Industry	740
		Skilled Technicians at General Manufacturing and Construction Companies	700
		Shipbuilding Welder	7430
		Aircraft Mechanic	7521
		Halal Butcher	7103

Source: Ministry of Employment and Labour.

ORGANISATION FOR ECONOMIC CO-OPERATION AND DEVELOPMENT

The OECD is a unique forum where governments work together to address the economic, social and environmental challenges of globalisation. The OECD is also at the forefront of efforts to understand and to help governments respond to new developments and concerns, such as corporate governance, the information economy and the challenges of an ageing population. The Organisation provides a setting where governments can compare policy experiences, seek answers to common problems, identify good practice and work to co-ordinate domestic and international policies.

The OECD member countries are: Australia, Austria, Belgium, Canada, Chile, the Czech Republic, Denmark, Estonia, Finland, France, Germany, Greece, Hungary, Iceland, Ireland, Israel, Italy, Japan, Korea, Latvia, Lithuania, Luxembourg, Mexico, the Netherlands, New Zealand, Norway, Poland, Portugal, the Slovak Republic, Slovenia, Spain, Sweden, Switzerland, Turkey, the United Kingdom and the United States. The European Union takes part in the work of the OECD.

OECD Publishing disseminates widely the results of the Organisation's statistics gathering and research on economic, social and environmental issues, as well as the conventions, guidelines and standards agreed by its members.

OECD PUBLISHING, 2, rue André-Pascal, 75775 PARIS CEDEX 16
(81 2018 81 1 P) ISBN 978-92-64-30786-5 – 2019

www.ingramcontent.com/pod-product-compliance
Lightning Source LLC
LaVergne TN
LVHW080654011026
849160LV00014B/1422
* 9 7 8 9 2 6 4 3 0 7 8 6 5 *